IMAGERY IN SPORTS AND PHYSICAL PERFORMANCE

Editors

Anees A. Sheikh, Ph.D.

*Department of Psychology, Marquette University and
Department of Psychiatry and Mental Health Sciences,
Medical College of Wisconsin*

Errol R. Korn, M.D.

*Scripps Memorial Hospital, Chula Vista, California and
Chula Vista Community Memorial Hospital, Chula Vista, California*

Imagery and Human Development Series

Series Editor: Anees A. Sheikh

Baywood Publishing Company, Inc.
AMITYVILLE, NEW YORK

Library of Congress Catalog Card No. 94-47
ISBN Number: 0-89503-079-9 (Paper)
             0-89503-080-2 (Cloth)

Library of Congress Cataloging-in-Publication Data

Imagery in sports and physical performance / editors, Anees A. Sheikh
    and Errol R. Korn.
        p.   cm. - - (Imagery and human development series)
    Includes bibliographical references and index.
    ISBN 0-89503-080-2. - - ISBN 0-89503-079-9 (pbk.)
    1. Sports- -Psychological aspects.   2. Imagery (Psychology)
I. Sheikh, Anees A. II. Korn, Errol R. III. Series: Imagery and
human development series (Unnumbered)
GV706.4.I53 1994
796' .01- -dc20   94-47
                                                    CIP

Table of Contents

Chapter

Preface

I never hit a shot, not even in practice, without having a very sharp, in-focus picture of it in my head. It's like a color movie. First I "see" the ball where I want it to finish, nice and white and sitting up high on bright green grass. Then the scene quickly changes and I "see" the ball going there: its path, trajectory and shape, even its behavior on landing. Then there is sort of a fade-out, and the next scene shows me making the kind of swing that will turn the images into reality. (Jack Nicklaus, *Golf My Way,* Simon & Schuster, New York, p. 79, 1974)

Imagery techniques had been utilized extensively for decades in training world-class athletes in the former Eastern-block countries. But in the United States the use of imagery to enhance athletic performance had received only limited attention. Recently this has changed and reactions to this application of imagery range from total faith in its efficacy to absolute denial that it may hold promise for our athletes.

Fortunately, a considerable body of research on the relationship between imagery and athletic performance has emerged in the last decade. Although many questions have been answered, many more require further scrutiny. Both experimental and anecdotal evidence clearly demonstrate that imagery techniques can be a valuable tool in improving athletic performance; however, they must be applied with care. Research has demonstrated that they also can have deleterious effects when used inappropriately.

This book represents the first comprehensive attempt to focus on the use of imagery in sports. All its contributors are experts in their area, and together they have assembled the most relevant data produced by recent research and offer a wealth of practical suggestions. Researchers, coaches, and athletes at every level of performance will find the information very helpful.

The editdors would like to thank all contributors for their invaluable chapters. Also they would like to express their appreciation to Stuart Cohen, president of Baywood Publishing Company for his encouragement and patience, and Li Tan and Katie Janusz for their timeless assistance in the preparation of this manuscript.

Anees A. Sheikh, Ph.D.
Errol R. Korn, M.D.

v

CHAPTER 1

Enhancing Athletic Performance Through Imagery: An Overview

JEFFREY J. JANSSEN
AND ANEES A. SHEIKH

"Higher, Stronger, Faster," the Olympic motto, embodies the goal of athletes since the origin of competition. To help them in their quest, athletes have turned to a variety of programs, such as aerobics, nautilus, plyometrics, cybex, and isometrics. Ergogenic aids such as anabolic steroids, blood doping, and carbohydrate loading also have been used. Equipment is constantly being developed and modified to facilitate optimal performance. Athletic apparel has been scientifically designed to improve performance and minimize injuries, and sports medicine has developed rehabilitative techniques to accelerate recovery.

However, at the elite level, it often is not the physical difference that determines who succeeds. These athletes usually possess similar physical abilities, and it is often the psychological difference that makes the winner. Mark Spitz, winner of seven gold medals in the Montreal Olympics, says, "At this level of physical skill, the difference between winning and losing is 99 percent psychological" [1, p. 124].

Nevertheless, the psychological aspects of sport generally had been ignored, and it was not until the early part of the twentieth century that scientists began to investigate them. Coleman Griffith, known as the father of North American sport psychology, was one of the first to examine the psychological aspects of sport [2], and now sport psychologists employ such techniques as goal setting, self-talk, relaxation, concentration, stress management, and imagery to help athletes train for performance. Imagery, which also has been called mental rehearsal, mental practice, and visualization, "refers to all those quasi-sensory or quasi-perceptual experiences of which we are self-consciously aware, and which exist . . . in the absence of stimulus conditions" [3, p. 2]. Although not conclusive, most research has shown that imagery can be an effective means of enhancing athletic performance.

Research involving the effects of imagery on performance and various theories to explain the relationship are briefly reviewed in this chapter. The

1

specific aspects of imagery that lead to improved performance are discussed, and finally practical guidelines for coaches and athletes and ideas for further research are proposed.

RESEARCH INVOLVING IMAGERY AND PERFORMANCE

Early Research

One of the first hypotheses concerning mental practice was proposed by Washburn in 1916 [4]. She contended that slight muscle movements were made when a person imagined himself/herself to be engaged in activity. In addition, she believed that the movements which resulted from imagining an activity were identical to the movements of actual activity, except that they were of much smaller magnitudes. Jacobson was the first to substantiate this hypothesis [5]. He was able to show, through the use of electromyography, that actual muscle contraction occurred when a person imagined an activity. Jacobson reported that the minute muscle contractions occurred only in the muscles that were involved in the imagined activity. Freeman likewise showed that concomitant muscle activity was produced during an imagined activity [6]. In 1934, Sackett conducted a study that investigated the effects of mental practice versus physical practice [7]. Sackett found that physical practice was superior to mental practice, but that mental practice was effective in improving performance. Vandall, Davis, and Clugston investigated the role of mental practice on dart throwing [8]. They concluded that mental practice improved performance almost as much as physical practice.

Results of Research Reviews

Since these early studies, several researchers have investigated the role of mental practice in enhancing performance. The results of these studies have been somewhat equivocal. Therefore, in 1967, Richardson conducted an extensive review of the previous research examining the effects of mental practice on performance [9]. He concluded that, overall, mental practice was effective in improving performance. A short time later Corbin also reviewed the mental-practice literature and cautiously concluded that mental practice was preferable to no practice at all [10]. Weinberg conducted a more recent review of the mental-practice research [11]. He, too, found that the majority of studies showed that mental practice was an effective means of improving performance. The most recent and extensive analysis of the mental practice research was conducted by Feltz and Landers [12]. A total of sixty studies were reviewed according to the criteria they established. They employed a statistical method of analysis called meta-analysis which is able to combine the results of several individual studies so that an overall effect can be established and examined. They found, in agreement with Richardson, that "mentally practicing a motor skill influences performance somewhat better than no practice at all" [9, p. 41]. In light of these reviews, we can conclude that mental practice seems to be an effective method for improving performance.

THEORIES ON HOW IMAGERY FUNCTIONS TO ENHANCE PERFORMANCE

It is still unclear exactly how imagery serves to facilitate performance. Several theories have been proposed, but none of them is comprehensive enough to encapsulate the imagery-performance relationship [13]. The explanations of the mechanism of imagery seem to depend on several variables including intent, perspective, experience, nature of task, and skill level in the sport as well as in imagery.

Psychoneuromuscular Theory

One of the more prevalent explanations is the psychoneuromuscular theory. This theory holds that during the imaging of an activity, the brain sends out low levels of impulses through the nerves to the muscles that are being activated in one's imagination. These impulses are similar to those emitted during overt activity, but they are so slight that they are almost undetectable. These low level nerve impulses help to establish a mental blueprint of what is required to perform the activity, making this movement easier to execute.

The theory is based on Carpenter's [14] ideo-motor principle and is supported by Jacobson's results [5]. Carpenter posited that low-level nerve impulses are produced during imagined movement and that these impulses are identical to those of actual movement but reduced in magnitude [12]. Jacobson was able to support this by monitoring muscle activity by inserting electrodes into the target muscles. When subjects were instructed to imagine contracting their right arm, increased action potentials occurred in the muscles of the arm, showing that low-level innervation actually took place. Jacobson's research was later supported and extended by Hale [15]. Eccles showed that slight neural firings help to create a mental blueprint that facilitates future performance [16].

In 1980, Suinn tested the theory, using the imagery technique that he developed called visuo-motor behavior rehearsal or VMBR [17]. By attaching electrodes from an EMG to the legs of a skier and having him imagine skiing a downhill race, he discovered that the recorded muscle patterns were strikingly similar to the muscle patterns of a skier who actually skied the course. He states, "By the time he finished the psychological rehearsal of the downhill race, his EMG recordings almost mirrored the course itself" [17, p. 310]. Bird conducted a similar study with athletes in various sports (riding, rowing, swimming, water skiing, and basketball)

[18]. She, too, found that the EMG pattern was highly similar to the imagined sport activity. She was able to show a congruency between the EMG of an imagined sport activity and the EMG of the actual sport activity. In addition, the imagined time to complete the sport activity and the actual time to complete the sport activity were alike.

Feltz and Landers [12] and Hecker and Kaczor [19] remain skeptical in regard to the psychoneuromuscular theory. Feltz and Landers cite a lack of controlled investigation to assess the quantitative effects of the muscle activity and also a lack of direct evidence showing localized innervation in the muscle that was imaginally moved. They point to a study conducted by Shaw showing increased muscle action potentials that occurred throughout the body rather than just in a particular muscle [20]. Hecker and Kaczor believe the psychoneuromuscular theory is deficient in explaining the role of feedback in improving performance. They consider the theory a "description of an important aspect of imagery rehearsal . . ., rather than an explanation of the processes involved in improved performance" [19, p. 364].

Symbolic Learning Theory

The symbolic learning theory represents another attempt to explain how imagery functions to improve performance. The theory holds that movement patterns are symbolically coded in our central nervous system. Imagery facilitates the coding of movements into symbols which makes the movement easier to execute. The better a movement is symbolically coded, the easier it is to make. Skills that are more cognitive in nature are more easily coded than pure motor skills, according to the theory.

Sackett was the first to propose the symbolic learning theory [7]. He was able to show that performance improved with mental rehearsal in a finger maze, a more cognitive task that could easily be symbolized. Morrisett [21], Minas [22], Wrisberg and Ragsdale [23], and Ryan and Simons [24, 25] supported Sackett's original proposal by showing that mental rehearsal had a greater positive effect on cognitive (symbolic) tasks than on motor tasks. Feltz and Landers also conclude that the data "provide strong support for the symbolic learning explanation" [12, p. 45].

The symbolic learning theory, however, leaves some questions unanswered. It is easy to see how early skill acquisition is enhanced by the encoding of movement patterns through imagery, but the theory does not explain how performance is enhanced in experienced athletes who already have the movement pattern well established. Also, it is nearly impossible to classify movements as strictly cognitive or strictly motor, rather they should be considered to be a cognitive-motor continuum [19].

Bioinformational Theory

A third and more recent theory on the facilitating effects of imagery on performance is Lang's bioinformational theory [26]. The theory holds that an image is composed of a specific set of organized propositions in the brain. The propositions are able to access information about behavior prototypes that are found in long-term memory. The propositions are divided into two different types: stimulus and response. Stimulus propositions transmit information about the imagined environmental stimuli, while response propositions relay information regarding behavioral activity. With the help of an EMG, the processing of response propositions can be detected. All imagined behavior involves assessing stimulus propositions and reacting with response propositions. Vivid images allow for a great deal of stimulus and response propositions to be processed. Mental rehearsal enhances performance by activating and altering response propositions that determine the behavior prototype which dictates the pattern of muscle movement [19].

Mahoney and Avener [27] found that internal imagery is better than external imagery in enhancing performance [27]. (A detailed explanation of internal versus external imagery is provided later.) This finding is consistent with bioinformational theory: internal imagery more readily facilitates the processing of response propositions because the person images actually doing the activity rather than merely watching it. Hale [15] and Harris and Robinson [28] similarly demonstrated that imagery from an internal perspective brings about more muscle activity as recorded by an EMG, than imagery from an external perspective.

Further support for the theory comes from Suinn [29]. He found that "encouraging subjects to process response information during imagery is associated with improved performance" [19, p. 366]. Also, the studies that found low-level innervation of the muscles during imagery, lend support to the theory by demonstrating physiologically that response information is being processed.

In addition, the bioinformational theory is bolstered by the finding that experienced athletes benefit more from imagery than do novices [11, 12, 30, 31]. It is expected that experienced athletes have a well-established behavior prototype of muscle movement. Imagery improves performance by accessing the prototype information and activating the correct response propositions. A less experienced athlete would have a more vague behavior prototype allowing extraneous and deleterious response propositions to be processed and rehearsed in imagery, which would ultimately interfere with the desired performance.

Finally, Hecker and Kaczor found that a person's heart rate increases during imagined scenes from the person's past experience [19]. The increased heart rate was related to the activation of response propositions and thus supported the theory. Hecker and Kaczor suggest that "the strength of Lang's [26] theory lies in its heuristic value since it provides a conceptual model that can guide research into imagery rehearsal" [19, p. 367].

Attention-Arousal Set Theory

A fourth explanation of how imagery functions to enhance performance is the attention-arousal set theory. It is believed that there is an optimal state of arousal for each athlete that allows him/her to achieve peak performance, and that imagery facilitates an athlete's attempt to set his/her arousal at an optimal level. Also, imagery can help to focus an athlete's attention on the task-relevant cues needed for optimal performance, thereby screening out potential distractions. Lee found that task relevant images were important but that imagery effects were not a result of affecting mood states [32]. This theory is quite new and there is very little empirical data to support it [19].

Other Theoretical Approaches

In addition to the foregoing approaches, a few other theories on how imagery functions to enhance physical performance have been offered. These include: covert-conditioning theory [33], self-efficacy theory [34], and triple-code theory [35, 36].

According to the covert-conditioning theory, covert and overt responses influence the body similarly and obey the same set of principles of learning and conditioning. Repeated and positively reinforced practice of an end result image is expected to create the desired change in performance. The self-efficacy theory proposes that imagery practice heightens an athlete's expectation of success which in turn enhances motor performance. The triple-code theory, in addition to recognizing the significance of psychophysiology in mental practice, emphasizes the role of meaning that an image has for a given subject. So any given image cannot be expected to have the same effect on all subjects. It appears that while all theories have a kernel of truth, none of them, in its present state, is sufficiently developed or detailed with respect to sport psychology.

ASPECTS OF IMAGERY AND THEIR INFLUENCE ON ATHLETIC PERFORMANCE

Combining Physical and Mental Practice

After concluding that imagery seems to be a valid technique for enhancing performance, researchers attempted to determine which aspects of imagery are most effective in enhancing performance. Initially, Stebbins found that a combination of mental and physical practice is the best method for improving performance [37]. Similarly, Trussell [38], Riley and Start [39], and Whitley [40] found that alternating between physical and mental practice was more effective than physical practice or mental practice alone [11]. However, more recent studies have shown that pure physical practice is better than any combination of physical and mental practice [41, 42]. A study by Hird, Landers, Thomas, and Horan used varying ratios of physical and mental practice for cognitive and motor tasks [42]. The subjects were assigned to one of six groups: 100 percent physical practice, 75 percent physical/25 percent mental, 50 percent physical/50 percent mental, 25 percent physical/75 percent mental, 100 percent mental practice, and control. The results indicated that pure physical practice is superior to any combination of physical and mental practice or mental practice alone. However, one should not conclude that mental practice has no merits. The authors of the study noted that physical practice often may be limited due to expense, time constraints, fatigue, or injury. Since the researchers also found that mental practice was better than no practice at all, they too recommended that imagery be used as a supplement to sport training.

Internal versus External Imagery

It appears that internal imagery may be more effective than external imagery for enhancing performance, especially for elite athletes. Internal imagery sometimes is called kinesthetic imagery, and it involves imagining an activity as if you are actually performing it, seeing everything as if you were in your own head. External imagery, on the other hand, involves seeing yourself perform an activity as if you were watching yourself perform on television. To demonstrate the difference, we will use the image of putting a golf ball. If you viewed it internally, you would see the ball in front of your feet and your club and arms stretched downward toward the ball. When putting, your focus would be on the ball, as you feel your club go back and come forward to hit the ball. If you viewed the sequence externally, you would be removed from your body and would see yourself performing the entire activity from an outside, third-person perspective.

Jacobson [5] and Shaw [20] were the first to postulate that internal imagery elicits more muscle activity than external imagery [11]. Jacobson found that when subjects were asked to think of performing a biceps curl (external imagery), eye activity occurred. But when they were told to imagine experiencing a biceps curl (internal imagery), localized muscle activity took place. Similarly, research conducted by Davidson and Schwartz [43] showed that internal imagery produced "greater somatic arousal and less visual activity" than external imagery [11, p. 201]. Mahoney and Avener were the first to categorize images into the internal and external classifications [27]. They discovered that gymnasts who qualified for the Olympics used predominantly internal imagery; whereas, those who had not qualified relied more on external imagery.

However, Epstein found no significant difference between internal and external imagery in her research on dart throwing [44]. Additional studies [45-47] have found no difference in imagery perspective for elite athletes [14]. Epstein contends that a person's imagery perspective is highly transitory due to individual and scene differences, and thus it is difficult to delineate the perspectives in research and arrive at a definitive answer.

More recently, Hale found that subjects who employed internal imagery on a weight-lifting task produced more localized muscle activity than those who employed external imagery [15]. As mentioned earlier, some researchers questioned the validity of this finding because the studies failed to monitor other muscle activity that tended to show a more generalized effect. Harris and Robinson followed up with a study that addressed this problem by monitoring general as well as specific muscle activity [28]. They found that internal imagery did produce more muscle efference than external imagery and that the efference was localized in subjects who were experienced in karate. However, Harris and Robinson concluded that "the influence of internal/external imagery perspective is unclear" and warrants further research [28, p. 109]. They acknowledged that a person's image perspective is highly dynamic and cannot be adequately controlled to yield conclusive results. The choice and ability to adopt a particular perspective may be related to how well the skill is learned [48]. Beginners may rely more on external images; whereas, experienced performers may utilize predominantly internal images. The external perspective is probably easier for beginners since they have little idea of the mechanics of the movement. Experienced athletes have actually performed the skills or a variation of them and this prior experience can be more easily transferred to imagery.

Cognitive versus Motor Skills

Most research has shown that tasks that are very cognitive or symbolic in nature benefit from imagery more than tasks that involve pure motor skills [12]. This finding supports Sackett's symbolic-learning theory, which holds that imagery enhances tasks that contain movements that can be readily symbolized [7]. It is important to view tasks to be on a cognitive-motor continuum and not classified into mutually exclusive categories. Morrisett [21] compared cognitive and motor tasks to test Sackett's theory. Morrisett found that cognitive tasks benefited more from imagery. Wrisberg and Ragsdale conducted a similar study and found that mental practice improved performance to the same degree as physical practice on highly cognitive tasks [23]. On motor tasks, they found mental practice to have the same effect as no practice at all, while physical practice improved performance. Ryan and Simons [24, 25] confirmed Wrisberg and Ragsdale's finding. But Ryan and Simons contend that most skills contain at least some cognitive elements and therefore could be improved through imagery.

Experienced versus Novice Athletes

The research suggests that imagery yields better results in experienced than in novice athletes. Clark found that varsity and junior-varsity basketball players improved their shooting more than novices using imagery [49]. Start [50] and Whitley [40] found similar results. Hall and Erffmeyer concluded that the foul shooting of highly skilled athletes benefited from imagery [31]. Similarly,

Harris and Robinson concluded that "skill level appears to influence the degree of efference" [28, p. 109] because they found that experienced karate students displayed more low-level innervation than novice students.

However, Weinberg, in his review of the literature concludes,

> It appears that MP (mental practice) can facilitate performance in both the early or latter stages of learning although some subjects need to have some minimal amount of physical practice before MP can be effective, especially in a complex skill [11, p. 199].

According to Feltz and Landers, novice performers may be able to benefit from imagery because it could aid them in developing a rough schema of the cognitive elements that are required for the task [12]. They conclude in their meta-analysis, "It appears then that mental practice effects are found in both the initial and later stages of learning" [12, p. 47]. Thus, imagery appears to be very beneficial to experienced performers and somewhat beneficial to novice performers.

Positive versus Negative Imagery

Powell, in an experiment with dart throwing, discovered that positive, success-oriented images improved performance, while negative images adversely affected performance [51]. Gould, Weinberg, and Jackson [52] and Woolfolk, Parrish, and Murphy [53] found similar results. Woolfolk, Murphy, Gottesfeld, and Aitken concluded that "briefly imaging the outcome of athletic activity immediately prior to performing that activity has greater influence on subsequent performance than does brief mental performance, again prior to performance, of the motor movements that make up the task itself" [54, p. 196]. In addition, it appears that the detrimental effect of negative images is stronger than the advantage brought about by positive images.

Duration of Mental Rehearsal

Unestahl remarked that for a program to be effective, it needs to be long enough so that the response becomes easy flowing, but brief enough so that the performer does not cease to be interested or motivated [55]. Researchers have attempted to determine the optimal amount of time spent on mental rehearsal. Ryan and Simons [24] and Schmidt [56] discovered that mental practice conducted too frequently or for lengthy periods has decreasing effect or even deleterious effect on performance. Twining suggested that after five minutes, it was difficult to maintain concentration [57]. Likewise, Richardson hinted that massed imagery practice could be deleterious to performance [9]. Corbin noted that distributed practice was more effective than massed practice in the execution of motor skills [10]. Shick found that three-minute sessions of mental practice improved performance more than a one-minute session [58]. Other authors suggest that five to ten minutes of imagery are optimal [59, 60]. Weinberg cautions that individual and task differences should be considered in determining the optimal duration of imagery sessions [11].

Role of Vividness and Control

Start and Richardson examined the role of vividness and control in imagery [61]. Vividness refers to how clearly the person sees the image and how detailed the image appears. Control pertains to how well the person can manipulate and direct what is being imaged. They found that subjects who had high vividness and high control improved performance the best. They were followed by those with low vividness and high control, then by those with low vividness and low control, and finally by those with high vividness and low control (which actually may be detrimental to performance). Uncontrolled images lead the mind and body to rehearse movements and situations that may have negative consequences; therefore, it is important for athletes to learn to control their images. For instance, an athlete shooting a free throw in basketball may be able to see the image very vividly in his mind, he/she may picture clearly the backboard and rim, the pebbled grain of the leather and the black seams of the ball, the players lined up along the free throw lane, and the spectators in the background. But then he/she may imagine the ball sailing over the backboard and into the top row of the bleachers. The inability to control the image so that it achieves the desired outcome can obviously be detrimental to performance. Hinshaw reviews a number of more recent studies on the topic of vividness and control of mental images [62]. Starker [63] discovered that "an individual may have more control over a spontaneous vivid image than over an induced vivid image" [62, p. 13]. Highlen and Bennett reported that skilled athletes seem to have both better control and better vividness than the less skilled athletes [64].

Imagery and the Senses

It seems that imagery is most effective when it incorporates all sensory modalities [36]. Athletes should not just visualize doing the activity, but should feel it kinesthetically, and hear the accompanying sounds, smell the accompanying odors, and, if possible, taste the accompanying tastes. For instance, a golfer should visualize the scene from an internal perspective: the lie of the ball, the fairway in front, and the green off in the distance. He/she should imagine the smell of the outdoor air and the freshly cut grass. On the backswing, he/she should feel that club going back and the weight transfer to the back foot. On the swing he/she should feel the club coming down and the weight transfer to the front foot. He/she should hear the sound of the club striking the ball. On the follow-through, he/she should feel the rotation of the hips. Then he/she should see the flight of the ball and its landing on the green a few feet from the hole. Incorporating as many senses as possible makes the image more real and life-like. This is important since it is thought that the mind cannot easily distinguish between a real and an imagined event.

Role of Relaxation

Relaxation prior to imagery is often recommended. Kolonay [65], Suinn [66], and Weinberg, Seaborne, and Jackson [67] found that relaxation preceding imagery is more effective than imagery alone [68]. Relaxation aids imagery by reducing distracting somatic tension and also eliminates cognitive distractions by calming and centering the mind. This allows for the emergence of right hemispheric activity which is associated with imagery. Relaxation provides a peaceful state that is conducive to producing vivid and controlled images. There are several methods used to achieve a relaxed state. Among them are Jacobson's [69] progressive relaxation, meditation, and autogenic training [36].

It must be noted that opposing views concerning the role of relaxation have been voiced. Qualls suggests that the "directive to relax and the stress created by biofeedback are inherently in conflict with the desired natural relaxation process itself; the body becomes physiologically 'confused' given the conflicting directions" [70]. Gray, Haring, and Banks contend instead that

> relaxation may have a negative effect on performance because it inhibits possible transfer effects of training; the individual would not be relaxed during the actual performance situation so that a conditioning in relaxation through VMBR techniques may actually be detrimental to later performance" [62, p. 9].

Obviously, the role of relaxation needs to be examined more closely. However, it seems that relaxation prior to imagery practice would make it more vivid and better controlled, which, in turn, would render it more effective. It should be kept in mind that the aim is not to keep the subject totally relaxed throughout mental practice, but instead relaxation is used to "launch" the subject into vivid and controlled imagery.

Nature of the Image

There is considerable evidence in the literature indicating that a subject's response is dependent upon the nature of the image itself [71-73]. For example, Quallis [70] and Hecker and Kaczor [19] demonstrated that the physiological consequences of images were influenced by the personal relevance of the imagined scene. Whether the subjects will employ an internal or external imaginal style also appears to depend on the nature of the image [44, 62]. "Familiar scenes may be imagined internally based on experience while unfamiliar scenes might be viewed from an outside, external perspective" [62, p. 14].

Applied Research

Much of the research on imagery and sports has been conducted in laboratory settings. This method has not yielded entirely reliable results. Often the researchers have monitored performance after only a minimal amount of imagery training [48, 74]. In addition, motivation for performing in a laboratory setting probably does not compare to performing in a high-stakes athletic contest.

Little applied research has been reported [74-76]. Only a few studies have examined the effects of an imagery training program in actual sport settings. One such study with figure skaters found that imagery skills could be improved with practice [77]. Unfortunately, the imagery intervention program had no significant effect on performance. However, Isaac found that an imagery program did improve trampoline performance, especially for subjects who were classified as having high imagery skills [74]. These findings suggest that imagery ability can be enhanced with practice and perhaps that greater imagery ability yields more positive effects on performance. Finally, a comprehensive program using imagery, relaxation, and self-talk with basketball players enhanced defensive performance [75]. Perhaps these studies will be an impetus for more field-based applied research in which athletes receive comprehensive, long-term imagery training and performance is monitored.

APPLICATIONS OF IMAGERY RESEARCH TO SPORT

Based on the research, imagery can be utilized in sport for a variety of purposes. Several of Vealey's recommendations have been incorporated here [68].

Acquiring and Practicing Skills

Coaches and athletes can utilize imagery to enhance performance in a variety of ways. One of these ways is the acquisition of new sport skills [68]. This could be done by first having the coach demonstrate the physical skill. The athletes could then develop an image of themselves performing the activity. This imagery may help to code the movement into the mind so that it may be more easily recognized and easier to perform physically (symbolic learning theory).

Once a skill is learned, imagery can help to strengthen the movements of the skill so that they become more fluid and automatic (psychoneuromusclar and bioinformational theories). For many right-handed basketball players, left-handed lay-ups feel awkward, and thus many players use the right-handed form on all lay-ups. This does not have to be the case, if athletes practice left-handed lay-ups both physically and mentally.

Acquiring and Practicing Strategies

Imagery also can be employed when learning new strategies in sports [68]. The strategies first would be demonstrated and then the athletes would imagine executing them. Lou Henson, the men's basketball coach at the University of Illinois, encourages the use of imagery with his team when they are learning his offensive system [68]. The players imagine themselves going through the plays from each different position. Also coaches could have their athletes imagine various situations and their reactions to them. If players have experienced pressure situations in their mind and handled them effectively, they will be more likely to confidently handle the same situations if they arise in real life. Often sports officials and referees are encouraged to use imagery to provide added experience in handling unexpected situations that may arise during a game [78].

Familiarizing Unknown Athletic Environments

Along these same lines, athletes can visualize sites that they have never visited but at which they must compete in the future. Harris and Harris cite an example [79]. The U.S. Women's Field Hockey Team was scheduled to play at Wembley Stadium in London, an unfamiliar site to them. They used a film of the stadium and imagery to become somewhat familiar with playing in such a large stadium in front of a crowd of 70,000 spectators.

Examining Performance Problems

Imagery also can be utilized to discover problems in performance [68]. If the athlete is not performing according to past or expected levels, imagery can be used to critically examine all the aspects of performance so that the potentially confounding factor might be found. For example, if a player who normally made 80 percent of his/her free throw attempts is now making only 50 percent, through imagery, he/she may discover that he/she has not been fully concentrating on the rim before shooting.

Setting Arousal

Imagery also can be used to set cognitive and somatic levels of arousal for optimal performance [68]. As demonstrated by biofeedback, imagery can be used to regulate physiological responses such as respiratory rate, heart rate, and skin temperature. Cognitively, athletes can help set their optimal level of arousal and more sharply focus their attention on the tasks needed for maximum performance (attention-arousal set formulation).

Providing Variety to Practices

Imagery can be used to add variety to practice when physical practice becomes tedious. Henschen advocates the use of imagery to break up the monotony and to provide time for physical recuperation [80]. He states that imagery has served this purpose for the University of Utah's women's gymnastic team.

Managing Pain

Injured athletes can employ imagery to cope with pain. Sometimes dissociative imagery can help an athlete to escape from the pain by imagining that he/she is in a pleasant surrounding. "Endurance athletes are frequently known to experience dissociative images that are the results of greater amounts of endorphins in the brain during prolonged activity" [81, p. 141]. Elite athletes also have been known to use associative imagery. Associative imagery allows athletes to monitor exactly what is happening to their bodies so that they can adjust their performance accordingly to avoid injury.

Accelerating the Healing Process

Imagery has been known to speed the healing process after injury [82-84]. This can be accomplished by providing the athlete with an anatomically detailed description of the injured area, preferably in color, and an explanation of the changes that need to occur for it to become healthy again. Then the patient should systematically visualize the healing process. Some have found it useful to conduct an inner dialogue with the injured area [85]. This dialogue involves instructing the injured body part to heal. Finally, the patient should imagine the area as fully healed and strong. Of course this is not to say that conventional sports medicine techniques should be ignored, but imagery can contribute to the healing process. In addition, injured athletes can utilize imagery while they are out of competition to mentally practice skills that their teammates are practicing physically. In this way their time off is not completely unproductive.

Practicing Psychological Skills

Imagery can be useful in practicing other psychological skills as well. Skills such as "attentional control, stress management, energizing, goal setting, self-confidence and interpersonal skill" can be practiced through imagery [68, p. 221].

Perhaps the most intriguing but least understood aspect of imagery is its ability to activate a person's conscious and unconscious resources toward the attainment of a specified goal. Goal images tend to act as a self-fulfilling prophecy. The internal images that a person has of himself/herself tend to motivate and guide his/her overt behavior. An athlete who sees himself/herself as one who chokes under pressure will most likely do just that in game situations. However, athletes who have successful images of themselves, usually do come through in the clutch. When a goal image is formulated, the unconscious mind is activated toward trying to fulfill it. The mind begins to notice all of the opportunities that lead toward the goal. Without a specific goal image, the mind cannot direct itself toward discovering the resources available for goal attainment. It is very important that athletes create and foster realistic but challenging goal images. It is often true that you achieve what you expect.

Times to Use Imagery

Imagery can and should be used throughout the season on a systematic basis. The type and content of imagery will vary depending on whether it is during practice, prior to competition, during competition, or after competition.

Imagery during Practice. Imagery used during practice should be primarily geared toward the learning and practicing of skills and strategies. It can also be used to set arousal levels prior to practice. In addition, pain coping and/or healing imagery can be used during practice.

Precompetition Imagery. Precompetition imagery should be designed to promote confidence. The images should encourage focusing on the task and should be either energizing or relaxing. Athletes should devise "trigger" words that elicit certain desired images. Self-talk words, such as "relax," "nice and easy," and "concentrate" can be paired with images that focus the athlete's attention and set arousal. Music also has been known to produce images that relate to different states of arousal. Images of certain animals, machines, and forces of nature can be used to energize athletes whose arousal levels are too low [86]. If needed, pain-coping imagery can be used prior to competition. A quick overview of strategy also can be done through imagery.

Imagery during Competition. During competition, imagery can be used to redirect an athlete's attention, if he/she is not performing well. It can be used to adjust or maintain arousal levels. If there are small breaks in the performance, imagery can be used to mentally rehearse an upcoming skill. For example, Greg Louganis, the Olympic gold medalist in diving, mentally rehearses each dive before executing it [87]. Again, imagery can be used for pain management during competition.

Postcompetition Imagery. Postcompetition imagery can be used to review positive and negative aspects of the past performance. When reviewing the positive aspects, athletes should remember to be aware of what contributed to making them so. They should examine their arousal level, their focus of attention, and their confidence level. When reviewing the negative aspects, athletes should try to determine why they occurred and what could have been done to prevent them. It is important then to revisualize the experience and substitute the correct response, so that the mind can build on it. Injuries sustained during competition also can be alleviated using imagery.

Implementing an Imagery Program

The following framework for implementing an imagery program has been adapted from Vealey [68].

Convincing the Athletes. To be effective, imagery programs need to be organized, systematic, and supported [48]. Athletes who are skeptical about using imagery as a regular part of their practice, need to be convinced of its worth. Some athletes will be persuaded by the research findings that were presented earlier. Others may need more "proof" before adopting imagery as a performance enhancement technique. They may be satisfied by learning about the numerous coaches and athletes who have used imagery in a variety of sports; for example, the U.S. Women's Field Hockey team, University of Arizona's softball team, the University of Utah's gymnastic team, Lou Hensen, Greg Louganis, Jack Nicklaus, Arnold Palmer, O. J. Simpson, Fran Tarkenton, Bill Russell, Chris Evert, Billie Jean King, Dwight Stones, Steve Cram, Jean Claude Killy, Jackie Stewart, Michael Jordan, Jim Courier, Joe Carter, and Nancy Kerrigan. Hemery conducted in-depth interviews of sixty-three of the world's top sports performers [88]. He found that 80 percent considered visualization (imagery) to be a great asset. This should help to convince the rest of the skeptics.

It is important that coaches not force their athletes into using imagery if they resist it. The coach should encourage the athlete to use imagery rather than making it mandatory. This can be accomplished by introducing the imagery technique to the entire team and urging them to at least try it for a short period of time. If after that time, the athlete is still uncomfortable using imagery, he/she should be excused from it. In addition, athletes and coaches should form realistic expectations regarding the potential benefits of imagery [48]. It should be acknowledged that imagery is not a mystical or miracle gimmick but a skill to develop much like physical skills.

Assessing the Athlete's Imaging Ability. After the athlete is convinced of the power of imagery, the next step is to assess his/her imaging ability. Tests such as Bett's QMI (or Sheehan's shortened version) are able to assess vividness and dominant sense modalities, and Gordon's test indicates degree of imagery control [36]. Also, Martens has developed the Sport Imagery Questionnaire which assesses both vividness and control of images [89].

Practicing Imagery Skills. After the athlete's imaging ability has been determined, it can be enhanced by practice in controlling images and making them more vivid [77]. The athletes should be encouraged to focus on past performances and the associated bodily sensations and emotions in as much detail as possible. The next step is to incorporate them into future images [89]. Different exercises have been developed for improving control of images. These involve the conscious manipulation of the image. Other exercises work on enhancing the vividness of images. Martens [89], Harris and Harris [79], Nideffer [87], Vealey [68], and Syer and Connolly [90] provide an excellent variety of exercises designed to improve control and vividness of imagery.

Incorporating the Imagery Program. The imagery program should be designed to meet the specific needs of the athlete. Factors such as skill level, position, optimal level of arousal, and the nature of the sport must be considered. Programs for individual sports tend to be relatively easy to develop, because they are highly specific and involve closed skills which are not dependent on the actions of teammates. This is not to say that those in team sports cannot benefit from imagery; for, imagery can be practiced very effectively with groups. The group sessions are geared more toward learning and practicing skills and strategies, and directing attention, while individual sessions can make use of the full spectrum of imagery applications. Imagery scripts can be generated by the coach, the athletes themselves, or purchased programs can be used. Whatever the case, the athlete should feel comfortable using the program and be sure that it is fulfilling his/her needs.

Program Evaluation. Finally, coaches and athletes should evaluate the program and record successes as well as the problems with it. This can be accomplished by keeping an imagery journal. The journal can be used to monitor progress and to single out images which are associated with peak performance. The journal can also help to make the program more systematic and thus increase commitment.

CONCLUDING REMARKS

Based on what is currently known in the scientific literature, it seems that imagery can be an effective method for enhancing athletic performance. This conclusion is further supported by a substantial body of anecdotal accounts. However, it also seems quite clear that imagery practice, when used inappropriately has the potential of producing significant decrements in performance, and we must be extremely cautious in the application of imagery techniques [91]. A complex relationship seems to exist between factors that have an impact on the effectiveness of imagery practice, and numerous aspects of this issue need further attention. These include an examination of: the effects of sex differences and various imaginal style, cognitive style and other individual difference variables; detailed self-reports by the subjects to determine what they actually imagine when given imagery instructions; longitudinal effects of intensive imagery training in laboratory and field settings; the use of imagery in areas that indirectly affect an athlete's performance, such as management of the stress of competition, alleviation of pain and fatigue, increasing stamina, and controlling arousal level [92].

REFERENCES

1. J. M. Williams, Psychological Characteristics of Peak Performance, in *Applied Sport Psychology: Personal Growth to Peak Performance*, J. M. Williams (ed.), Mayfield, Palo Alto, California, pp. 123-132, 1986.
2. D. K. Wiggins, The History of Sport Psychology in North America, in *Psychological Foundations of Sport*, J. M. Silva and R. S. Weinberg (eds.), Human Kinetics, Champaign, Illinois, pp. 9-22, 1984.
3. A. Richardson, *Mental Imagery*, Springer, New York, 1969.
4. M. F. Washburn, *Movement and Mental Imagery*, Houghton, Boston, 1916.
5. E. Jacobson, Electrophysiology of Mental Activities, *American Journal of Psychology, 44*, pp. 677-694, 1932.
6. G. L. Freeman, The Facilitation and Inhibitory Effect of Muscular Tension Upon Performance, *American Journal of Psychology, 45*, pp. 17-52, 1933.
7. R. S. Sackett, The Influences of Symbolic Rehearsal Upon the Retention of a Maze Habit, *Journal of General Psychology, 10*, pp. 376-395, 1934.
8. R. A. Vandall, R. A. Davis, and H. A. Clugston, The Function of Mental Practice in the Acquisition of Motor Skills, *Journal of General Psychology, 29*, pp. 243-250, 1943.
9. A. Richardson, Mental Practice, *Research Quarterly, 38*, pp. 59-107, 263-273, 1967.
10. C. B. Corbin, Mental Practice, in *Ergogenic Aids and Muscular Performance*, W. P. Morgan (ed.), Academic Press, New York, pp. 93-118, 1972.
11. R. S. Weinberg, The Relationship Between Mental Preparation Strategies and Motor Performance: A Review and Critique, *Quest, 33*, pp. 190-213, 1982.
12. D. L. Feltz and D. M. Landers, The Effects of Mental Practice on Motor Skill Learning and Performance: A Meta-analysis, *Journal of Sport Psychology, 5*, pp. 25-57, 1983.
13. G. E. Schwartz, Psychophysiology of Imagery and Healing: A Systems Perspective, in *Imagination and Healing*, A. A. Sheikh (ed.), Baywood, New York, pp. 38-50, 1983.
14. W. B. Carpenter, *Principles of Mental Physiology*, (4th Ed.), Appleton, New York, 1984.
15. B. D. Hale, The Effects of Internal and External Imagery on Muscular and Ocular Concomitants, *Journal of Sport Psychology, 4*, pp. 379-387, 1982.
16. J. Eccles, The Physiology of Imagination, *Scientific American, 199*, p. 135, 1958.
17. R. M. Suinn, Body Thinking: Psychology for Olympic Champions, in *Psychology in Sports: Methods and Applications*, R. M. Suinn (ed.), Burgess, Minneapolis, pp. 306-315, 1980.
18. E. Bird, EMG Quantification of Mental Rehearsal, *Perceptual and Motor Skills, 59*, pp. 899-906, 1984.
19. J. E. Hecker and L. M. Kaczor, Application of Imagery Theory to Sport Psychology: Some Preliminary Findings, *Journal of Sport Psychology, 10*, pp. 363-373, 1988.
20. W. Shaw, The Distribution of Muscle Action Potentials During Imaging, *The Psychological Record, 2*, pp. 195-216, 1938.
21. L. N. Morrisett, *The Role of Implicit Practice in Learning*, unpublished doctoral dissertation, Yale University, 1956.
22. S. C. Minas, Mental Practice of a Complex Perceptual-motor Skill, *Journal of Human Movement Studies, 4*, pp. 102-107, 1978.
23. C. A. Wrisberg and M. R. Ragsdale, Cognitive Demand and Practice Level: Factors in the Mental Rehearsal of Motor Skills, *Journal of Human Movement Studies, 5*, pp. 201-208, 1979.

24. D. E. Ryan and J. Simons, Cognitive Demand, Imagery, and Frequency of Mental Rehearsal as Factors Influencing Acquisition of Motor Skills, *Journal of Sport Psychology, 3*, pp. 35-45, 1981.
25. D. E. Ryan and J. Simons, What is Learned in Mental Practice of Motor Skills, *Journal of Sport Psychology, 5*, pp. 419-426, 1983.
26. P. J. Lang, Imagery in Therapy: An Information Processing Analysis of Fear, *Behavior Therapy, 8*, pp. 862-886, 1977.
27. M. J. Mahoney and M. Avener, Psychology of the Elite Athlete: An Exploratory Study, *Cognitive Therapy and Research, 1*, pp. 135-141, 1977.
28. D. V. Harris and W. J. Robinson, The Effects of Skill Level on EMG Activity During Internal and External Imagery, *Journal of Sport Psychology, 8*, pp. 105-111, 1986.
29. R. M. Suinn, Imagery Rehearsal Applications to Performance Enhancement, *The Behavior Therapist, 8*, pp. 155-159, 1985.
30. R. C. Noel, The Effect of Visuo-motor Behavior Rehearsal on Tennis Performance, *Journal of Sport Psychology, 2*, pp. 221-226, 1980.
31. E. G. Hall and E. S. Erffmeyer, The Effect of Visuo-motor Behavior Rehearsal with Videotaped Modeling on Free Throw Accuracy of Intercollegiate Female Basketball Players, *Journal of Sport Psychology, 5*, pp. 343-345, 1983.
32. C. Lee, Psyching Up For a Muscular Endurance Task: Effects of Image Content on Performance and Mood State, *Journal of Sport and Exercise Psychology, 12*, pp. 66-73, 1990.
33. J. R. Cautela and L. Samdperil, *Applied Sport Psychology, 1*, pp. 82-97, 1989.
34. A. Bandura, Self-Efficacy: Toward a Unifying Theory of Behavioral Change, *Psychology Review, 84*, pp. 191-215, 1982.
35. A. Ahsen, ISM: The Triple Code Model for Imagery and Psychophysiology, *Journal of Mental Imagery, 8*, pp. 15-42, 1984.
36. A. A. Sheikh (ed.), *Imagery: Current Theory, Research, and Application,* John Wiley and Sons, New York, 1983.
37. R. J. Stebbins, A Comparison of the Effects of Physical and Mental Practice in Learning a Motor Skill, *Research Quarterly, 39*, pp. 714-720, 1968.
38. E. M. Trussel, *Mental Practice as a Factor in the Learning of a Complex Motor Skill,* unpublished master's thesis, University of California, 1952.
39. E. Riley and K. B. Start, The Effect of Spacing of Mental and Physical Practices on the Acquisition of a Physical Skill, *Australian Journal of Physical Education, 20*, pp. 13-16, 1960.
40. G. Whitley, *The Effect of Mental Rehearsal on the Acquisition of Motor Skill,* unpublished diploma in education dissertation, University of Manchester, 1962.
41. D. L. Feltz, D. M. Landers, and B. J. Becker, A Revised Meta-analysis of the Mental Practice Literature on Motor Skill Learning, in *Enhancing Human Performance: Issues, Theories, and Techniques,* D. Druckman and J. Swets (eds.), National Academy Press, pp. 1-65, 1988.
42. J. S. Hird, D. M. Landers, J. R. Thomas, and J. J. Horan, Physical Practice is Superior to Mental Practice in Enhancing Cognitive and Motor Task Performance, *Journal of Sport and Exercise Psychology, 8*, pp. 281-293, 1991.
43. R. J. Davidson and G. E. Schwartz, Brain Mechanisms Subserving Self-generated Imagery; Electrophysiological Specificity and Patterning, *Psychophysiology, 14*, pp. 598-602, 1977.
44. M. L. Epstein, The Relationship of Mental Imagery and Mental Rehearsal to Performance of a Motor Task, *Journal of Sport Psychology, 2*, pp. 211-220, 1980.

45. P. Highlen and B. Bennett, Psychological Characteristics of Successful and Non-successful Elite Wrestlers: An Exploratory Study, *Journal of Sport Psychology, 1,* pp. 123-137, 1979.
46. A. W. Meyers, C. J. Cooke, J. Cullen, and L. Liles, Psychological Aspects of Athletic Competitors: A Replication Across Sports, *Cognitive Therapy and Research, 3,* pp. 361-366, 1979.
47. R. J. Rotella, B. Gransneder, B. Ojala, and J. Billing, Cognitions and Coping Strategies of Elite Skiers: An Exploratory Study of Young Developing Skiers, *Journal of Sport Psychology, 2,* pp. 350-354, 1980.
48. D. Smith, Conditions that Facilitate the Development of Sport Imagery Training, *The Sport Psychologist, 1,* pp. 237-247, 1987.
49. L. V. Clark, Effect of Mental Practice on the Development of a Certain Motor Skill, *Research Quarterly, 31,* pp. 560-569, 1960.
50. K. B. Start, The Influence of Subjectively Assessed Games Ability on Gain in Motor Performance After Mental Rehearsal, *Journal of General Psychology, 67,* pp. 169-172, 1962.
51. G. E. Powell, Negative and Positive Mental Practice in Motor Skill Acquisition, *Perceptual and Motor Skills, 37,* pp. 423-425, 1973.
52. D. Gould, R. S. Weinberg, and A. Jackson, Effect of Mental Preparation Strategies of Muscular Endurance, *Journal of Sport Psychology, 2,* pp. 329-339, 1980.
53. R. L. Woolfolk, W. Parrish, and S. M. Murphy, The Effects of Positive and Negative Imagery on Motor Skill Performance, *Cognitive Therapy and Research, 9,* pp. 335-341, 1985.
54. R. L. Woolfolk, S. M. Murphy, D. Gottesfeld, and D. Aitken, Effects of Mental Rehearsal of Task Motor Activity and Mental Depiction of Task Outcome on Motor Performance, *Journal of Sport Psychology, 7,* pp. 191-197, 1985.
55. L. E. Unestahl, Inner Mental Training for Sport, in *Mental Training for Coaches and Athletes: Proceedings of ISSP 5th World Sport Psychology Congress,* T. Orlick, J. Partington, and J. Sanela (eds.), Coaching Association of Canada, Ottawa, Ontario, 1982.
56. R. A. Schmidt, *Motor Skills,* Harper & Row, New York, 1975.
57. W. E. Twining, Mental Practice and Physical Practice in Learning a Motor Skill, *Research Quarterly, 20,* pp. 432-435, 1939.
58. J. Schick, Effects of Mental Practice in Selected Volleyball Skills for College Women, *Research Quarterly, 51,* pp. 88-94, 1970.
59. J. Vedelli, Mental Rehearsal in Sport, in *Sport Psychology: Psychological Considerations in Maximizing Sport Performance,* L. K. Bunker, R. J. Rotella, and A. S. Reilly (eds.), McNaughton & Nunn, pp. 256-259, 1985.
60. B. J. Cratty, *Psychological Preparation and Athletic Excellence,* Movement Publications, Ithaca, New York, 1984.
61. K. B. Start and A. Richardson, Imagery and Mental Practice, *British Journal of Educational Psychology, 34,* pp. 85-90, 1964.
62. K. E. Hinshaw, The Effects of Mental Practice on Motor Skills Performance: Critical Evaluation and Meta-Analysis, *Imagination, Cognition and Personality, 11,* pp. 3-35, 1991-92.
63. S. Starker, Two Modes of Visual Imagery, *Perceptual and Motor Skills, 38,* pp. 649-650, 1974.
64. P. S. Highlen and B. B. Bennett, Elite Divers and Wrestlers: A Comparison between Open- and Closed-Skill Athletes, *Journal of Sport Psychology, 5,* pp. 390-409, 1983.

65. B. J. Kolonay, *The Effects of Visuo-motor Behavior Rehearsal on Athletic Performance,* unpublished master's thesis, Hunter College, The City University of New York, 1977.
66. R. M. Suinn, Behavioral Rehearsal Training for Ski Racers, *Behavior Therapy, 3,* p. 519, 1972.
67. R. S. Weinberg, T. J. Seaborne, and A. Jackson, Effects of Visuo-motor Behavior Rehearsal, Relaxation, and Imagery on Karate Performance, *Journal of Sport Psychology, 3,* pp. 228-238, 1981.
68. R. S. Vealey, Imagery Training for Performance Enhancement, in *Applied Sport Psychology: Personal Growth to Peak Performance,* J. M. Williams (ed.), Mayfield, Palo Alto, California, pp. 209-231, 1986.
69. E. Jacobson, Electrophysiology of Mental Activities, *American Journal of Physiology, 94,* pp. 22-34, 1930.
70. P. J. Qualls, The Physiological Measurement of Imagery: An Overview, *Imagination, Cognition and Personality, 2*:2, pp. 89-101, 1982.
71. G. E. Schwartz, S. L. Brown, and G. L. Ahern, Facial Muscle Patterning and Subjective Experience during Affective Imagery: Sex Differences, *Psychophysiology, 17,* pp. 75-82, 1980.
72. R. B. Tower, Imagery Training: A Workshop Model, *Imagination, Cognition and Personality, 2*:2, pp. 153-162, 1982.
73. A. Sheikh and R. Kunzendorf, Imagery, Physiology and Psychosomatic Illness, in *International Review of Mental Imagery,* Vol. 1, A. Sheikh (ed.), Human Sciences Press, New York, pp. 95-138, 1984.
74. A. R. Isaac, Mental Practice: Does It Work in the Field?, *The Sport Psychologist, 6,* pp. 192-198, 1992.
75. G. Kendall, D. Hrycaiko, G. Martin, and T. Kendall, The Effects of an Imagery Rehearsal, Relaxation, and Self-Talk Package on Basketball Game Performance, *Journal of Sport and Exercise Psychology, 12,* pp. 157-166, 1990.
76. N. Wollman, Research on Imagery and Motor Performance: Three Methodological Suggestions, *Journal of Sport Psychology, 8,* pp. 135-138, 1986.
77. W. Rodgers, C. Hall, and E. Buckolz, The Effect of an Imagery Training Program on Imagery Ability, Imagery Use, and Figure Skating Performance, *Journal of Applied Sport Psychology, 3,* pp. 109-125, 1991.
78. R. S. Weinberg and P. Richardson, *Psychology of Officiating,* Human Kinetics, Champaign, Illinois, 1990.
79. D. V. Harris and B. L. Harris, *The Athlete's Guide to Sports Psychology: Mental Skills for Physical People,* Leisure Press, Champaign, Illinois, 1984.
80. K. Henschen, Athletic Staleness and Burnout, in *Applied Sport Psychology: Personal Growth to Peak Performance,* J. M. Williams (ed.), Mayfield, Palo Alto, California, pp. 347-342, 1986.
81. T. Kubistant, *Performing Your Best,* Leisure Press, Champaign, Illinois, 1986.
82. R. J. Rotella and S. R. Heyman, Stress, Injury, and the Psychological Rehabilitation of Athletes, in *Applied Sport Psychology: Personal Growth to Peak Performance,* J. M. Williams (ed.), Mayfield, Palo Alto, California, pp. 343-364, 1986.
83. L. Ievleva and J. Orlick, Mental Links to Enhanced Healing: An Exploratory Study, *The Sport Psychologist, 5,* pp. 25-40, 1991.
84. L. B. Green, The Use of Imagery in the Rehabilitation of Injured Athletes, *The Sport Psychologist, 6,* pp. 416-428, 1992.
85. O. C. Simonton, S. Matthews-Simonton, and J. Creighton, *Getting Well Again,* J. T. Tharcher, Los Angeles, 1978.

86. D. V. Harris, Relaxation and Energizing Techniques for Regulation of Arousal, in *Applied Sport Psychology: Personal Growth to Peak Performance,* J. M. Williams (ed.), Mayfield, Palo Alto, California, pp. 185-207, 1986.
87. R. M. Nideffer, *Athlete's Guide to Mental Training,* Human Kinetics, Champaign, Illinois, 1985.
88. Hemery, *The Pursuit of Sporting Excellence,* Human Kinetics, Champaign, Illinois, 1986.
89. R. Martens, *Coaches Guide to Sport Psychology,* Human Kinetics, Champaign, Illinois, 1982.
90. J. Syer and C. Connolly, *Sporting Mind, Sporting Body,* University Press, Cambridge, Great Britain, 1984.
91. A. J. Budney and R. L. Woolfolk, Using the Wrong Image: An Exploration of the Adverse Effects of Imagery on Motor Performance, *Journal of Mental Imagery, 14,* pp. 75-86, 1990.
92. S. M. Murphy, Models of Imagery in Sport Psychology: A Review, *Journal of Mental Imagery, 14,* pp. 153-172, 1990.

CHAPTER 2

Visualization in Sports

RICHARD M. SUINN

INTRODUCTION

The reliance upon imagery techniques to achieve peak performance in sports is readily noticed among a number of world famous competitive athletes. The Olympic high jumper Dwight Stones is frequently seen, eyes closed, head bobbing, as he develops the image of his approach to and clearing the bar. Alpine ski racer, Jean Claude Killy, is known for his exceptional achievement of winning a gold medal in three Olympic events. Yet an equally important achievement was his ability to prepare for one race with only mental practice, as a result of an injury preventing on-snow practice. Killy believes that this race turned out to be one of his very best performances, despite the lack of physical practice and possibly because of the use of imagery as a substitute. Jack Nicklaus, certainly one of the world's best golfers, provides instruction on his use of imagery as follows:

> I never hit a shot, not even in practice, without having a very sharp, in-focus picture of it in my head. It's like a color movie. First I 'see' the ball where I want it to finish, nice and white and sitting up high on bright green grass. Then the scene quickly changes and I 'see' the ball going there: its path, trajectory and shape, even its behaviour on landing. Then there is a sort of a fade-out, and the next scene shows me making the kind of swing that will turn the images into reality [1, p. 79].

Tennis champion, Chris Evert Lloyd, well respected for her consistent ground strokes, revealed in a radio interview that she painstakingly rehearses before a tournament match. She identifies her opponent's strategies, then prepares herself by visualizing herself countering with her own approach [2]. Bruce Jenner, gold medalist in the decathlon, has also attributed some of his success to the use of mental rehearsal approaches; similarly, Bill Russell in basketball and Dick Fosbury in track have referred to the value of imagery [3, 4]. Bill Glass, former defensive end for the Cleveland Browns football team, concluded that mental imagery aided him to reach the honor of being an All-Pro selection. He visualized himself as in a "motion picture" practicing the quick moves, throwing off the offensive tackle, and aggressively charging the quarterback [5]. In some cases, as with Glass, the athlete's discovery of imagery rehearsal has been through the help of a consultant; on the other hand, many well-known athletes have evolved such techniques on their own initiative during their search for ways of enhancing their levels of performances. With the systematizing of visualization, and with the new research available, visualization has now become not only a standard but a widespread technique employed by athletes and teams. Following the next section on mental practice and definitions, this chapter will focus on one such visualization method.

Mental practice and mental rehearsal are the terms used in early studies of psychological techniques for sport enhancement, and were coined to distinguish such techniques from physical or motor practice. Inasmuch as it was obvious that physically rehearsing a motor skill led to improvements, the question was whether adding mental rehearsal would lend any more to skill acquisition. In 1972, Corbin defined mental practice as the "repetition of a task, without observable movement, with the specific intent of learning" [6, p. 94]. This broad definition considers the term as a generic one, covering a diverse set of activities, which might include closing one's eyes and thinking about a motor movement but without any visual/proprioceptive components, all the way to full-blown imaginal rehearsal with auditory-visual-proprioceptive-emotional elements. Possibly because of the broadness of the term, research on mental practice over a thirty-year period can best be summarized as not always consistent nor conclusive [6-10]. There is some agreement that mental practice frequently has a beneficial effect on either the learning of a new skill or the betterment of performance of an existing skill, although gains were not proven in all research reports. Tentative findings also suggest that experienced athletes profit more from mental practice than novices, that simple motor tasks may be improved more than complex tasks and that distributing mental practice is more useful than massed practice. Unfortunately, one reason for the failure of prior studies to be more conclusive may be related to issues of research design. Different studies have involved different mental practice techniques rather than a standard one, hence the diverse results may be due more to the diverse methods. Standardization has also been missing in even the type of instructions given subjects, for instance, regarding what subjects should be rehearsing in their mental practice (a single movement, a coordinated swing, a visual component, the muscular feeling, the total gestalt, etc.). Finally, what has been needed, is improvement in controls over certain factors under study, such as the level of experience of the subjects, the nature of the task being learned or performed, or the amount and sequence of the practice [11]. One set of researchers drew the conclusion that: "If there is a real difference it is probably due to the *quality* of the mental rehearsal rather than to the *quantity*" [12].

Others have explored the question of whether mental practice is of greater influence in motor tasks with a strong cognitive component (e.g., learning a maze that has been rotated in space) as compared with those with a stronger motor component (e.g., performance on a stabilometer) [13-15]. Thus far, the results are yet inconclusive, with some studies lending support to the special value of mental practice with tasks with a strong cognitive component, while other studies show equally "large effect sizes" with motor-based tasks [7, p. 46]. As a final example of the type of factors needing further control and study is the involvement of internal/external orientation in the application of imagery. As part of a report, Hale briefly summarized some of the research, showing equivocal results [16]. Internal imagery involves "an approximation of the real-life phenomenology such that a person actually images being inside his/her body and experiencing those sensations which might be expected in the actual situation," while external imagery involves "a person view(ing) himself from the perspective of an observer (much like in home movies)" [17]. While some research argues for the reliance upon internal imagery, others either fail to support such a position, or suggest that the locus of the imagery may be influenced by "the individual doing the imagining, but also of the scene being imagined" [16, p. 380, 18-21]. Further, it is possible that taking an external imagery approach leads to the subject also assuming the role of an external, critical-evaluational observer; this in turn may produce distraction or negative self-conscious responses. Finally, the value of an internal or an external orientation could be dependent upon the subject's level of experience with mental rehearsal and resistance to distracting experiences [19].

Overall, theories regarding why mental practice should have an effect on motor performance are yet to be completed. Initial theorizing by Sackett referred to mental practice as affecting skills where there is an "ideational representation of the movement" [22]. Morrisett, expanded on this by proposing that such ideation refers to the associative processes which intervene between the stimulus to the subject and active responding [23]. In one version of this explanation, elements of motor learning are *tried out* during the mental practice. Thus, Schmidt proposed that the subject during mental practice, "can think about what kinds of things might be tried, . . . and the learner can perhaps rule out inappropriate courses of action" [24, p. 520]. Also, mental practice enables the subject to rehearse images or subvocal responses to cue off temporal or spatial sequences involved in the skill ("toss up with the left hand, then bring up the racquet . . .").

A social learning analysis of the effects of modeling in improvement of learning offers a slightly different explanation of the role of cognition [25]. It is hypothesized that learning involves both a step of coding and a step of matching. An overt event, such as a model demonstrating a motor skill, is initially transformed or coded symbolically and stored centrally. The subject then attempts to perform the skill, comparing this performance against the internally stored model, making judgments and correcting errors in further replication efforts. This "conception-matching" process is completed at the point that the performance feedback matches the internally coded model. By this explanation, the coding may rely upon either verbal coding or by visual imagery coding [26]. Mental practice thereby becomes a method for enhancing coding, either through rehearsal of the verbal or the visual systems. Jowdy and Harris interviewed jugglers as they used imagery for training and received reports that "Many subjects . . . created the image of a particular action and then tried to duplicate the imaged action . . . like copying the image" [20, p. 197].

One other explanation deserves attention regarding mental practice, and this can be called the ideo-motor or neuromuscular innervation theory. Carpenter postulated that imagined movements are transformed into low level neuromuscular responses; further, that these responses are identical to those involved in actual physical practice except in magnitude [27]. Therefore, mental practice would be said to actually include a level of physical practice (and thus include more activity than simply symbolic trials or coding behaviors). Some case studies have illustrated EMG activity that seems to mirror the motor actions being mentally imagined; however, there is still question regarding whether such activity is restricted only to the bodily sites innervated during true physical activity or is more generalized [7, 20, 28-30]. Harris and Robinson reported EMG activity during imagery that was "specific to the muscle (normally) . . . activated in overtly executing the task" [31, p. 109], with such localized muscle innervation being greater for advanced skill subjects. An interesting speculation is the possibility that certain forms of mental practice, such as to be described later may actually be a means of accessing the right hemisphere. Hatfield, Landers, and Ray discovered that marksmen shift from left to right hemisphere activity during competitive shooting [32]. The question has been raised, entirely speculatively by Suinn, regarding whether mental practice extends physical practice through storing or otherwise involving the right hemisphere in acquisition-storage that might lead to *automatic* performance. Peak performances are often described as involving such automatic behaviors; mental practice through visualization has been applied to enhance such peak performance; research could well explore the possible relationships among mental practice, locus of brain involvement during such practice, automatic behaviors, and associations with enhanced performance.

DEFINITIONS AND DISTINCTIONS

As indicated earlier, the terms mental practice and mental rehearsal were initially coined to distinguish a variety of methods from physical practice. These terms might best be defined as a more embracing, generic category of any form of covert practice or symbolic rehearsal, such as simply thinking through a motor action. In this chapter, the term imagery rehearsal shall be used to represent a more narrow version of mental practice. Specifically, it shall mean covert practice whereby imagery is the dominant mode of the mental practice experience. In this mode, the mental practice emphasizes having persons actually try to realistically capture all of the sensory-proprioceptive-emotional aspects of the task and the environment. Imagery rehearsal is involved when a person undergoes a hypnotically induced reintegration of a prior experience. When an athlete reports a flashback memory of a disastrous fall and injury, imagery may be inferred.

Drug-induced hallucinatory experiences that appear realistic, or sensory memories reproduced through direct stimulation of brain cells may be viewed as examples of imagery. Unlike other forms of mental practice, imagery rehearsal goes beyond the more sparse, unidimensional process of intellectually recalling an event. In contrast to the mental practice instruction of "Close your eyes and think about making the free throw," imagery techniques actually seek a full-dimensional re-experiencing of the event: "Be there in the situation again . . . so that you are aware of where you are, what's around you, who's with you . . . you're actually on the basketball court again, score is all tied, the crowd is especially vocal, you have the ball in your hands, can feel the firmness as you bounce it several times. . . ." One useful analog is to consider imagery as more similar to dreams than to attempts to retrieve an experience through thinking it over. Dreams appear so realistically that sometimes the dreamer actually is surprised that they are not real. In dreams, it is possible to be swept up in the activities, in the events that are evolving, in the awareness of the environment. On the other hand, imagery rehearsal differs from dreams in the amount of control. Dreams appear to have their own life and not only resist being manipulated, but the dream topic also seems to appear randomly. In contrast, imagery rehearsal events are selected ahead of time by the person, and the sequence of activities are under control and direction. It is as if the athlete were able to select a specific portion of a movie in which he/she was filmed, switch on the projector, be instantly transported into the movie so as to re-experience the entire scene, but yet retain the control of a movie director who could alter the script or ask for an instant replay.

One of the most systematically described and researched versions of imagery rehearsal is called *visual motor behavior rehearsal* (VMBR) [33]. VMBR follows specific steps, including relaxation followed by the use of imagery to practice aspects of motor performances. In common with imagery rehearsal, generally, VMBR is a covert activity which involves sensory-motor sensations that reintegrate reality behaviors, and which include neuromuscular, physiological, and emotional involvement. Elsewhere I have described the VMBR activity as follows:

> The imagery of visuo-motor behavior rehearsal apparently is more than sheer imagination. It is a well-controlled copy of experience, a sort of body-thinking similar to the powerful illusion of certain dreams at night. . . . This imagery is more than visual. It is also tactile, auditory, emotional, and muscular. One swimmer reported that the scene in her mind changed from black and white to color as soon as she dove mentally into a pool, and she could feel the coldness of the water. A skier who qualified for the U.S. Alpine ski team experienced the same "irritability" that she felt during actual races, when she mentally practiced being in the starting gate. Without fail, athletes feel their muscles in action as they rehearse their sport. One professional racer who took the training actually moved his boots when skiing a slalom course in his mind" [34, pp. 40-41].

The advantage of imagery rehearsal over other versions of mental practice is in the principle governing learning: that learning is enhanced to the degree that the conditions of practice are similar to those of (game) conditions, under which the performance is to be later exhibited. If we consider a continuum of degree of similarity, then thinking about making a free throw is somewhat similar to the actual free throw during a game; imagining making a free throw *as if* the crowd were present would be much more similar than thinking, and using imagery rehearsal would be the closest to actually making the free throw during the real game itself.

There are several advantages of VMBR as a form of imagery rehearsal. First, VMBR is a standardized training method that is subject to description and therefore replication. Secondly, the use of VMBR does not seem to demand special skills such as required, for instance, in the development of imagery using hypnosis. Finally, VMBR has been subject to research and there are now available published reports on its efficacy. For these reasons, the rest of the chapter will be devoted to in-depth description of VMBR, its various applications (goals for which VMBR can be used), and a summary of the research on its usage.

VISUAL MOTOR BEHAVIOR REHEARSAL

Visual Motor Behavior Rehearsal has its origins in the techniques used in behavior therapy, which rely upon imagery rehearsal for anxiety reduction. Desensitization and Anxiety Management Training both begin with relaxation training, followed by imagery related to anxiety to phobic situations. The goal of each is to train the client to be in anxiety-related settings but with the achievement of a relaxed, rather than an anxiety, state. In essence, these behavior therapies emphasize retraining of the emotional aspects of the situations [35-37]. Because of my experience with these methods, an executive sought help for his problem of presenting poorly when faced with his routine reports to his superiors. Although having a medical history involving surgical treatment of his vocal cords, the weakness he experienced during such presentations was not considered a factor by his physician. Desensitization was considered as a treatment; however, this executive did not report any anxiety or tension. For this reason, I decided to alter the traditional desensitization technique, retaining the concept of using imagery, but changing the procedures and goals so as to strengthen correct public speaking skills, instead of dealing with anxiety. Essentially, the imagery portion of desensitization was revised to become a form of mental practice. With the successful application of this approach to mental practice, the procedure was refined and applied to other cases involving skill enhancement, such as music performance [38]. Simultaneously, members of an Alpine ski racing team sought consultation for competitive performance enhancement, a research study was organized, and the term visual motor behavior rehearsal coined to reflect this approach with athletic teams [39]. For the next number of years, VMBR was used with various

Olympic team members, and further refined and studied, until it appeared to deserve attention as a meaningful type of imagery rehearsal technique.

VMBR can be provided in either an individual or a group format. The individual format shall be described here (for information on the group approach, see [34]). As an overview, VMBR involves a set of training steps in addition to decisions about the content of the imagery, based upon goals. Although the minimum number of training sessions depends upon the goals and the pace of learning the technique of the athlete, initial benefits of VMBR probably would not be expected until three to four sessions are completed. Each session runs forty-five to sixty minutes at the start, with later sessions being tailored to the athlete and circumstances; such later sessions may be as brief as a few minutes (similar to the visualization preparation taken by Stones, Nicklaus, etc., while in the competitive event itself). The main training should take place in a quiet locale, typically with recliners or comfortable mats; however, later applications with athletes experienced with VMBR can take place at the competition site. In general, a VMBR session begins with a preinterview, goes to specific relaxation/imagery exercises, ends with a postinterview, and assigns homework. Since VMBR involves the development of a skill, namely in relaxation and imagery rehearsal, the homework is intended to enable practice and therefore improvement of the skill.

The preinterviews will cover several topics at different stages of training: to determine the athlete's past experience with relaxation training, to deal with questions and possible misunderstandings or expectations, and later to determine how well the athlete is acquiring the ability to relax and to develop controlled imagery, to monitor homework practice and possible problems, and to seek progress information on recent competitive experiences. Postinterviews at the end of each VMBR session are essentially used to trace the progress during the session: was relaxation readily achieved, what procedures seem to expedite such relaxation, how useful was the imagery-scene for the goal being sought, how controlled were the scenes (in vividness, clarity)? Some common issues surfacing during the preinterview concerns the fact that VMBR is not a form of hypnosis, that the training involves development of a skill which is under the control of the athlete, and that practice is an important contributor to VMBR gains. Postinterview topics that are common include the reassurance that imagery will occasionally be incomplete for some athletes in early sessions (but should improve with practice), that an internal perspective ("being in your body") is preferred to an external or observer perspective, and that athletes should select and remain with the single imagery scene that is best associated with the goals of the session.

Session One

Session One will involve three phases: selection of imagery scenes, relaxation exercise, and visualization exercise. Two types of scenes are used—a scene to cue off relaxation responses, and a competition scene involving a successful event. Scenes are discussed with the athlete with emphasis on specificity and concreteness. The relaxation scene, for example, must be a real circumstance: "an activity, an event, that is familiar to you, a real situation, which was characterized by relaxation." One athlete might recall a meadow during a backpacking trip, taken in the fall in the Rockies—the specific time when he/she was sitting in the shade listening to a brook and gazing at the clouds. Elements of the scene would identify location, time, activity, surroundings, and "any and all sensory experiences that help make this scene realistic." In the same way, a successful competition is recalled; it may be one involving a personal best or a peak experience or a performance that was satisfying in some other way, such as, where the athlete felt especially focused or concentrated well, or particularly free and loose, etc. These scenes are described in detail by the athlete; writing the descriptions on a 3 x 5 index card can enable later examination to insure that the details confirm the description to be that of a real experience, rather than a fantasized one, or an ideal one, or a composite of several experiences.

Relaxation training follows the identification of scenes. To facilitate training, the athlete reclines on an adjustable chair (or on a floor mat), has the exercise explained, and is then instructed to close his/her eyes and to follow the relaxation exercise instructions. Since a brief form of the Jacobsen deep muscle relaxation exercise is used, it is appropriate to explain that this procedure is an isometric exercise, whereby muscle groups are first tensed, then released [40]. To focus attention and thoughts, the athlete is told to note the contrast effect between the feelings of tensing versus the feelings after muscles are released. This aspect of training normally takes from twenty to thirty minutes, and is the foundation for the next phase, visualization.

Visualization begins with the instruction to "switch on" the relaxation scene, as clearly as possible, "so as to really be there again, using all the sensory experiences to be in that circumstance again, noticing the sense of further relaxation." A hand signal is called for to indicate when "any part of this scene is clear." The scene is retained for about thirty to forty-five seconds before the instruction is given to switch off the scene and to return to continuing the muscle relaxation, through "continuing to let each muscle relax even further . . . the right hand . . . forearm . . . right upper arm . . . etc." A deep breath is requested as a further method for controlling the relaxation, and eventually as a future cue for initiating relaxation. The relaxation scene is again initiated, with the request to "signal when you're into the scene." The relaxation scene serves two functions: a means of further enhancement of the athlete's level of relaxation, and a method for introducing the athlete to visualization. Care should be taken to have the relaxation scene as one that is truly relaxing rather than effortful. To be avoided would be situations involving sleeping, being relaxed after strenuous exercise (that is, being tired), or relaxed sensations attributed to alcohol or drugs. Useful scenes involve activities such as quiet reading of a favorite story, lounging on the beach, or a peaceful stroll down a comfortable path. For some athletes, a recreational scene might be acceptable where a quiet scene is unavailable, such as free skiing down a favorite slope, or easy swimming around a lake.

The next scene involves a successful competitive experience. This scene makes the transition from the relaxation scene to the first athletic scene. By using a successful event, the experience begins with a favorable one and avoids distracting responses. As with the relaxation scene, this scene is drawn from a real experience, and the visualization should be such that the athlete is re-experiencing the event in a first-person way, and not as an observer who is watching a film. Signals are used to denote the onset of the scene, the scene is repeated twice, and after each repetition muscle relaxation review is conducted, along with the deep breath. Upon completion of the last repetition, the athlete is instructed to sit up in preparation for the postinterview.

The postinterview collects information about progress and on topics to enhance future progress. Covered are items such as how well the relaxation proceeded, what parts of the exercise helped, how clear and controlled were the scenes, etc. It occasionally occurs that a particular athlete may experience partial relaxation, or have difficulty with a muscle group seeming to remain tight, or have some scene drifting or changing of scenes. Reassurances should be given that complete relaxation of all muscles is less important than the total level of overall relaxation, that relaxation homework should help in bettering this level, and that scene control should improve with later sessions (but should be monitored). Sometimes, the drifting or the changing of scenes is prevented through more thorough preinterview describing of the scene details, and through the athlete's making a clear choice regarding the one relaxation and the one competition scene that is the most relevant. Homework involves practicing the tension relaxation exercise five times during the next seven days, without visualization of any scenes. To prevent rushing through the exercise, the athlete is told to set aside forty-five minutes of uninterrupted time in a quiet locale, such as during the evening while in bed.

Session Two

Session Two builds on the first session and is dependent upon the progress made at the first session and during homework practice. There are six steps involved: identification of a new competition scene, relaxation exercise, use of relaxation scene, use of successful competition scene, use of new competition scene, and end of session with the successful competition scene again. As with all sessions, pre and postinterviews are conducted to determine progress. The new competition scene is one that is selected to match the goals of the VMBR training. Such goals will be elaborated upon later in this chapter. Briefly, VMBR may be aimed at technique enhancement, error analysis and correction, preparation for competition, and confidence enhancement. The specific new scene selected should be one which enables achieving whichever of these goals were selected.

For instance, if technique enhancement is the intended outcome, then the new scene would involve one whereby the technique in question was emphasized. For a ski racer who wishes to improve the technique involved in starts, the scene would involve being at a meet at the moment of preparing and going through the starting gate. For a gymnast who wishes to improve the dismount off the balance beam, the scene would be the moments prior to and including the movements of the dismount. A tennis player may wish to include a scene practicing a cross-court return of serve. As before, the scene selected must be a real event and not a fantasized one. Given the homework involving practicing relaxation, the athlete should have good control of the muscle relaxation exercise. Therefore, the relaxation instructions initiated in this session will be briefer. This is accomplished through elimination of the tensing steps. Instead the athlete is simply instructed to sit back on the recliner, close the eyes, and direct attention to "letting each muscle group become more relaxed . . . starting with the right hand . . . letting the muscles become loose and relaxed . . . as they had been in the prior session . . . then moving to the right forearm and upper arm, letting the tension be replaced by increased relaxation. . . " The pace of the instruction should be such that the athlete has sufficient time to hear what muscle group is to be involved, and to have about thirty to forty seconds to focus attention on relaxation of that muscle. When the entire body has been covered, the deep breath can be called for, and a general instruction used, such as "continue to relax your entire body . . . if there are any areas you want to further relax, take a few moments to do so . . . use the deep breath also as a further way of increasing the level of your relaxation."

Following the relaxation, the relaxation scene is then used for two repetitions. This is followed by two repetitions of the successful competition scene, with instructions to be more aware of "bodily sensations associated with the successful performance," such as ease and fluidness, the sense of confidence in one's skills, and what the athlete keyed on that was contributing to the successful performance. At various times following the completion of a successful competition or the new competition scene, a brief review of the muscle groups to insure the retention of relaxation is desirable. Finally, the new competition scene is covered, using two repetitions. As before, all scenes are retained for thirty to forty-five seconds for each repetition. The content of the scene remains a function of the goals. Scenes may involve a lengthy sequence or repeats of a short sequence of activities. As an example, in order to improve on retaining concentration throughout, a tennis player might visualize playing out a point—from the serve to the end of that point. However, another tennis competitor, whose goal is to change the ball toss, will visualize only the service—visualizing the preparation for the serve, the toss of the ball, the full swing, and the completion of the serve—without necessarily completing the point. In this latter case the athlete will repeat this part of the scene as many times as fits into the thirty to forty-five seconds. The time allotted does not follow a hard and fast rule; for the lengthier sequence scene, the athlete should be given the instruction, "switch on the new competition scene . . . the one involving . . . you will be focusing on . . . when you have completed that scene, signal me." For scenes involving repetition of segments of the activity, the thirty to forty-five second timing is a reasonable approximation. The session ends with repeat of the successful competition scene so as to provide the athlete with an ending to the session that is a positive one. Homework involves practicing relaxation without the tensing, for about one to five minutes several times during the day.

Session Three

This session covers the same steps as in the prior session, except for the initial relaxation. Instead of the muscle review being conducted by the trainer, the athlete is told to initiate the relaxation on his/her own, using whatever methods seems to best cue off the relaxation (such as the deep breath, a relaxation scene, focusing on some muscles, etc.), and to signal the achievement of a comfortable level. A relaxation scene is repeated twice, followed by the successful competition scene, the other competition scene to achieve VMBR goals, and terminating the session with use again of the successful competition scene. Session Three will typically run thirty to forty-five minutes. Homework expands the application of relaxation such that the athlete now initiates it on the field/gymnasium during practice or prior to competition. Brief visualization of the sport skill is also used prior to performances if the athlete has demonstrated good control during sessions, and seems prepared for the use of visualization during competition. For most athletes, a few more training sessions along the content of Session Three will provide the foundation for such transfer to the in vivo environment. I have conducted twenty minutes of VMBR the evening before an Olympic event, and about five minutes of visualization immediately prior to the actual event. Well trained athletes can initiate visualization themselves as part of their warm-up procedures. The eventual total number of VMBR sessions will be a function of the progress of the athlete toward each goal, and the total number of goals set for the training. As the competitive season moves along, goals may change along with the physical progress and competitive experience of the athlete, and further sessions may be tailor-made to accommodate such change.

GOALS OF VMBR TRAINING

As indicated earlier, the types of goals will determine the content of the VMBR experience. In essence, VMBR is a tool that is only as valuable as its proper application. The value of VMBR probably derives from two factors. First, performance may be enhanced due to visualization activities precipitating neuromuscular and possibly central nervous system correlates. As hypothesized earlier, this may be related to encoding, to matching, or even possibly to direct neuromuscular innervation, leading possibly to storing the results as muscle memory or in right brain hemisphere locations. In case illustrations of VMBR, I have demonstrated the similarity of EMG activity within muscle groups to that anticipated by the imagery scenes being rehearsed by the athlete [29, 41]. In one case, the athlete visualized racing a downhill course, going over jumps, rough areas, and skidding to a halt at the finish line. The EMG recordings appeared to duplicate the level of intense motor activity that one would expect at various places on the course. In another demonstration, EMG readings during noneffortful visualization was compared with that of an effortful scene. Once more, the EMG activity appeared to match that expected of the particular scene—with bursts of activity occurring during the effortful, running scene, and none during the quiet-activity scene.

A second factor influencing performance with VMBR practice is the content of the scenes. Consider the possibility that VMBR is similar to entering a program into the human body as if it were a computer. Then the nature of the results would be a reflection of the adequacy of the program being entered. If the scenes being rehearsed are improper, then the eventual performance would in all likelihood be poor. In one study, one group of golfers was instructed to visualize correct putting, while another visualized incorrect responses [42]. Results showed that the correct practice group improved over a no-visualization group, while the incorrect practice group showed performance deterioration. In effect, the principle of VMBR appears to be that *correct practice makes perfect* while *incorrect practice makes for imperfection.* Avoidance of such imperfect use of VMBR argues strongly for careful analysis during goal setting. The psychologist must be well trained in behavioral analysis of sport activities, breaking down the broad concerns of the athlete into specific behaviors. What does *losing concentration* mean, or what actions are represented by the term "being more aggressive"? Where the athlete lacks accurate understanding of the variables involved in his/her performance, consultation with others may be essential, such as with coaches, biomechanists, or kineseologists.

The various goals of VMBR deserve elaboration. Regarding *technique enhancement*, VMBR is used to improve a motor skill. The motor-skill may be acquiring a new gymnastic or ice skating routine, putting together a new dive, improving on a golf or tennis follow-through, quickening the timing on a start or power move or move off the ball, or practicing fluidity of ease or gracefulness in a dance step or karate form. The visualization of the golf stroke by Nicklaus, and the quick-step by Glass, are examples of technique enhancement. The rehearsal may be for the purpose of acquiring a new skill or of strengthening an existing skill to the point of it being second nature. In some circumstances, the technique rehearsed may be a "key" associated with a pattern of motions, such as attending to the rhythm of movements, or focusing on the sense of driving the shoulder through a spot or even rehearsing the idea of funneling force into a lift or outward on a throw. Certainly the technique may be more of the nature of being strategies. Chris Evert Lloyd's rehearsal of counter-moves to her opponent's strength would be a form of strategy. I have involved a runner in rehearsing different strategies if the field is wet or dry, or with a headwind or in the absence of such wind. Further, I have trained cross-country runners in monitoring their physical condition, then adjusting with the appropriate change to meet adverse conditions (such as altering stride in response to energy depletion). Even simple strategies can be visualized and rehearsed, such as practicing taking a moment to slow down and recover after a stressful point or to reestablish calmness instead of continuing to feel rushed.

A second goal of VMBR is its use for error analysis and correction. The visualization involved goes beyond the intellectual activity of thinking about or attempting to recall and reconstruct an event. Instead, when the athlete "switches on" a competition scene, it is as if a movie switch were turned on, activating the complete and exact details of the event. Unlike a movie, the athlete is not sitting and watching, but is actually experiencing the event in a first-person way. However, it *is* possible to call into action active monitoring and an observer role. In this approach, VMBR becomes a type of instant replay enabling the athlete to closely attend to what went on. A major application is the re-experiencing of a recent competition that did not go well, such as a skating or gymnastic routine or slalom race or ski jumping event in which a fall occurred. Certainly athletes will have their own remembrance of what they think happened, and in some cases athletes will be adamant about the accuracy of the recall, until being shown a videotape replay! VMBR can be another method for re-analyzing an event in order to identify the problem. In one instance, a ski racer was absolutely certain that his fall on the seventh gate was because the snow conditions were slightly different at that point. However, using VMBR the racer observed instead that he had actually had his weight on the wrong ski and that it was not the snow conditions that had been at fault. Following such VMBR analysis, it is always important to provide for error correction. Thus, the skier was instructed to repeat the same race, but this time to keep his weight on his downhill edge. In a similar fashion, another skier used VMBR to eliminate a prior weekend's error—she had identified her fall as due to an unanticipated bump that affected her rhythm. VMBR was then utilized whereby she "pushed off" the bump, using it in her favor as a means of accelerating to the next gate. This error correction not only makes prior competitive events into experiences for further learning, but also goes a long way toward enabling an athlete to put aside a poor competitive performance and look ahead positively to the future.

A third goal of VMBR is the preparation of the athlete for a forthcoming competitive event. Physical preparation on a practice field or practice court, or against a practice opponent tends to fall short of replicating the exact conditions of the actual competition. The practice court does not replicate the environment when a spectator crowd joins in, nor can the practice field anticipate the weather at game time. Football teams assign their second string players the task of running plays of the opposition, and boxers rely upon sparring partners; but everyone realizes that such opponents do not duplicate even the personalities, much less the skill levels of real opponents. VMBR can help an athlete to prepare for conditions, for opponents, and for circumstances. Regarding weather conditions, it is possible to visualize performing in wind, rain, snow, humid weather, etc. Since an athlete is not able to control such conditions, he/she must be prepared psychologically to cope with whatever weather occurs at the time. Ski jumpers become worried about wind gusts, nevertheless they must accept the judges' signal to take the jump. Regarding opponents, VMBR was used with a volleyball team in preparation for facing the usually intimidating UCLA team, as well as to prepare to cope with the awesome noise of the Paley Pavilion. Similar preparation was underway for the U.S. Women's Track and Field Team for the 1980 Moscow Olympic Games. I have also used VMBR with a fencer in anticipation of facing an opponent with a unique style, or the hazards of biased judges that interfere with concentration. VMBR can not only present the athlete with the external factors likely to be present but can also enhance internal preparation through improved emotional control, and strategic planning. This goal is particularly relevant for those athletes who seem to do well on the practice court/field but who are not able to transfer their training to the demands of real competition.

A fourth goal of VMBR is confidence enhancement. In some aspects, confidence becomes a byproduct of proper preparation. One runner used VMBR to practice what he would do under different weather conditions and different competitive circumstances, such as if the pace of the race was faster than he anticipated. He also practiced visualizing the course itself in order to have a firmer memory of it. He later reported that he felt extremely confident inasmuch as he had practiced for every possible contingency, and had run the race "in my mind so many times" that nothing could go wrong. In a more direct approach, VMBR can also aid in confidence through the use of the successful competition scene. This repetition provides the athlete with evidence of his/her abilities and accomplishments. Further, when the successful scene is used as a means of focusing on what factors contribute to such success (proper training, personal talent, experience, practice, concentration on certain "keys," etc.), the athlete is able to acknowledge a readiness to compete well. Finally, for some athletes, the concept of positive affirmations may be of some help. Coaches have often introduced positive self-statements as a method of training. Current beliefs among cognitively oriented behavioral psychologists confirm that thoughts and self-statements can influence performance. In this way, VMBR can also be used for rehearsal of positive affirmations, such as "I have trained hard and well, I'm better prepared for any conditions than anyone else, I'm going to have the best day of my career."

RESEARCH FOUNDATIONS OF VMBR

VMBR research began more from case study illustrations, but has become sophisticated, perhaps because the technique is methodologically systematic and more subject to research. Several conclusions seem supported by a series of studies by different researchers:

• VMBR training does appear to contribute to enhancement of sport performance, across a variety of different sports. Single-case designs as well as group studies have examined the efficacy of VMBR with tasks ranging from basketball to tennis to diving [43-46]. Gravel, Lemieux, and Ladouceur [47]; Hall and Erffmeyer [48]; Kolonay [49]; Nideffer [50]; Noel [51]; Prediger [52]; Suinn [39]; Suinn, Morton, and Brammell [53]. Weinberg and his colleagues [54] have added research using a placebo controlled group and further confirmed the value of VMBR.

• The VMBR approach to mental practice does seem to require the synergistic effect of relaxation plus mental imagery. As cited earlier, VMBR differs from other versions of mental rehearsal in its reliance upon the two elements of relaxation training followed by visualization. As early as 1977, Kolonay conducted a component analysis study, whereby VMBR was contrasted with groups using relaxation alone or mental imagery alone. Results with accuracy of basketball free throws across several varsity teams supported the combination relaxation and imagery, i.e., the VMBR approach. With karate students, Weinberg et al. also confirmed this same finding. Furthermore, Weinberg et al. were able to demonstrate that, although VMBR does also reduce anxiety, the performance enhancement effects are not simply because of anxiety reduction [55]. The content of VMBR scenes is important since VMBR appears to be a powerful tool. Noel discovered that VMBR did in fact lead to improvements in the service accuracy of skilled tennis players. However, novices actually worsened. One probable interpretation of this is the notion that VMBR involves practice, and imperfect practice might be expected to lead to imperfect performance. Woolfolk et al. were able to demonstrate that visualizing incorrect putting caused performance deterioration, in contrast to visualizing correct golf strokes. Such findings are also consistent with those of others who conclude that mental practice can not only enhance, but also has the potential for worsening motor performance [42, 56, 57].

CONCLUDING STATEMENTS

This chapter has centered on the use of mental practice as a means of improving on sport performance. Emphasis has been placed upon visual motor behavior rehearsal as a specific, systematic approach to such practice—a technique which has become a standard method for sport psychology training [58]. In closing, several comments deserve attention [59]:

1. VMBR has been subject to sufficient research and applications as to be considered a reasonable procedure for mental rehearsal or visualization

training. By reason of the existence of a standard description of the technique, VMBR might also be a valid base for future research aimed at understanding the mechanisms and variables affecting mental practice.

2. VMBR is in itself no more than a tool [60]. As a tool, its application will be influenced by a number of variables. Primary is the varying goals which the athlete seeks to achieve through the application of VMBR. Additionally, the design of the scenes to reach such goals would be determined by careful analysis of steps needed to achieve such goals. Experienced, insightful athletes might be competent at such analysis with the aid of a qualified sport psychologist. The involvement of coaches, other professionals (such as a kinesiologist), on-site observations, and other modes for achieving such analyses might all be necessary.

3. VMBR is a type of practice, specifically mental practice. Physical practice or training programs do not remain unchanged, but are adjusted to the needs of the athlete, the competitive experience, and the amount of time before the next event. Some athletes may require greater use of VMBR sessions for confidence enhancement. Prior to the season, during the learning phase, VMBR might address the acquisition of a new move to add to the athlete's competition routine. As the season wears on, VMBR may shift to briefer "booster" sessions to strengthen a technique, or sessions aimed at preparing for the next opponent's characteristics. Regarding the influence of time prior to the next event, one pattern might be: first session following last competition might focus on error analysis and correction; next session might focus on strengthening the corrected actions as well as preparation for the forthcoming competition; next session might focus on the one goal considered essential for enhanced performance at the next competition; night before might emphasize a brief VMBR followed by emphasis on relaxation; day of competition could emphasize brief relaxation exercises to maintain composure and comfort, along with a brief visualization just prior to the event; etc.

4. VMBR is a skill, and training is essential. As noted in the description of the VMBR training steps, relaxation is shortened and the visualization content is altered as the athlete shows progress. As a skill, VMBR demands practice. As a skill that builds on each step, the successful achievement of one step permits the movement to the next step. Over-night and dramatic changes in performance levels would be no more realistically expected of VMBR than following the first day of weight training or a new diet.

5. Performance enhancement of athletic skills is the end product of a number of factors [29]. Among these are the level of physical skill, the amount of prior experience as a competitor, the presence of incorrect responses, and the availability and strength of correct psychological responses. Extensive psychological training procedures have been designed, which include VMBR. Among such procedures are basic relaxation, stress management,

thought management, energy management, concentration training, and self-regulation training [58]. In effect, VMBR alone may not be the sole factor in improved performance. However, in the context of other training, VMBR can be one factor of importance.

REFERENCES

1. J. Nicklaus, *Golf My Way,* Simon & Schuster, New York, 1974.
2. A. Lazarus, *In the Mind's Eye,* Rawson, New York, 1977.
3. W. Russell and L. Branch, *Second Wind: The Memoirs of an Opinionated Man,* Random House, New York, 1979.
4. R. Fosbury, Fosbury on Flopping, *Track Technique, 55,* pp. 1749-1750, 1974.
5. W. Furlong, Coping, the Power of Imagination, *Quest,* pp. 95-96, May 1979.
6. C. Corbin, Mental Practice, in *Ergogenic Aids and Muscular Performance,* W. Morgan (ed.), Academic Press, New York, 1972.
7. D. Feltz and D. Landers, The Effects of Mental Practice on Motor Skill Learning and Performance: A Meta-analysis, *Journal of Sport Psychology, 5,* pp. 25-57, 1983.
8. J. Oxendine, *Psychology of Motor Learning,* Meredith, New York, 1968.
9. A. Richardson, Mental Practice: A Review and Discussion, Part I, *Research Quarterly, 38,* pp. 95-107, 1967a.
10. A. Richardson, Mental Practice: A Review and Discussion, Part II, *Research Quarterly, 38,* pp. 263-273, 1967b.
11. R. Suinn, Imagery and Sports, in *Imagery, Current Theory, Research and Application,* A. Sheikh (ed.), John Wiley and Sons, New York, 1982.
12. E. D. Ryan and J. Simons, What is Learned in Mental Practice of Motor Skills: A Test of the Cognitive-motor Hypothesis, *Journal of Sport Psychology, 5*:4, pp. 419-426, 1983.
13. D. Housner, The Role of Visual Imagery in Recall of Modeled Motoric Stimuli, *Journal of Sport Psychology, 6*:2, pp. 148-158, 1984.
14. E. D. Ryan and J. Simons, Cognitive Demand, Imagery, and Frequency of Mental Rehearsal as Factors Influencing Acquisition of Motor Skills, *Journal of Sport Psychology, 3,* pp. 35-45, 1981.
15. C. Wrisberg and M. Ragsdale, Cognitive Demand and Practice Level: Factors in the Mental Rehearsal of Motor Skills, *Journal of Human Movement Studies, 5,* pp. 201-208, 1979.
16. B. D. Hale, The Effects of Internal and External Imagery on Muscular and Ocular Concomitant, *Journal of Sport Psychology, 4*:4, pp. 379-387, 1982.
17. M. Mahoney and M. Avener, Psychology of the Elite Athlete: An Exploratory Study, *Cognitive Therapy and Research, 1,* pp. 135-141, 1977.
18. L. A. Doyle and D. M. Landers, *Psychological Skills in Elite and Subelite Shooters,* unpublished manuscript, 1980.
19. M. L. Epstein, The Relationship of Mental Imagery and Mental Rehearsal to Performance of a Motor Task, *Journal of Sport Psychology, 2*:3, pp. 211-220, 1980.
20. D. P. Jowdy and D. V. Harris, Muscular Responses During Mental Imagery as a Function of Motor Skill Level, *Journal of Sport and Exercise Psychology, 12,* pp. 191-201, 1990.
21. S. M. Murphy, D. P. Jowdy, and S. K. Durtschi, *Report on the United States Olympic Committee Survey on Imagery Use in Sport: 1989,* U.S. Olympic Training Center, Colorado Springs, Colorado, 1989.

22. R. Sackett, The Influence of Symbolic Rehearsal upon the Retention of a Maze Habit, *Journal of General Psychology, 10,* pp. 376-395, 1934.
23. L. Morrisett, *The Role of Implicit Practice on Learning,* unpublished doctoral dissertation, Yale University, 1956.
24. R. Schmidt, *Motor Control and Learning: A Behavioral Emphasis,* Human Kinetics, Champaign, Illinois, 1982.
25. W. Carroll and A. Bandura, The Role of Visual Monitoring in Observational Learning of Action Patterns: Making the Unobservable Observable, *Journal of Motor Behavior, 14,* pp. 152-167, 1982.
26. R. Jeffrey, The Influence of Symbolic and Motor Rehearsal in Observational Learning, *Journal of Research in Personality, 10,* pp. 116-127, 1976.
27. W. Carpenter, *Principles of Mental Physiology* (4th Edition), Appleton, New York, 1984.
28. D. MacKay, The Problem of Rehearsal or Mental Practice, *Journal of Motor Behavior, 13,* pp. 274-285, 1981.
29. R. Suinn, Psychology and Sports Performance: Principles and Applications, in *Psychology in Sports: Methods and Applications,* R. Suinn (ed.), Burgess Publishing, Minneapolis, Minnesota, 1980a.
30. R. Suinn, *Visuo-motor Behavior Rehearsal: A Demonstration,* Videotape Demonstration, ABC Television, Long Beach, California, 1984a.
31. D. V. Harris and W. J. Robinson, The Effects of Skill Level on EMG Activity during Internal and External Imagery, *Journal of Sport Psychology, 8,* pp. 105-111, 1986.
32. B. Hatfield, D. Landers, and W. Ray, Cognitive Processes during Self-paced Motor Performance: An Electroencephalographic Profile of Skilled Marksmen, *Journal of Sport Psychology, 6,* pp. 42-59, 1984.
33. R. Suinn, Visual Motor Behavior Rehearsal: The Basic Technique, *Scandinavian Journal of Behavior Therapy, 13,* pp. 131-142, 1984b.
34. R. Suinn, Body Thinking for Olympic Champs, *Psychology Today, 36,* pp. 38-43, 1976a.
35. R. Suinn, *Anxiety Management Training: A Behavior Therapy,* Plenum Press, New York, 1990.
36. R. Suinn and F. Richardson, Anxiety Management Training: A Non-specific Behavior Therapy Program for Anxiety Control, *Behavior Therapy, 4,* p. 498, 1971.
37. R. Woolfolk, S. Murphy, D. Gottesfeld, and D. Aitken, Effects of Mental Rehearsal of Task Motor Activity and Mental Depiction of Task Outcome on Motor Skill Performance, *Journal of Sport Psychology, 7,* pp. 191-197, 1985.
38. R. Suinn, Visual Motor Behavior Rehearsal for Adaptive Behavior, in *Counseling Methods,* J. Krumboltz and C. Thoresen (eds.), Holt, New York, 1976b.
39. R. Suinn, Behavior Rehearsal Training for Ski Racers, *Behavior Therapy, 3,* p. 519, 1972.
40. R. Suinn, Muscle Relaxation Exercise, in *Psychology in Sports: Methods and Applications,* R. Suinn (ed.), Burgess, Minneapolis, Minnesota, 1980b.
41. R. Suinn, Imagery and Sports, in *Imagery, Current Theory, Research and Application,* A. Sheikh (ed.), John Wiley and Sons, New York, 1983.
42. R. Woolfolk, S. Murphy, and M. Parrish, *The Effects of Imagery on Motor Skill Performance,* presented at World Congress of Behavior Therapy, Washington, D.C., 1983.
43. J. D. Andre and J. R. Means, Rate of Imagery in Mental Practice: An Experimental Investigation, *Journal of Sport Psychology, 7,* pp. 124-128, 1986.

44. B. K. Bennett and C. M. Stothart, *The Effects of a Relaxation-based Cognitive Technique on Sports Performances,* paper presented at the Congress of the Canadian Society for Motor Learning and Sport Psychology, Toronto, Canada, 1978.
45. O. Desiderato and I. B. Miller, Improving Tennis Performance by Cognitive Behavior Modification Techniques, *The Behavior Therapist, 2*:4, p. 19, 1979.
46. D. Gough, Improving Batting Skills with Small College Baseball Players Through Guided Visual Imagery, *Coaching Clinic, 27,* pp. 1-6, 1989.
47. R. Gravel, G. Lemieux, and R. Ladouceur, Effectiveness of a Cognitive Behavioral Treatment Package for Cross-country Ski Racers, *Cognitive Therapy and Research, 4,* pp. 83-90, 1980.
48. E. G. Hall and E. S. Erffmeyer, The Effects of Visuo-motor Behavior Rehearsal with Videotaped Modeling on Free Throw Accuracy of Intercollegiate Female Basketball Players, *Journal of Sport Psychology, 5,* pp. 343-346, 1983.
49. B. J. Kolonay, *The Effects of Visuo-motor Behavior Rehearsal on Athletic Performance,* unpublished Master's thesis, City University of New York, 1977.
50. R. M. Nideffer, Deep Muscle Relaxation: An Aid to Diving, *Coach and Athlete, 24,* p. 38, 1971.
51. R. C. Noel, The Effect of Visuo-motor Behavior Rehearsal on Tennis Performance, *Journal of Sport Psychology, 2*:3, pp. 220-226, 1980.
52. Prediger, Performance Enhancement Through Visualization, *Research Quarterly for Exercise and Sport,* Fall 1988.
53. R. Suinn, M. Morton, and H. Brammell, *Psychological and Mental Training to Increase Endurance in Athletes,* Final Report to U.S. Olympic Women's Athletics Developmental Subcommittee, 1979.
54. R. Weinberg, T. Seabourne, and A. Jackson, Effects of Visuo-motor Behavior Rehearsal, Relaxation Imagery on Karate Performance, *Journal of Sport Psychology, 3,* pp. 238-328, 1981.
55. R. Weinberg, T. Seabourne, and A. Jackson, Effects of Visuo-motor Behavior Rehearsal on State-trait Anxiety and Performance: Is Practice Important? *Journal of Sport Behavior, 5,* pp. 209-219, 1982.
56. D. Gould, R. Weinberg, and A. Jackson, Mental Preparation Strategies, Cognition and Strength Performance, *Journal of Sport Psychology, 2,* pp. 329-339, 1980.
57. A. Meyers, R. Schleser, C. Cooke, and C. Cuvillier, Cognitive Contributions to the Development of Gymnastics Skills, *Cognitive Therapy and Research, 3,* pp. 75-85, 1979.
58. R. Suinn, *The Seven Steps to Peak Performance: Manual for Olympic Teams,* Colorado State University, Department of Psychology, Fort Collins, Colorado, 1985.
59. R. Suinn, Future Directions in Sport Psychology Research: Applied Aspects, in *Future Directions in Exercise/Sport Research,* J. Skinner et al. (eds.), Human Kinetics Books, Illinois, 1989.
60. R. Suinn, Psychological Techniques for Individual Performance Enhancement: Imagery, in *Handbook on Research in Sport Psychology,* R. Singer, M. Murphey, and L. Tennant (eds.), Macmillan, New York, 1992.

CHAPTER 3

Developing Self-Talk to Facilitate the Use of Imagery Among Athletes

LANCE B. GREEN

The emphasis in sports psychology during the 1980s has been the impact of what the athlete is thinking on performance. This includes the use of mental imagery to facilitate performance. Indeed, meta-analyses of research conducted in this area indicate that the use of mental imagery enhances motor performance [1, 2].

This chapter will address the interdependence between the processes of self-talk, imagery, and motor programming in sport performance. It is hypothesized that the interplay of an athlete's self-talk and imagery influences the triggering of specific motor programs used in sport performance. The use of self-talk and imagery during pre-competition training as well as the pre-execution phase of movement is the focus of this treatise.

SELF-TALK, IMAGERY, AND MOTOR PROGRAMS

Self-Talk

Self-talk is the conversation that one has with one's self. It may be of a covert nature or it may actually be overt, where individuals actually speak to themselves verbally, outwardly. Within the context of athletics, the frequency and content of self-talk develops a mind set within which an athlete performs. It has been suggested that the mind set created by cognitive strategies has a dynamic influence on the quality of performance. Thus, athletes are encouraged to develop the skill of "intentional thinking." For example, Bunker and Williams [3] have discussed irrational and distorted types of thinking which include catastrophizing, perfectionism, one-trial generalizations, and self-worth being determined by athletic achievement [3].

Various mind sets are also created by self-talk which falls into polarized categories of cognition such as self-defeating thoughts versus self-enhancing thoughts [4], winners versus losers [5], descriptive versus judgmental [6], or process versus product thinking [7]. It is relatively easy to intuitively imagine the mind sets that these different thought patterns create within the athlete. Thus, the ultimate objective of addressing the content of the athlete's self-talk is to develop a process-oriented type of thinking. This form of thought includes a vocabulary of trigger words used to facilitate 1) concentration on the task at hand, 2) the formation of appropriate images associated with performance, 3) the proper mind set for performance, and 4) the formation of motor programs.

Imagery

Richardson describes a continuum of imagery types which includes after imagery, eidetic imagery, memory imagery, and imagination imagery [8]. Use of all types of imagery by athletes may occur, but this chapter will address the place of eidetic imagery and memory imagery in performance enhancement. The characteristics which have been used to describe eidetic imagery include: its percept-like nature, that is, as if one were looking at a picture and describing it in its totality; it persists longer than after imagery and does not require a fixed gaze; its vivid details are described in the present tense; its clarity of detail; and the fact that it persists for a much longer time than does after imagery, that is, weeks, months, years after the fact [8].

The eidetic image, as described by the athlete, is a multi-dimensional experience. It may be described from a cognitive perspective with the description of people present, environmental surroundings, colors, for example, what color uniforms are being worn, the color of the dirt, the color of fence signs, etc. Also, eidetic imagery may be expressed affectively as the athlete describes the motivational state, feelings, or spiritual characteristics associated with an experience. In addition, Doob has identified how eidetic imagery can provide greater confidence and greater vividness to the experience [9]. From a psychomotor perspective, Kluver has discussed the manner in which the parts in the picture seem to move, which lends the experience nicely to the athletic setting [10]. Thus, the eidetic form of imagery, as used by athletes, recreates a multi-dimensional experience that encourages the integration of all sensory modalities.

Memory imagery is different from the eidetic experience in that it is more of a hazy, incomplete image, and usually of a very brief duration. It is common and used in everyday life by most individuals; applicable to events from the past, for ongoing processes of the present, and even in terms of anticipating events of the future; and it is amenable to voluntary control [8]. In essence, an athlete could voluntarily control the image that he or she wishes to use before or after skill execution in order to facilitate performance. The potential for memory imagery occurring as a spontaneous accompaniment to performance during the course of competition is very applicable to athletics [11].

In addition, the works of Richardson [12], Botman and Crovitz [13] with personal and autobiographical memories appear to be quite applicable to an athletic population. Personal memories are said to be a sub-category of auto-biographical memories due to the following distinctive qualities: 1) "they consist in a brief moment of one's personal past that is experienced, again, in the present," 2) "seems to be like the reliving of that past moment," and 3) "is affectively stronger than an autobiographical memory" [12, pp. 53-54]. The use of cue events [14], cue words [15, 16], or contact senses such as touch, taste, or smell [17] is said to elicit both autobiographical and personal memories.

The use of imagery by athletes is dynamic because it has the potential to synthesize all sensory modalities at different points in time, for example, preparation before a contest, as well as during actual competition.

Motor Programs

By definition, a motor program is an abstract representation of movement, a mini-film of a psychomotor skill; a neuropsychological process which culminates in psychomotor execution [18]. If one were to view a film of a baseball game, isolate one swing of a particular batter, then cut those frames out of the film, the result would represent the motor program of "the swing" that is stored within the psychoneurological processes. In essence, the athlete develops appropriate motor programs for his/her sport which are stored within the body-mind. It is similar to programming a computer, but instead of programming words and numbers, the athlete programs motor skills.

In order to illustrate how a motor program is developed, Schmidt uses the analogy of shifting gears in a car [18]. Initially, the skill is broken down into seven different movements, each isolated but included within the overall task: accelerator up, clutch down, shift forward, shift right, shift forward, accelerator down, clutch up. With limited experience, an individual can group these numerous steps into three consolidated movements, referred to as "output chunking" [19]. In other words, the first two movements could be joined as one and triggered by the word "feet." Steps three, four, and five could be chunked and triggered by the word "hand." The last stage involves the chunking of steps six and seven which could be triggered by a single word, "feet." Thus, with limited experience, an individual could break these seven skills down into three movements, each initiated by trigger words, such as "feet," "hand," "feet."

At this point the motor program is composed of three separate movements. With extended practice, these separate movements become chunked into one, resulting in one fluid, very coordinated movement that can be triggered by one word, for example, "shift." The gear shift analogy illustrates what a motor program is, how it might be formed, and what it entails once the motor skill becomes reflexive. It also demonstrates the use of imagery and self-talk composed of trigger words [20], as well as the manner in which the two working interdependently facilitate the formation of mental blueprints called motor programs [2, 21-23].

By describing the neuropsychological processes involved with motor programs, the foundation is laid for developing imagery programs for different classifications of motor skills (e.g., closed, open, continuous, and serial skills). In this manner, the works of Schmidt [18], Greene [24], and Pribram [25] provide the neuropsychological framework with which imagery training can facilitate the development of motor programs associated with "unconscious" performances.

According the Schmidt there are three types of neuropsychological systems that control motor programs [18]. The first is a closed loop system composed of a reference mechanism, feedback, and an executive level. Feedback from the environment is interpreted by a reference of correctness with which adjustments in initial motor programs are possible. For example, a baseball player fielding a ground ball that takes a bad hop would receive feedback from the environment that his hands are in the wrong place in order to properly field the ball. Within the closed loop system, the opportunity exists for making corrections based on feedback from the environment. Once a motor program is in the process of being executed, an adjustment program can be triggered as a result of feedback from the environment in order to make corrections.

An open loop system is another form of control within the neuropsychological system. It does not include feedback and possesses no reference for correctness. An open loop system is composed of an executive level and an effector mechanism. According to the open loop system, if that same baseball player were to field the same ground ball, there would be no adjustment made based on feedback. The athlete would merely carry out the original motor program to field the ground ball and consequently would not make appropriate adjustments. Thus, once the motor program has been triggered, the program runs with no adjustment.

The third system is a synthesis of the previous two in which an open loop system is imbedded within a closed loop system and works together in a coordinated fashion [24]. It is referred to as the hybrid system, a multi-level hierarchical control system that is very similar to the coordinated concept of structure advanced by Fitch, Tuller, and Turvey [26], and Turvey [27]. Greene notions that, with the hybrid system, there is a ball-park response that gives the general idea of the movement to be executed, such as, field the ground ball.

Once the ball-park response has been triggered, refinement of that movement occurs which takes into account a multitude of variables associated with the environment and individual biomechanics. The interaction between these feedback and feedforward systems determines most of the details of the movement and defines which motor units are to be fired at the musculature level. Thus, corrections prompted by adjustment programs occur during a program's execution so that the movement can meet the requirements of the task.

Pribram's two-process model of imagery addresses these same functions [25]. It includes neuropsychological processes that identify two classes of neural codes, such as those involving discreet impulse characteristics of nerve discharge and those involving steady state, slow potential micro-structures just below the threshold for continuous excitation. These slow potentials are characterized by a spontaneous discharge of receptors whose output interacts with current input, such as adjustment programs executed during *unconscious* play.

He also suggests that images have knowledge of ideas that are unbeknownst to the individual. In other words, a motor program may have a mind of its own. An adjustment program or slow potential may be triggered without a conscious thought being associated with it. The possibility of this phenomenon lends credence to the athlete's ability to play in a literal state of *unconsciousness*. A state wherein stored motor programs are triggered during performance and the necessary, spontaneous adjustments are made during execution without conscious attention being devoted to them.

Pribram's model also describes the TOTE and TOTEM systems. The TOTE (test-operate-test-exit) system refers to the exchange between the environment and the organism. It suggests that output fibers, or the efferents, regulate the receptor and sensory functions of an organism as well as its movements. Within the TOTE system, feedback and feedforward mechanisms are included which are similar to Greene's multi-hierarchical system. This system accounts for potential adjustment programs that are carried out during execution in an overt sense. The TOTEM (test-operate-test-exit-mental) system is an application of the TOTE model specifically to the mental level, for example, the process by which images conduct TOTE operations on each other within the mental environment. It is this system that is utilized with mental rehearsal used during non-execution times in an athlete's training and performance.

OBSTACLES IN THE USE OF IMAGERY

Given the interplay of self-talk, imagery and the psychoneurological processes associated with motor programming, it is somewhat surprising that positive self-talk and appropriate images are not more pervasive in sport performance. This may be due, in part, to certain obstacles athletes encounter. Athletes wishing to use imagery need to overcome the socialization processes associated with ontogenetic development as well as the application of imaging to different classifications of sport skills (e.g., open vs. closed sport skills).

Ontogenetic Development

According to Piaget [28] and Kuhlman [29], ontogenetic development proceeds from percept to imagery and, then, to verbal storage. And Doob has concurred that it includes a transition from pre-verbal to post-verbal imagery [30].

In early childhood, individuals use a great deal of imagery. Because of a limited vocabulary, imagery is very useful for young children. As they grow into the adult world, they are socialized into using verbal communication in everyday living. Imagery is left behind. The images of life give way to verbal representation of experience. In essence, just as a child is taught to push certain buttons on a calculator without having to learn the processes of multiplication and division, he/she is also socialized toward verbal cognition rather than multi-sensory images.

Richardson notes that the ability to use eidetic imagery in those who once possessed it begins to wither away from lack of use [8]. Doob has also noted that a reason for partial or complete disappearance of imagery use is that language is usually more efficient than imagery [30]. It is much less time consuming and more economical to say, "I lost the serve at 3-2 in the second set," than to re-see, re-hear, and re-feel the experience when communicating it to others. Thus, individuals are socialized into using words that *might* create a vivid explanation, but often do not.

However, the use of imagery in the world of athletics *is* economical and efficient as indicated by Sheehan as he noted that people use imagery because of its usefulness to them [31]. Instead of engaging in a time consuming discourse concerning performance, an athlete may use split-second imagery to flash into what has just happened or to anticipate what might happen. In truth, as an athlete develops his/her skills toward the reflexive level, self-talk becomes less and less frequent [3]. An athlete must, however, overcome the obstacle of socialization that fosters the notion that the use of imagery is neither economical nor functional. For an athlete to enhance performance by using imagery, he or she must be guided in overcoming the socialization outcomes of ontogenetic development and encouraged to revert to the child-like inclusion of multidimensional processing.

Classification of Skills

Another obstacle to the use of imagery by athletes lies in the development of imagery rehearsals that are sport specific. The type of sport one plays influences what kind of imagery program needs to be developed and practiced. Different sports utilize a variety of skills classified as open, closed, discreet, continuous, or serial.

Open skills are those for which the environment is constantly changing so that the performer cannot effectively plan a response, such as wrestling and punt returning. It is very difficult for a football player to program exactly what he is going to do on a punt return. While he may start the return to the right, once the play develops it is hard to predict exactly what might happen after that. It proves difficult to plan for the unknown, thus, open skills do not seem, intuitively, to be open to mental rehearsals. On the other hand, closed skills are those where the environment is predictable (e.g., archery, bowling). The use of imagery is more easily applied to a closed, very repetitive skill that the athlete wants to perform virtually the same way every time.

Other classifications of skills present obstacles to the use of imagery in training and during competition. Discreet skills are those with a recognizable beginning and end, the end being defined by the skill in question (e.g., throwing or kicking). Continuous skills are those that have no recognizable beginning or end with the behavior continuing until the response is arbitrarily stopped (e.g., swimming or running). Serial skills are those in which a number of discreet skills are linked together, such as a gymnastics floor exercise [18].

The classification of motor skills presents issues that need to be addressed in the formation of imagery programs for athletes, such as the development of experientials applicable to open skills. The works of Greene [24] and Pribram [25] facilitate the development of imagery with open skills. They lay the neuropsychological groundwork for adjustment programs, so that an athlete may be guided through a mental rehearsal that adds to the stored inventory of programs available for *unconscious* use.

The individual guiding the athlete through mental rehearsals of open and/or serial skills must be very knowledgeable of what potential options exist for a particular sport. With open skills, the facilitator must be aware of potential, unexpected environmental input and what the counters are to those particular scenarios. Those counters then become the focus of imagery experientials. Serial skills require that the specific discreet skills that are sequenced be isolated and then reassembled. The facilitator must then develop imagery rehearsals depicting both the *parts* and the *whole* [32, 33].

For example, the baseball player may be guided through scenarios that include bad hops; a coach leading a wrestler through preparation for a particular match may indicate that an opponent has particular tendencies and then identify possible counters for each move; tennis players could isolate specific shots used in various sequences such as returns of serve. The inclusion of possible adjustment programs in mental rehearsals require a formidable technical knowledge of a particular sport. Furthermore, once an athlete reaches a level of mechanical efficiency commensurate with advanced play, imagery programs should focus on the desired outcome of a particular skill, such as a line drive in baseball hitting rather than the mechanics of a swing; the location of an overhead in tennis rather than the mechanics of the stroke.

THE IMAGERY PROGRAM

An imagery program should facilitate the use of imagery by athletes on a daily basis. It should become part of daily practices as well as pre-competition rehearsals away from the competitive cite. The objective is to incorporate imagery into daily routines both on and off the field, as well as before, during, and after competition. The total program should include the development of self-awareness in athletes about their use of imagery, the quantification of imagery abilities, and the application of imagery as a tool to be used daily.

Self-Awareness

Developing awareness of the many uses of imagery with athletes and coaches is part of selling the program. Without motivated participants, the program is doomed from its inception. In introducing the art of imagery, sport and non-sport related experientials can be used either at the practice cite or in a more clinical setting. In addition, the use of multi-sense experientials initiate the athlete as to the potential positive outcomes associated with imagery such as concentration, relaxation, and the identification of problematic areas in their performance.

Another part of the initial phase of the program includes the identification of preferred sense modalities of athletes by applying the works of Syer and Connally [34] and Griffitts [35]. What are the preferred modalities of a particular athlete? Is the athlete more visually oriented, kinesthetically oriented, auditory, etc.? What are the primary and secondary modalities used by the athletes? Isaksen et al. indicated that there is a general preference for using visual imagery [36]. It, therefore, is important to understand which modality the athlete prefers so that imagery experientials can be developed which provide for a match with the athlete.

The development of self-awareness also includes identifying the content and tendencies of the athlete's self-talk. Is it process or product oriented, descriptive or judgmental, self-enhancing or self-defeating? Are there recurring situations in a contest which trigger a negative form of self-talk? What kind of self-talk occurs during good performances?

Quantification of Imagery Abilities

Developing awareness of imagery abilities can also be addressed with the use of psychometric instruments. These may include Gordon's Test of Visual Imagery Control [37] or Bett's Vividness of Imagery Scale [38]. In addition, Paivio and Harshman have applied the theory of symbolic representations by using the Individual Differences Questionnaire (IDQ) to differentiate between visual imagers and those who use verbalization as their preferred mode of processing [39].

However, there are other instruments that are applicable specifically to sport (see Issac, Marks, and Russell's Vividness of Movement Imagery Questionnaire (VMIQ) [40]; Hall and Pongrac's Movement Imagery Questionnaire (MIQ) [41]; and Martens' Sport Imagery Questionnaire [42]). In addition, Hall, Rodgers, and Barr developed the Imagery Use Questionnaire (IUQ) that addresses when athletes use imagery, how often they use it, and the types of skills for which they use imagery [43].

Imagery as an Applied Tool

The inclusion of imagery experiences in an athletic program can be accomplished in the following ways: 1) during daily practice sessions, 2) as a part of pre-event routines, 3) instead of physical practice during parts of seasons where fatigue is high, 4) away from the practice site, and, 5) in an applied sense during pre-execution phases of competition. In this manner, the ontogenetic obstacle of use can be reversed and the second obstacle of adapting the use of imagery to different classifications of skills can be addressed.

In a more specific sense, imagery can be applied to any movement that can be analyzed from its preparation, execution, and follow-through phases. Its preparation phase occurs during two distinct periods of time: pre-competition and pre-execution. The pre-competition component occurs away from the competitive site, during non-execution times of practices, just prior to competition, or at other times and places prior to contests. The pre-execution component occurs during the time immediately preceding execution of a sport skill during competition and/or practice. For example, a baseball pitcher is in a state of pre-execution from the time he/she releases a pitch and the completion of the subsequent play until the time of the next pitch.

Pre-Competition

During the pre-competition phase, eidetic rehearsals that elicit multi-modality images can be used to enhance confidence and to identify problem areas. For example, a coach or a sport psychologist in a clinical setting such as an office might facilitate a *Peak Performance* experiential in which the athlete describes his or her best performance in a multi-sensory fashion. The re-experiencing of emotions and vivid details associated with optimum performance often lays the foundation for future performance and encourages appropriate motor program formation.

Athletes can also develop adjustment programs by rehearsing appropriate skills that might serve to counter different scenarios within their sport. This actually may enhance the spontaneous control of memory imagery and add to an inventory of stored programs at the slow potential level as described by Pribram [25]. For example, a hitter in baseball could practice kinesthetic hitting whereby he/she engages in and feels the execution of the swing associated with a fast ball or curve ball in certain locations. Or, a tennis player could imagine certain returns of serve.

The use of pre-competition imagery may also include the use of mechanistic rehearsals of memory images. This may foster the athlete's transition from thinking in words to thinking in pictures prior to execution. For example, a mechanistic rehearsal such as "The Play by Play" may be used with baseball pitchers during practice. This involves rehearsals where a pitcher works a number of innings mentally, breaking each inning down pitch by pitch. In this fashion, the athlete uses imagery to condition his/her thinking process during pre-execution and to practice fundamentals such as the drop step, balance point, and release point.

During practices, a viable use of imagery is with the use of station teaching. For example, in a baseball practice you may have various stations where the athletes practice soft-toss hitting drills, engage in conditioning, hit live pitching, as well as a station for mental practice. At this station they can go through different sport specific mental rehearsals (e.g., kinesthetic hitting in baseball, pre-play routines). Other sports may focus on simulated swimming starts for swimmers or pre-dive routines for divers. Incorporating the use of sport specific imagery during actual practices on a daily basis through the use of station teaching is an excellent way of enhancing the imagery program.

Pre-competition mental rehearsals are also facilitated by the making of mastery cassette tapes. The purpose of making a mastery tape is to help the athlete develop the process-oriented thinking associated with optimum concentration as well as enhancing the use of senses other than the visual, for example, the kinesthetic and emotive qualities associated with peak performance. The sport psychologist may facilitate this process by engaging the athlete in "The Ideal Performance" experiential. In this, the athlete describes an ideal on-site preparation and performance. Pertinent trigger words are identified from the dialogue that elicit desired motor programs. The athlete then relives the scenario using only the trigger words extracted from the transcript of his/her description of the ideal competition.

For example, a mastery tape for a swimmer competing in the 100 meter free style could include triggers that describe both the warm-up and race. During the warm-up, the athlete mentally rehearses the process of warming up which is detailed by these triggers: focused stretching, the pencil dive, warm up, dives and turns, get away. Each of these words elicits an image (in any modality) of what is actually being accomplished behaviorally.

Focused stretching indicates that the athlete is going through a series of stretching exercises using controlled breathing techniques. The *pencil dive* describes the first feel of water as he or she dives in. *Dives and turns* indicate what mechanics are desired for the dive and for turns. *Warm-up* facilitates the images associated with doing 500 meters free style, hard kicking, 200 build-ups, and sprints. *Get away* refers to the relaxation method of isolation whereby the athlete sits away from everybody else with a walkman listening to music or mastery tapes of the event.

For the race itself, trigger words are identified that indicate what happens at the start, for example, walk to blocks, climb blocks, listen, explode, dive out, hit, head pop, kick hard. The race itself is triggered by desired strategies and techniques. *Fast pace* may be the trigger-mantra as this individual swims the first 25 meters. As the first turn is approached, trigger words associated with the turn are used, such as *through the wall, head pop, kick hard.* The second 25 meters are focused on *control,* indicating the strategy to control strokes mechanically. The turns are repetitive, for example, *through the wall, head pop, kick hard.* The third 25 meters are facilitated with the trigger *pick it up,* indicating the need to increase stroke count. For the final turn the triggers are the same, *through the wall, head pop, kick hard.* The last 25 meters entails *where am I?, no breath, touch through.*

This is an example of a mental rehearsal for the 100 meter free style that is put on tape. What the athlete actually hears on tape is her/her own voice and emotions throughout the preparation, the start, and the actual race. On one side of the tape the athlete has an experiential describing the event. The only words and emotions that are recorded are those associated with the actual thought processes that the trigger words have established. This facilitates the use of total focus on the task at hand during the race and during pre-competition mental rehearsals.

On the flip side of this mastery tape, the athletes use whatever type of music is best suited for their arousal needs. If they wish to get energized for a race, they may want fast-paced or crescendo-like music. If the individual is usually excited and aroused due to the event itself, he/she may need music to calm down. They might wish to elicit a more calming effect with their music. The master tape can be used by the athlete away from the site, on road trips, or whenever they see fit to engage in mental rehearsal on their own.

Pre-Execution

During competition the athlete also has the opportunity to use imagery and self-talk immediately prior to skill execution (i.e., during pre-execution). For example, a pitcher who is getting ready to deliver a pitch can rehearse what he would like to have happen immediately prior to delivery. Images that are elicited by nonverbal communication with the catcher might include: ". . . selection . . . location . . . picture it . . . breathe . . . go." Once he has assessed the situation, selected the pitch and location, he may *picture it* prior to actually delivering the pitch.

Or, a tennis player who is receiving a serve can use imagery immediately prior to the opponent's serve. He/she can image a forehand return to a particular spot on the court, or a backhand return to a particular part of the court. In this fashion, the receiver prepares the adjustment programs at the slow potential level for use during the point.

During pre-execution, an athlete may integrate the use of self-talk and imagery to facilitate concentration immediately prior to a play by using process trigger words to elicit appropriate pre-play mind sets [44-47]. He or she may also apply Cautella's athletic triad, a form of covert cognitive conditioning [48]. These are examples of the application of Hill's [49] use of imagery pegs and Paivio's [50] conceptual pegs that are used in the same sense as mnemonic systems.

The use of trigger words as imagery pegs that trigger a motor program before a play can be developed through mental rehearsal. By mentally rehearsing an instant pre-play via trigger words, the athlete becomes somewhat conditioned to think in that manner just prior to execution. Ultimately, the athlete attempts to eliminate as much self-talk as possible so that he/she thinks exclusively in images. This is an application of what Walter referred to as a combination of habitual verbalizing and habitual visualizing [51]. Indeed, additional research indicates that elite performers use internal/kinesthetic imagery rather than the external/visual imagery used by less skilled athletes [1, 52-54]. At the very least, the process of imaging during pre-execution promotes process oriented thinking that enhances focused concentration, game state relaxation and helps to eliminate counter-productive verbiage [45].

SUMMARY

This treatise has traced the influence of self-talk and imagery on the formation of motor programs used in sport performance. An athlete who develops the arts of self-talk (e.g., intentional thinking that includes a vocabulary of process-oriented trigger words) and imagery is said to progress from thinking in words to thinking in pictures just prior to the execution of specific skills. While all forms of imagery are probably used by elite athletes at some point in time, eidetic and memory types have been described within this text as being suitable for training and performance.

In addition, the description of specific neuropsychological systems (e.g., the multi-hierarchical and two-process models) laid the foundation for imagery training suitable for all classifications of motor skills. Heretofore, imagery training has been used primarily with closed skills, while open, serial, and continuous skills have not received respective attention.

It was established that prior to implementing an imagery program with athletes, it is important to recognize potential obstacles to its success. These obstacles include, but are not limited to, ontogenetic development, classification of skills, and awareness on the part of coaches and athletes as to the many uses of imagery in training and performance. Once these obstacles are taken into consideration, the imagery program should focus on developing the athlete's awareness of his/her imagery abilities and the application of imagery to pre-competition and pre-execution phases of preparation.

This might entail the use of eidetic experientials, the development of adjustment programs applicable to open skills, mechanistic rehearsals, as well as covert conditioning using the athletic triad. In addition, athletes can become vested in the application of trigger words just prior to execution in the manner of imagery pegs and what Walter referred to as combining habitual verbalizing with habitual visualizing [51]. Coaches are also encouraged to implement imagery training during daily practices with the use of station teaching. Coaches and athletes are also encouraged to develop and use mastery cassette tapes in order to facilitate mental rehearsal during pre-competition preparation.

In conclusion, the use of imagery by athletes is a natural process, especially among elite performers. It is, however, interesting to recognize the lack of appropriate self-talk and imagery used by less skilled athletes [43, 52, 54, 55]. Athletes wishing to become more consistent and effective in their performances should seriously consider the inclusion of imagery training in their preparation for competition.

From the perspective of researchers interested in investigating not only the psychoneurological processes associated with imagery, but the use of it in health practices, educational processes, and other related practices, the use of a so-called healthy population of athletes seems to have been untouched.

REFERENCES

1. K. E. Hinshaw, The Effects of Mental Practice on Motor Skill Performance: Critical Evaluation and Meta-analysis, *Imagination, Cognition and Personality, 11*:1, pp. 3-35, 1991-92.
2. D. L. Feltz and D. M. Landers, The Effects of Mental Practice on Motor Skill Learning and Performance: A Meta-analysis, *Journal of Sport Psychology, 5,* pp. 25-27, 1983.
3. L. Bunker and J. M. Williams, Cognitive Techniques for Improving Performance and Building Confidence, in *Applied Sport Psychology: Personal Growth to Peak Experience,* J. M. Williams (ed.), Mayfield, Palo Alto, California, 1986.
4. D. Meichenbaum, *Cognitive Behavior Modification: An Integrative Approach,* Plenum, New York, 1977.
5. D. Waitley, *The Psychology of Winning,* Berkley Books, New York, 1979.
6. W. T. Gallwey, *The Inner Game of Tennis,* Random House, New York, 1974.
7. R. M. Nideffer, Concentration and Attention Control Training, in *Applied Sport Psychology: Personal Growth to Peak Experience,* J. M. Williams (ed.), Mayfield, Palo Alto, California, 1986.
8. A. Richardson, *Mental Imagery,* Routledge and Kegan Paul, London, 1969.
9. L. W. Doob, Exploring Eidetic Imagery Among the Kamba of Central Kenya, *Journal of Social Psychology, 67,* 1965.
10. H. Kluver, An Experimental Study of the Eidetic Type, *Genetic Psychology Monograph, I,* 1926.
11. G. D. Hicks, On the Nature of Images, *British Journal of Psychology, 15,* pp. 121-148, 1924.
12. A. Richardson, Personal Memories: An Exploratory Investigation, *Imagination, Cognition and Personality, 11*:1, pp. 53-74, 1991-92.
13. H. I. Botman and H. F. Crovitz, Dream Reports and Autobiographical Memory, *Imagination, Cognition and Personality, 9*:3, pp. 213-224, 1989-90.
14. R. Brown and J. Kulik, Flashbulb Memories, *Cognition, 5,* pp. 73-99, 1977.
15. D. Rubin, On the Retention Function for Autobiographical Memory, *Journal of Verbal Learning and Verbal Behavior, 21,* pp. 21-38, 1982.
16. D. C. Rubin and M. Kozin, Vivid Memories, *Cognition, 16,* pp. 81-95, 1984.
17. E. G. Schachtel, *Metamorphosis: On the Development of Affect Perception, Attention, and Memory,* Basic Books, New York, 1959.
18. R. A. Schmidt, *Motor Control and Learning,* Human Kinetics, Champaign, Illinois, 1988.
19. S. W. Keele, *Attention and Human Performance,* Goodyear, Pacific Palisades, California, 1973.
20. J. M. Silva III, Competitive Sport Environments: Performance Enhancement Through Cognitive Intervention, *Behavior Modification, 6,* pp. 443-463, 1982.

21. J. Eccles, The Physiology of Imagination, *Scientific American, 199,* p. 135, 1958.
22. R. M. Suinn, Psychology and Sports Performance: Principles and Applications, in *Psychology in Sports: Methods and Applications,* R. M. Suinn (ed.), Burgess, Minneapolis, Minnesota, pp. 26-36, 1980.
23. S. Goss, C. Hall, E. Buckolz, and G. Fishburne, Imagery Ability and the Acquisition and Retention of Movements, *Memory and Cognition, 14,* pp. 469-477, 1986.
24. P. H. Greene, Problems of Organization of Motor Systems, in *Progress in Theoretical Biology* (vol. 2), R. Rosen and F. M. Snell (eds.), Academic Press, New York, 1972.
25. K. Pribram, *Languages of the Brain,* Prentice-Hall, Englewood Cliffs, New Jersey, 1971.
26. H. L. Fitch, B. Tuller, and M. T. Turvey, The Bernstein Perspective: III. Tuning to Coordinative Structures with Special Reference to Perception, in *Human Motor Behavior: An Introduction,* J. A. S. Kelso (ed.), Erlbaum, Hillsdale, New Jersey, 1982.
27. M. T. Turvey, Preliminaries to a Theory of Action with Reference to Vision, in *Perceiving, Acting, Knowing,* R. Shaw and J. Bransford (eds.), Erlbaum, Hillsdale, New Jersey, 1977.
28. J. Piaget, Le Point de Vue de Piaget, *International Journal of Psychology, 3,* pp. 281-299, 1968.
29. C. Kuhlman, *Visual Imagery in Children,* unpublished doctoral dissertation, Harvard University, 1960.
30. L. W. Doob, The Ubiquitous Appearance of Images, in *The Function and Nature of Imagery,* P. W. Sheehan (ed.), Academic Press, New York, 1972.
31. P. W. Sheehan, *The Function and Nature of Imagery,* Academic Press, New York, 1972.
32. M. Denis, Imagery and the Use of Mental Practice in the Development of Motor Skills, *Canadian Journal of Applied Sport Sciences, 10,* pp. 4s-16s, 1985.
33. A. Paivio, Individual Differences in Coding Processes, in *Cognitive Research in Psychology: Recent Approaches, Designs and Results,* F. Klix, J. Hoffman, and E. Vander Merr (eds.), Elsevier, North Holland, Amsterdam, 1980.
34. J. Syer and C. Connally, *Sporting Body: Sporting Mind,* Cambridge University Press, Cambridge, 1984.
35. C. H. Griffitts, Individual Differences in Imagery, *Psychology Monograph, 37,* Whole No. 172, 1927.
36. S. G. Isaksen, K. B. Dorval, and G. Kaufman, Mode of Symbolic Representation and Cognitive Style, *Imagination, Cognition and Personality, 11*:3, pp. 271-277, 1991-92.
37. R. Gordon, The Gordon Test of Visual Imagery Control, in *Mental Imagery,* A. Richardson (ed.), Routledge and Kegan Paul, London, 1969.
38. G. H. Betts, The Betts QMI Vividness of Imagery Scale, in *Mental Imagery,* A. Richardson (ed.), Routledge and Kegan Paul, London, 1969.
39. A. Paivio and R. Harshman, Factor Analysis of a Questionnaire on Imagery and Verbal Habits and Skills, *Canadian Journal of Psychology, 37*:4, pp. 461-483, 1983.
40. A. Isaac, D. F. Marks, and D. G. Russell, An Instrument for Assessing Imagery of Movement: The Vividness of Movement Imagery Questionnaire, *Journal of Mental Imagery, 10*:4, pp. 23-80, 1986.
41. C. R. Hall and J. Pongrac, *Movement Imagery Questionnaire,* University of Western Ontario, London, Ontario, 1983.
42. R. Martens, *Sport Imagery Questionnaire,* personal correspondence with author, October 1987.
43. C. R. Hall, W. M. Rodgers, and K. A. Barr, The Use of Imagery by Athletes in Selected Sports, *The Sport Psychologist, 4,* pp. 1-10, 1990.

44. D. McCluggage, *The Centered Skier,* Warner Books, New York, 1977.
45. L. B. Green, Developing Concentration: How to Use the Time Between Plays, *Athletic Journal,* 67:9, April 1987.
46. J. B. Shea, J. P. Hunt, and S. T. Zimny, Representational Structure and Strategic Processes for Movement Production, in *Differing Perspectives in Motor Learning, Memory and Control,* D. Goodman, R. B. Wilberg, and I. M. Franks (eds.), North Holland, Amsterdam, 1985.
47. R. A. Magill, *Motor Learning Concepts and Applications,* W. C. Brown, Dubuque, Iowa, 1985.
48. J. Cautella, *Imagathletics: The Application of Covert Conditioning to Sport Performance,* presentation to the Association for the Advancement of Applied Sport Psychology, Annual Conference, Nashua, New Hampshire, October 12-16, 1988.
49. D. S. Hill, An Experiment with an Automatic Mnemonic System, *Psychology Bulletin, 15,* pp. 99-103, 1918.
50. A. Paivio, Learning of Adjective-noun Paired-associates as a Function of Adjective-noun Word Order and Noun Abstractions, *Canadian Journal of Psychology, 17,* pp. 370-379, 1963.
51. W. G. Walter, *The Living Brain,* Norton, New York, 1953.
52. M. J. Mahoney and M. Avener, Psychology of the Elite Athlete: An Exploratory Study, *Cognitive Therapy and Research, 1,* pp. 135-142, 1977.
53. B. Mumford and C. R. Hall, The Effects of Internal and External Imagery on Performing Figures in Figure Skating, *The Canadian Journal of Applied Sport Sciences, 10,* pp. 171-177, 1985.
54. T. Orlick and J. Partington, *Psyched,* Coaching Association of Canada, Ottawa, 1986.
55. W. P. Morgan and M. L. Pollack, Psychological Characterization of the Elite Distance Runner, *Annals of the New York Academy of Sciences, 301,* pp. 382-403, 1977.

CHAPTER 4

The Role of Imagery in Perfecting Already Learned Physical Skills

NEIL McLEAN
AND ALAN RICHARDSON

In recent years, it has become relatively common for coaches to include some form of mental practice in the training programs of their athletes. Given this trend, it is of concern that our understanding of the effectiveness and process of mental practice is not more advanced.

Many studies looking at mental practice have used subjects who were either unfamiliar with the task or at relatively low levels of skill. In this chapter the focus is on the use of mental practice[1] by athletes with well established skills.

Essentially, mental practice involves the manipulation of sensory-like or percept-like experiences of objects or events, that a person can voluntarily produce and maintain in awareness. These thought images, as they have been called [10], vary in vividness, controllability, location, and modality; and, as will be noted later, each of these major dimensions is of relevance to the kinds of improvement that may be expected from mentally practising different types of physical task. Some attention will also be paid to the part played by verbal imagery (i.e., self-talk) in the performance of selected skills.

Most of the work in this area has focused on closed skills, where the environment is relatively constant (e.g., ten pin bowling or high board diving) and the activity is self-paced. Less work has been reported with open skills, where the performance occurs in a constantly changing environment, often involving an opponent, and requires the athletes to react to the changing task demands.

---

[1] Synonyms of mental practice used by different investigators include: symbolic rehearsal [1] imaginary practice [2]; implicit practice [3]; mental rehearsal [4]; conceptualizing practice [5]; cognitive rehearsal [6]; behavior rehearsal [7]; psychomotor rehearsal [8]; covert rehearsal [9].

Finally, consideration must be given to what might be meant by perfecting an already learned skill. For closed skills, at least, there is an important sense in which an internalized model of the task movements must be established, before mental practice can be effective. Until a reasonably accurate template, model or motor program is available, improvement in actual performance should not be expected. In fact, four studies are known that bear upon an important implication of this assumption: that to mentally practice an inaccurate model may lead to a decrement in performance. In the first by Samuels [11] cited in Smyth [12], it appears that no effect was obtained, while in the second by Powell [13], the design makes it difficult to draw any firm conclusions. In the third study, the mental practice of inaccurate dart throws appears to have made no difference to actual accuracy [14]. Only in a study by Woolfolk, Parrish, and Murphy, was it found that negative practice had an effect [15]. Inexperienced golfers, who mentally practiced just missing the hole when putting, suffered a decrement in actual performance when compared with a matched group, who mentally practiced accurate putting. Reports by those taking part, suggest that this difference in outcome, between the two groups, may be due to effects on the motivational system; while positive outcomes appear to have increased self-confidence, the opposite effect occurred for negative outcomes. Moreover, there is evidence to suggest that attempts to mentally practise difficult, unfamiliar tasks are unlikely to lead to any improvement. Phipps and Morehouse [16], for example, found that it was only on the easiest of three unfamiliar gymnastic skills (viz. the hock swing to the horizontal bar), that a significant improvement in actual performance resulted from mental practice [16].

Problems that arise during the easier stages of learning a skill, may be less likely to apply to the performer who has already advanced to a relatively high level. At this later stage, it can be assumed that a clear, internalized model of the skill exists. The performer knows precisely how to execute the appropriate movements; the problem now is to increase the probability that the movements will be executed perfectly whenever required.

The first section contains a discussion of studies, in which relatively high-level performers have been instructed to mentally practice closed skills under both actual practice and actual competition conditions. The second section contains a discussion of individual differences in imagery abilities, as these relate to differential degrees of improvement in performance. In the third and last section, the probable mechanisms responsible for improved performance will be discussed.

THE ROLE OF IMAGERY INSTRUCTIONS, TO MENTALLY PRACTICE, IN THE PERFECTING OF WELL-LEARNED SKILLS

There are numerous anecdotal reports of top-level sports performers using mental practice to enhance their skills. For example, Jack Nicklaus reports using detailed mental rehearsal of both the action and outcome of his golf swing prior to every shot [17]. However, an evaluation of controlled investigations, of the effect of mental practice on established skills, is made difficult by the range of tasks investigated, the variety of mental practice techniques employed and differences between subject groups (e.g., extent of experience with the task). As noted earlier, researchers have tended to focus on closed, rather than open skills. In the investigations of open skill sports, discrete skills (e.g., serving in tennis, free throw in basketball, penalty kicking in football) have been extracted for study.

Notwithstanding the focus on closed skills, an impressive range of activities has been investigated. Many of these studies have focused on actual game skills, such as golf putting [15], dart throwing [18], and the service action in volleyball [19] and tennis [20]. Other studies have looked at perceptual-motor tasks not directly involved in sports performance, but representative of the types of skills that might be involved, such as tennis ball target throwing [21] and rotary pursuit tracking [22]. A third group of studies has been largely involved with strength and/or endurance, such as sit-ups [23], while a fourth category of studies focused on skills more reliant on cognitive abilities than motor skills (e.g., digit substitution, card sorting [2] and maze training [24]). Only a minority of the studies have been done on performance in actual competitive conditions. In the majority of studies, skill levels were recorded in practice settings or under specially arranged experimental conditions.

There is considerable variation between studies in terms of the mental practice procedures used. Whereas Suinn emphasizes the vivid re-creation of sensory-motor sensations experienced across the range of sense modalities involved [25], other studies have simply requested subjects to imagine themselves performing the target task [26].

Another variation is the imagery procedure termed "coping imagery," that the athlete is instructed to imagine and practice coping strategies associated with different aspects of the game [27]. The subject is encouraged to imagine game situations, ranging from successful performance through to failure, and is instructed to imaginally rehearse "coping" within these various scenes. In this procedure, the focus is more on the application of established skills, in the competition environment, rather than a focused rehearsal of the actual skills involved in the performance. The procedure reflects a recent trend where the imagery intervention includes a component best described as self-instructional training. For example, Meyers et al. [27] in their study with gymnasts, used an intervention that included not only rehearsal of the actual skills involved, but a series of self-statements stressing the individual's ability to cope with the task (self-efficacy instructions [28]), promoting positive expectations of success, and reinforcing the athlete for successful imaginal performance.

There is a variation, not only in terms of the type of mental practice, but also in length and number of trials and the timing of this practice. In the studies reviewed by Feltz and Landers [29], the number of practice sessions ranged from one to thirty-five, while the total length of sessions ranged from ten seconds [30, 31] to thirty minutes [32]. There was also considerable variation in the number of trials per session.

The initial skill levels, of those taking part in these studies, also varies a great deal. Whereas many of the case reports have been based on elite performers [17, 33], the majority of experimental investigations have used novices. In the Feltz and Landers review, 128 of the 146 studies were with novice subjects, where it might reasonably be assumed that the subject was either new to the task or at an early level of skill development. It has been generally assumed that imagery practice is of less benefit to the novice than to the performer with established skills [34-36]. However, relatively few studies have directly tested this assumption and when there has been an attempt to do so, level of ability has been very roughly estimated (e.g. [37]) or the skill levels attained by the subject prior to mental practice have been described in most general terms (e.g., experienced vs. novice). It is, perhaps, not surprising that considerable confusion surrounds these results. For example, Clark compared the effects of mental practice on the basketball free-throw accuracy of three groups (varsity, junior varsity, and novice) and concluded that mental practice was least effective for the novice group [39]. However, Feltz and Landers classified *all* of Clark's subjects as novices, possibly because they were high school students, rather than college or professional athletes [29]. There is clearly a need for more precise definition of the skill levels of subject groups.

Given the range of variables, which differ across studies, it is perhaps not surprising that the outcome data are mixed. In reviews of the mental practice literature, it has generally been concluded that mental practice is better than no practice, physical practice is better than no practice, physical practice is better than mental practice alone, and a combination of mental and physical practice yields results, as good as, or better than physical practice alone [34, 36]. However, it is difficult to be confident about these broad conclusions.

Several studies have reported no significant differences in skill enhancement between groups instructed in mental practice and no-treatment control groups. In a study focusing on tennis serving with subjects of high and low ability, Weinberg et al. compared the effects of three cognitive strategies (imagery, positive self-efficacy statements, and attentional focus) with a no-treatment control condition [26]. None of the cognitive strategies facilitated performance, although the authors noted that their instruction may have been insufficient to ensure that subjects were sufficiently practiced in using the various strategies.

Kelsey examined the effects of mental practice on an endurance task (sit-ups) and found no difference between subjects using mental practice and a group that did no practice at all [23]. Shick investigated the effects of mental practice (details of the procedure were not provided) on volley and service skills, in volleyball players [19]. Mental practice yielded an improvement in service skills in comparison with a no-treatment control group, but there were no differences between the groups on volleying skills.

It has been suggested that a combination of mental practice and physical practice may be the optimal training routine [36]. Trussell found that mental practice, followed by physical practice, yielded more improvement on a three-ball juggling task than physical practice alone [39]. However, although Egstrom [5] and Steel [40] found that a combination of mental and physical practice yielded significant skill improvements, the extent of improvement was not significantly better than groups receiving physical practice only.

More recent studies have yielded a similar pattern of confusion. Meyers et al. working with gymnasts, compared the effects of different combinations of mental and physical practice (physical practice; mental practice; combined physical and mental) and a no-practice control group [27]. They predicted that while mental practice would enhance performance on simple tasks and when the motor skill was well established, physical practice would be more effective when the skill was more complex and not so firmly established within the subject's skill repertoire. Contrary to prediction, the physical practice group outperformed the mental practice group on both simple and complex tasks. The combined mental/physical practice group improved significantly across all task levels, but the improvement of this group was not significantly different from the other groups. The mental practice group improved significantly from pretest to posttest on two of the three tasks, but again this improvement was no greater than that of the control group.

In a study of similar design focusing on dart throwing accuracy, Mendoza and Wichman found that their mental practice group outperformed the control group, but once again the physical practice group significantly outperformed the mental practice group and a combined physical/mental practice group [41].

As noted earlier, relatively few studies have looked at the effect of mental practice on performance in actual competitive settings. As Suinn points out, skill acquisition involves not only the strengthening of correct responses, but also the transfer of correct responses to competitive conditions [35]. In a study focused on transfer of skill, Meyers, Schleser, and Okwumabua investigated the effect of a cognitive behavioral intervention (a combination of imagery, coping strategies and self instruction) on free-throw and field goal accuracy of two female college basketball players [42]. They used a single subject, multiple baseline design with treatment reversal for one subject. Both subjects were experienced college team athletes; one player was a center (subject 1) and the other a forward (subject 2).

Baseline recording with the center revealed a 71.1 percent free throw accuracy during practice, with a 41.3 percent accuracy rate during game performance. This pretest performance, clearly indicated that the free-throw skill was well established, but was not being transferred to the game setting. After intervention, the practice performance stayed much the same (75.4%), but the game performance increased to 54.8 percent accuracy. When the subject was instructed to cease using the mental practice techniques, the game performance dropped to 28.6 percent accuracy, while the practice rate remained constant at 76.9 percent. For the second subject, field goal accuracy was targeted, with an increase from a baseline accuracy of 36.7 percent to a 52 percent accuracy rate during the intervention period.

The single subject design makes it difficult to generalize from these results. However, the study included several findings of interest. It is of note, that the practice free-throw accuracy rate of subject 1 did not improve with intervention. Meyers et al. suggested that this may indicate that the imagery based strategies ". . . do not directly improve physical skills but may facilitate physical performance" [27, p. 347]. They argued that this performance improvement is most likely a result of the athlete coping better with the demands of the game and suggested that improvement in coping is a result of better arousal control, positive expectations of success and an increase in self-efficacy.

Several other studies have examined the effect of imagery rehearsal on basketball free-throw accuracy. Kolonay assigned college basketballers to four groups: a no-treatment control group; relaxation only; imagery only; and visuo-motor behavioral rehearsal [43]. Visuo-motor behavioral rehearsal (VMBR) was developed by Suinn and combines relaxation with imagery rehearsal [25]. The 7 percent improvement in accuracy for the VMBR group was not only statistically significant, but it was claimed that this level of improvement meant the difference between winning and losing in eight games during the season. The relaxation only and imagery only groups did not change at all.

However, this finding was not replicated by Lane [44]; while his VMBR group showed more improvement in free-throw accuracy than no-treatment controls, the difference between the groups was not significant. Lane noted that the difference between the groups was more apparent in "away" games than "home" games. Assuming that "away" games occur in a more demanding environment, this finding further suggests that at least in some cases, mental practice may work by enhancing the athlete's ability to cope with the demands of the competitive environment, rather than via direct skill enhancement.

It may be that for the elite athlete with highly established skills, the positive effect of mental practice may have to do with maximizing the transfer of skills from practice to performance. However, as Feltz and Landers rightly point out, it is simplistic to view mental practice as operating at only one stage of learning [29]. For the novice athlete, mental practice may enhance skill by reinforcement of a template or schema of the task. However, it is likely that this template must be initially established by some actual experience with the task. At higher skill levels, mental practice may still serve to enhance the efficiency of the athlete by strengthening a cognitive template, but might also work by maximizing the cognitive focus of the athlete by improving concentration and reducing skill-disruptive levels of arousal. At elite levels of performance, skill level may well be close to a ceiling, leaving little room for actual skill enhancement. For these top-level performers, the value of mental practice may be mostly in ensuring transfer of skill from practice to performance; at this stage the cognitive focusing effect of imagery may be the most important.

IMAGING ABILITIES AND THEIR ROLE IN
MENTAL PRACTICE

There is some evidence that greater gains from mental practice may be expected among those performers who have the ability to form vivid images, than among those whose imagery ability is weak [45, pp. 182-184]. The assumption has been that this ability is always used during mental practice, but apart from a few anecdotal accounts no systematic inquiries have been undertaken to ensure that this is so.

Studies are required, which involve the selection of vivid and weak imagers to engage in mental practice and ratings of the vividness (life-likeness) of the images, achieved during such practice. It might be predicted that increases in performance level are more closely related to the level of vividness *achieved* during mental practice than to level of vividness, as indexed by scores on a standard test of imagery taken at another time.

What has been said for the imagery dimension of vividness, applies equally to that of control [46]. As the work of Start and Richardson suggested, the dimension of imagery control may interact with that of vividness, either to enhance or to reduce the benefit gained from mental practice [47]. As with vividness, so with control, it is desirable to obtain ratings of achieved control immediately following mental practice and not to rely on scores from a standard test of imagery control. At the moment, there is no more than anecdotal evidence concerning the degree of control achieved during actual mental practice. Clark provided us with the well-known anecdote of the basketball player who "reported mentally attempting to bounce the ball, preparatory to shooting, only to imagine that it would not bounce and stuck to the floor. This disturbed him to a point where he could not success-fully visualize the shooting technique" [38, p. 567]. Systematically obtained accounts of what is taking place during mental practice are needed in future research.

A third dimension of imagery, which requires investigation, has been called "orientation" [48]. No general measure of this dimension is available, but once again inquiry, as to the orientation employed, may provide an important insight into the effectiveness of mental practice for different individuals, when perform-ing different movement tasks.

The dimension of orientation refers to whether mental practice is undertaken from the performer's perspective or from the perspective of an external observer. Someone adopting the first orientation can experience the kinaesthetic sensations appropriate to the skill as well as the visual experience (imagery) of the apparatus, etc., that would be *seen* in actual performance. Someone adopting the second external orientation, will *see* him or herself engaged in the skilled activity as if from the perspective of an outsider, but will not experience kinaesthetic involve-ment. In an exploratory study of a *closed* skill, Mahoney and Avener found that successful Olympic level gymnasts tended to use internal rather than external imagery [49]. In a better controlled study reported by Neisser, the mental practice of dart throwing with an internal orientation was found to produce higher levels of accuracy in actual performance, than mental practice with an external orientation [14].

There may well be a relationship between perspective of imagery and type of skill; it seems plausible that closed skills would benefit more from an internal focus, while open skills may gain most benefit from an external orientation. It might seem obvious that this should be so, but no systematic research has yet been published to provide any convincing evidence on the relevance of this orientation variable.

That modality of imagery, may be of importance to effective mental practice, has been implied more often than it has been demonstrated. At least since Arnold's paper [50], the two modalities of imagery to receive most theoretical and empirical attention have been the visual and the kinaesthetic. In a study reported by Marks, it was found that in mentally practicing a two-handed rotary-pursuit-tracking-task, those with both vivid visual and kinaesthetic imagery improved significantly more than those with weak imagery in these two modalities [51]. White, Ashton, and Lewis [52] found that of all the modalities measured by the revised Bett's test of imagery vividness [53], only that for kinaesthetic imagery showed a significant correlation with improved performance of the *racing start* among swimmers, who had engaged in mental practice of this skill. This emphasis on kinaesthetic imagery is consistent with Jones' view that this modality is of special importance to effective mental practice, at least of closed skills [54]. On occasion, it may happen that other modalities are of significance to individual performers. For example, Suinn reports the case of a swimmer whose visual imagery became more lifelike (changed from black and white to color), when she mentally dived into a pool and "could feel the coldness of the water" [35, p. 512].

It may be that verbal imagery (self talk) has a special place in all forms of mental practice. More research attention needs to be given to this possibility. When a performer has decided upon the cue that will be used to initiate a mental practice trial, the first self instruction might take the form of a command to, "begin imaging the task now." This might be followed by the key phrase or sentence that most readily (for a given performer and task) suggests the action to be performed. For example, Annett mentions a squash coach who assists his pupils in adopting the correct stance for receiving service by telling them to imagine themselves in the stereotypic position of a "Red Indian on the war-path waving a tomahawk" [55, p. 196]. For those taking part, this sentence appears to have encapsulated "what would otherwise be much longer statements specifying the angles of virtually all the main body joints, as well as a feeling of tension and preparedness to act" [55, p. 197]. Not only can a player experience this body readiness (i.e., mentally practice it) at any time through the use of this command, but can use the command when waiting to receive a service during actual play. Verbal imagery may also be associated with self instructional interventions, when coping statements are rehearsed; for example, Meyers et al. coached their gymnasts in the use of statements such as, "That's an easy move. I know I can do it pretty well. . . . That was great. I really did a good front walkover" [27, pp. 76-77].

Given the importance of these different imagery characteristics, more needs to be known on the best way of training those who lack them. Only one published study is known, which has attempted to evaluate the effectiveness of different training procedures. This investigation was undertaken by Richardson and Patterson and aimed to enhance the vividness of imagery available to weak imagers [56]. The essential ingredient in effective training involves increased attention to the sensory qualities of objects and events, as these are experienced through all modalities; plus practice in forming appropriate images of these actual sensory-perceptual events. Attention and subsequent practice may be enhanced when the trainee is moderately relaxed and undistracted by other concerns. Martens describes a similar training program that he extended to include the controllability dimensions, but unfortunately no evaluation data is provided [57].

EXPLAINING IMPROVEMENTS IN PERFORMANCE ATTRIBUTABLE TO MENTAL PRACTICE

All major reviews of the literature have concluded that mental practice can be of benefit [29, 34-36, 45, 57-61]. However, as noted earlier, our understanding of the process of mental practice is limited. Why does it work?

Let us begin with a consideration of those closed skills that make up the bulk of all studies where the role of mental practice has been investigated.

IMPROVEMENT IN CLOSED SKILLS

Mental practice has been said to influence physical performance, via one or other of three mediating systems. For convenience of exposition, these will be called the motivational, cognitive, and learning systems. Unfortunately, there has been a tendency to approach the problem of explanation, as if all tasks for which mental practice has been found to be beneficial are essentially the same and as if ultimately, only one explanation can be correct. An alternative and potentially more useful approach is to consider how different explanations may apply under different task conditions.

Motivational System

The physical performance of a particular skill may be improved when mental practice is employed to achieve an optimum level of motivation. Sometimes motivation may need to be increased and sometimes decreased to achieve an optimum level, but it can be demonstrated that it is to this system, rather than any other, that we must turn for an explanation. An example is provided by Silva: a junior college basketball player had achieved a high level of accuracy in making free throws in non-competitive situations [9]. Why could he not perform equally well in competitive situations? In discussion with his coach, it became clear that he felt over aroused (anxious) under the stress of competitive play and had lost his self-confidence. Self-confidence (a motivational construct) was restored by a mental practice program designed to reduce anxiety and promote confidence. Under non-competitive conditions, he was instructed to visualize himself going to the foul line under *must make* circumstances. Then the "shot was rehearsed repeatedly for various real game situations; such as, a coach taking time-outs to freeze the shooting player or opponents distracting the subject with arm and hand movements or verbalizations" [9, p. 459]. He was also asked to imagine ". . . himself missing an important shot, but coming back and making the second shot" [9, p. 459] to further reinforce coping capacity under pressure. For mental practice at home and immediately prior to taking a free-throw in a competitive game, the words "relax" and "practice" were paired with an image of himself taking three dribbles, focusing and then calmly shooting the basket. As a result of these mental practice exercises, he improved his free-throw shooting accuracy from an average of 54 percent in the first seven games of the season to 75 percent in the final sixteen games.

Given that the skill level (learning) of this player was high to begin with, but that performance under stressful conditions was unrepresentative of what had been learned, the explanatory problem is to account for the improvement that followed mental practice. From the player's testimony, it appears that he had been over aroused when taking foul shots prior to seeking assistance, but that relaxation followed by mental practice served to reduce this arousal to near optimum levels, leading to more successful transfer of his skills to the competitive game setting.

Cognitive System

Where it happens that the motor movements of a task have been learned to a high degree of proficiency, but the order that they are to be executed have not, mental practice of the sequence of movements may be expected to facilitate the speed and accuracy of the final performance. If the task is a finger maze [1], a digit substitution task [62], a card sorting task [2], a finger dexterity test [63], or a sequence of ball throws [64], the motor movements may be readily available, but the sequence must also be learned.

Whether these sequences are learned and maintained by silent self-talk (e.g., "first left, then right, then right again," in a finger maze) or by their visually (and/or kinaesthetically) imaged counterparts, it is the cognitive system that is primarily involved in the learning and maintenance of such a movement sequence. Much of the benefit gained by a diver, a dancer, or a gymnast, when a complicated sequence of movements is mentally rehearsed prior to performance, may be attributed to this type of cognitive activity. However, as the smooth coordination of motor movements, in addition to their sequencing, becomes of increasing importance to high level performance, mental practice may also influence the motivational system by providing added reassurance to the performer.

Learning System

When mental practice of a well learned skill is carried out prior to performance, it may be used to influence the motivational system (e.g., reduce anxiety or promote self-confidence) or it may be used to influence the cognitive system by consolidating the accurate sequencing of a complex series of movements, especially but not exclusively, where the motor movements required are simple and repetitive (e.g., card sorting).

We now come to consider the way in which mental practice might lead to improved performance by acting more directly on the perceptual-motor learning elements of a skill. Many skills (e.g., dart throwing, putting) have relatively clear criteria for success (i.e., accuracy) and require some form of feedback or knowledge of results (K.R.) if improvement is to occur. Indeed, in writing about the physical practice of perceptual-motor skills, Bilodeau and Bilodeau concluded that, "there is no improvement without K.R., progressive improvement with it and a deterioration after its withdrawal" [65, p. 250].

If this is true, how is it possible for mental practice to produce any improvements? In the absence of any objective indication of deviation from perfect performance (i.e., K.R.), it might be thought that mental practice could not affect the learning system directly. The following facts suggest that a possible mechanism does exist by which mental practice could produce the feedback necessary for improvement in performing a perceptual motor skill.

1. There is a common experience of "knowing" whether or not an accurate performance will result, at a point after the relevant body movements are complete, but before the projected object (e.g., dart, ball) has been separated from the thrower or striker by more than a few centimeters. Is this experience supported by the facts? The answer appears to be, yes. In a study by Henderson, it was found that skilled dart players could predict the landing point of each throw, when the flight of the dart and its point of impact were made invisible, subsequent to the dart leaving the thrower's hand [66]. In this example, existence of an accurate motor program or template for the movement (i.e., high level of skill) was sufficient to provide a basis for feedback.

2. Not only do physical throws or other movements have kinaesthetic effects, but so do mentally imaged movements of the body. Though not necessarily as specific in their effects on the appropriate muscles, an imaged activity will produce detectable electromyographic activity. This finding was first

reported by Jacobson [67] and replicated with variations in procedure by Shaw [68, 69], Shick [19], and Suinn [35].

3. If an imaged action has actual physiological effects on the muscles involved in that action, both kinaesthetic feedback of relevant (usable) kind is available, plus the implicit "visual" information associated with it. In this mental practice situation it is important that the implicit "visual" information is represented at a level of intensity and accuracy that will provide a basis for correcting the next mentally practiced movement. Thus, the actual kinaesthetic feedback, which is likely to be below the threshold of conscious awareness, nevertheless brings with it an associated visual image of the movement's outcome, for example, a dart landing in an outer part of the board at 3 o'clock.

4. In earlier sections, evidence was presented suggesting that those who are already relatively skilled and who have vivid, controlled visual and kinaesthetic imagery available to them, benefit most from mental practice. Because such evidence has particular relevance to the importance of perceptual-motor skills, it is especially important that more of it be obtained. The time has come for more detailed studies, where the factors believed to mediate successful mental practice are examined in relation to a wide range of perceptual-motor tasks and in relation to different skill levels among the performers.

CONCLUSIONS

1. The majority of studies on the effects of mental practice have used subjects with relatively little experience of the skill being observed (i.e., novices). Relatively few studies have been reported where subjects have high levels of skill prior to the mental practice. In many studies, the level of skill of subjects is not adequately defined; broad categories such as "novice" and "experienced" need to be replaced by more precise definitions of base rate skill.

2. It is difficult to draw firm conclusions from research in this area, due to variation across studies in terms of the form of mental practice employed, the nature of the skill being investigated and the length and number of sessions of mental practice. In addition, there is a need for more rigorous assessment of the actual use of the mental practice procedure during practice and prior to and during actual performance.

3. The outcome data are confusing. Mental practice generally yields better results than no-practice, but adding mental practice to physical practice does not, in general, add significantly to the effect of physical practice alone.

4. With the elite athlete, there is a suggestion that the major effect of mental practice is to enable the efficient transfer of skills from practice to competition, rather than to directly enhance the level of skill.

5. Our understanding of the process of mental practice is limited. It seems likely that mental practice will have different effects for athletes of different skill levels. It is tentatively suggested, that for the elite athlete, mental practice is most likely to work via the motivational and/or cognitive systems rather than by affecting the learning process.

6. Research should routinely include measures of relevant individual difference variables, notably differences in imaging abilities [70].

REFERENCES

1. R. S. Sackett, The Influence of Symbolic Rehearsal upon the Retention of a Maze Habit, *Journal of General Psychology, 10,* pp. 376-395, 1934.
2. H. M. Perry, The Relative Efficiency of Actual and Imaginary Practice in five Selected Tasks, *Archives of Psychology, 34,* pp. 5-75, 1939.
3. L. N. Morrisett, Jr., *The Role of Implicit Practice in Learning,* unpublished doctoral dissertation, Yale University, 1956.
4. G. Whiteley, *The Effect of Mental Rehearsal on the Acquisition of Motor Skill,* unpublished diploma in education dissertation, University of Manchester, England, 1962.
5. G. H. Egstrom, Effect of an Emphasis on Conceptualizing Techniques during Early Learning of a Gross Motor Skill, *Research Quarterly, 35,* pp. 422-481, 1964.
6. R. G. Hall, *The Imaginal and Verbal Components in the Acquisition of a Perceptual-Motor Skill,* unpublished doctoral dissertation, Washington State University, 1971.
7. R. M. Suinn, Behavior Rehearsal Training for Ski Racers, *Behavior Therapy, 3,* pp. 519-520, 1972.
8. R. T. Sterner and L. Carpp, Psychomotor Rehearsal: Enhancement of Rotary Pursuit Tracking Using a Massed Training Schedule, *Perceptual and Motor Skills, 44,* pp. 243-248, 1977.
9. J. M. Silva III, Competitive Sport Environments: Performance Enhancement through Cognitive Intervention, *Behavior Modification, 6,* pp. 443-463, 1982.
10. A. Richardson, Imagery: Definition and Types, in *Imagery: Current Theory, Research and Application,* A. A. Sheikh (ed.), Wiley, New York, 1983.
11. T. E. Samuels, *The Effects of Mental Practice on the Acquisition of a Perceptual Motor Skill,* unpublished doctoral dissertation, Washington State University, 1969.
12. M. M. Smyth, The Role of Mental Practice in Skill Acquisition, *Journal of Motor Behavior, 7,* pp. 199-206, 1975.
13. G. E. Powell, Negative and Positive Mental Practice in Motor Skills Acquisition, *Perceptual and Motor Skills, 37,* p. 312, 1973.
14. U. Neisser, Toward a Skillful Psychology, in *The Acquisition of Symbolic Skills,* J. A. Sloboda (ed.), Plenum, New York, 1983.
15. R. L. Woolfolk, M. W. Parrish, and S. M. Murphy, The Effects of Positive and Negative Imagery on Motor Skill Performance, *Cognitive Therapy and Research, 9,* pp. 335-341, 1985.
16. S. J. Phipps and C. A. Morehouse, Effects of Mental Practice on the Acquisition of Motor Skills of Varied Difficulty, *Research Quarterly, 40,* pp. 773-778, 1969.
17. J. Nicklaus, *Golf My Way,* Simon & Schuster, New York, 1974.
18. M. L. Epstein, The Relationship of Mental Imagery and Mental Rehearsal to Performance of a Motor Task, *Journal of Sport Psychology, 2,* pp. 211-220, 1980.

19. J. Shick, Effects of Mental Practice on Selected Volleyball Skills for College Women, *Research Quarterly, 41*, pp. 88-94, 1970.
20. R. C. Noel, The Effect of Visuo-motor Behavioral Rehearsal on Tennis Performance, *Journal of Sport Psychology, 2*, pp. 220-226, 1980.
21. W. I. Steel, The Effect of Mental Practice on the Acquisition of a Motor Skill, *Journal of Physical Education, 44*, pp. 101-108, 1952.
22. E. I. Rawlings and I. L. Rawlings, Rotary Pursuit Tracking Following Mental Practice in the Acquisition of Rotary Pursuit Tracking, *Perceptual and Motor Skills, 38*, p. 302, 1974.
23. I. B. Kelsey, Effects of Mental Practice and Physical Practice upon Muscular Endurance, *Research Quarterly, 32*, pp. 47-54, 1961.
24. E. D. Ryan and J. Simons, What Is Learned in Mental Practice of Motor Skills: A Test of the Cognitive-motor Hypothesis, *Journal of Sport Psychology, 5*, pp. 419-426, 1983.
25. R. M. Suinn, Visual Motor Behavior Rehearsal for Adaptive Behavior, in *Counseling Methods*, J. Krumboltz and C. Thoresen (eds.), Holt, New York, 1976.
26. R. S. Weinberg, D. Gould, A. Jackson, and P. Barnes, Effect of Cognitive Strategies on the Tennis Serve of Players of High and Low Ability, *Perceptual and Motor Skills, 50*, pp. 663-666, 1980.
27. A. W. Meyers, R. Schleser, C. J. Cooke, and C. Cuvillier, Cognitive Contributions to the Development of Gymnastic Skills, *Cognitive Therapy and Research, 3*, pp. 75-85, 1979.
28. A. Bandura, Self Efficacy: Toward a Unifying Theory of Behavioral Change, *Psychology Review, 84*, pp. 191-215, 1977.
29. D. Feltz and D. Landers, The Effects of Mental Practice on Motor Skill Learning and Performance: A Meta-analysis, *Journal of Sport Psychology, 5*, pp. 25-57, 1983.
30. L. E. Smith and J. S. Harrison, Comparison of the Effects of Visual, Motor, Mental and Guided Practice upon Speed and Accuracy of Performance of a Simple Eye-Hand Coordination Task, *Research Quarterly, 33*, pp. 299-307, 1962.
31. J. E. Razor, *A Comparison of the Effects of Mental and Physical Practice as a Means of Increasing Strength*, unpublished doctoral dissertation, Indiana University, 1966.
32. J. O. Standridge, *The Effect of Mental, Physical, and Mental-Physical Practice in Learning the Whip Kick*, unpublished Master's thesis, University of Tennessee, 1971.
33. D. Fosbury, Fosbury on Flopping, *Track Technique, 55*, pp. 1749-1750, 1974.
34. A. Richardson, Mental Practice: A Review and Discussion, Part 1, *Research Quarterly, 38*, pp. 95-107, 1967.
35. R. M. Suinn, Imagery and Sports, in *Imagery: Current Theory, Research and Application*, A. A. Sheikh (ed.), Wiley, New York, 1983.
36. R. S. Weinberg, The Relationship between Mental Preparation Strategies and Motor Performance: A Review and Critique, *Quest, 33*, pp. 195-213, 1982.
37. K. B. Start, The Influence of Subjectively Assessed Games Ability on Gain in Motor Performance after Mental Practice, *Journal of General Psychology, 67*, pp. 169-172, 1962.
38. L. V. Clark, Effect of Mental Practice on the Development of a Certain Motor Skill, *Research Quarterly, 31*, pp. 560-569, 1960.
39. E. M. Trussell, *Mental Practice as a Factor in the Learning of a Complex Motor Skill*, unpublished Master's dissertation, University of California, 1952.
40. W. I. Steel, *Effect of Mental and Physical Practice on Endurance on a Bench Press Task*, unpublished research report, University of Manchester, 1963.

41. D. Mendoza and H. Wichman, "Inner" Darts: Effects of Mental Practice on Performance of Dart Throwing, *Perceptual and Motor Skills, 47,* pp. 1195-1199, 1978.

42. A. W. Meyers, R. Schleser, and T. Okwumabua, A Cognitive Behavioral Intervention for Improving Basketball Performance, *Research Quarterly for Exercise and Sport, 53,* pp. 344-347, 1982.

43. B. J. Kolonay, *The Effects of Visuo-Motor Behavior Rehearsal on Athletic Performance,* unpublished Master's thesis, City University of New York, 1977.

44. J. F. Lane, Improving Athletic Performance through Visuo-motor Behavior Rehearsal, in *Psychology in Sports: Methods and Applications,* R. Suinn (ed.), Burgess, Minneapolis, pp. 316-320, 1980.

45. A. Richardson, *The Experiential Dimension of Psychology,* University of Queensland Press, St. Lucia, Queensland, 1984.

46. A. Richardson, Voluntary Control of the Memory Image, in *The Function and Nature of Imagery,* P. W. Sheehan (ed.), Academic Press, New York, 1972.

47. K. B. Start and A. Richardson, Imagery and Mental Practice, *British Journal of Educational Psychology, 34,* pp. 280-284, 1964.

48. M. J. Mahoney, Cognitive Skills and Athletic Performance, in *Cognitive Behavioral Interventions: Theory, Research and Procedures,* P. C. Kendall and S. D. Hollon (eds.), Academic Press, New York, 1979.

49. M. H. Mahoney and M. Avener, Psychology of the Elite Athlete: An Exploratory Study, *Cognitive Therapy and Research, 1,* pp. 135-141, 1977.

50. M. B. Arnold, On the Mechanism of Suggestion and Hypnosis, *Journal of Abnormal and Social Psychology, 41,* pp. 107-128, 1946.

51. D. F. Marks, Imagery and Consciousness: A Theoretical Review from an Individual Difference Perspective, *Journal of Mental Imagery, 2,* pp. 275-290, 1977.

52. K. D. White, R. Ashton, and S. Lewis, Learning a Complex Skill: Effects of Mental Practice, Physical Practice and Imagery Ability, *International Journal of Sports Psychology, 10,* pp. 71-79, 1979.

53. P. W. Sheehan, A Shortened Form of Bett's Questionnaire upon Mental Imagery, *Journal of Clinical Psychology, 23,* pp. 386-389, 1967.

54. J. G. Jones, Motor Learning without Demonstration of Physical Practice, under Two Conditions of Mental Practice, *Research Quarterly, 36,* pp. 270-276, 1965.

55. J. Annett, Motor Learning: A Review, in *Motor Behavior: Programming, Control, and Acquisition,* H. Heuer, U. Kleinbeck, and K. H. Schmidt (eds.), Springer-Verlag, New York, 1985.

56. A. Richardson and Y. Patterson, An Evaluation of Three Procedures for Increasing Imagery Vividness, in *International Review of Mental Imagery* (Volume 2), A. A. Sheikh (ed.), Human Science Press, New York, 1986.

57. R. Martens, Imagery in Sport, *Sports Medicine, 8,* pp. 213-230, 1984.

58. A. Richardson, Mental Practice: A Review and Discussion, Part 2, *Research Quarterly, 38,* pp. 263-273, 1967.

59. S. M. Murphy, Models of Imagery in Sport Psychology: A Review, *Journal of Mental Imagery, 14,* pp. 153-173, 1990.

60. C. Corbin, Mental Practice, in *Ergogenic Aids and Muscular Performance,* W. P. Morgan (ed.), Academic Press, New York, 1972.

61. K. E. Hinshaw, The Effects of Mental Practice on Motor Skill Performance: Critical Evaluation and Meta-analysis, *Imagination, Cognition, and Personality, 11,* pp. 3-35, 1991-92.

62. D. Eggleston, *The Relative Value of Actual versus Imagery Practice in a Learning Situation,* unpublished Master's dissertation, Columbia University, 1936.

63. E. Ulich, Some Experiments on the Function of Mental Practice Training in the Acquisition of Motor Skills, *Ergonomics, 10,* pp. 411-419, 1967.
64. S. C. Minas, Mental Practice of a Complex Perceptual-motor Skill, *Journal of Human Movement Studies, 4,* pp. 102-107, 1978.
65. E. A. Bilodeau and I. M. Bilodeau, Motor Skills and Learning, *Annual Review of Psychology, 12,* pp. 243-280, 1961.
66. S. E. Henderson, Predicting the Accuracy of a Throw without Visual Feedback, *Journal of Human Movement Studies, 1,* pp. 183-189, 1975.
67. E. Jacobson, Electrophysiology of Mental Activities, *American Journal of Psychology, 44,* pp. 677-694, 1932.
68. W. A. Shaw, The Relation of Muscular Action Potentials to Imaginal Weight Lifting, *Archives of Psychology, 35,* pp. 1-50, 1940.
69. W. A. Shaw, The Distribution of Muscular Action Potentials during Imaging, *Psychological Record, 2,* pp. 195-216, 1938.
70. A. Richardson, *Individual Differences in Imaging: Measurement, Origins and Consequences,* Baywood, New York, 1994.

CHAPTER 5

Imagery Perspectives and Learning in Sports Performance

BRUCE D. HALE

There seems to be little doubt that mental practice can positively affect skilled motor performance, especially when practice conditions are "optimal." It is equally clear, however, that mental practice is not always an aid to performance and that factors such as practice type, the skill task, and the nature of the performer ultimately reflect the extent of behavior change resulting from mental practice [1, p. 115].

This conclusion aptly sums up the state of knowledge concerning the efficacy of mental practice as an ergogenic aid for motor performance. Most research has indirectly investigated mental practice by merely examining behavior changes resulting from short-term mental rehearsal periods [2]. Richardson has suggested that in order to precisely state the necessary conditions for beneficial mental practice effects to occur, scientifically controlled experiments must be undertaken to manipulate the following independent variables; clarity and control of visual and kinesthetic imagery, magnitude and location of muscle action currents, degree of task familiarity, and accuracy of anticipated outcomes [3,4]. Recent literature reviews have further suggested that the following variables also need to be closely examined to understand the mechanism of beneficial sport imagery; "cognitive-symbolic" versus "motor tasks," stages of learning, and motivational effects [2,5,6].

Within the last decade, another critical variable has emerged offering enormous potential for performance enhancement—imagery "perspective." Until 1931, individual differences in imagery types were explored under the categories of "visualizers" versus "motor imagers" versus "verbalizers." Jacobson first suggested within-subjects' utilization of different sensory modalities (visual, kinesthetic, auditory, etc.) during imagery might be a crucial variable affecting learning and performance [7].

But it was Mahoney and Avener who first explicitly categorized visual and kinesthetic images into an "internal-external" classification based on the individual's visual and somatic perception experienced during image generation

[8]. They defined internal imagery as "requiring an approximation of the real-life phenomenology such that a person actually imaging being inside his/her body and experiencing those sensations that might be expected in the actual situation" [8, p. 137]. In external imagery, "a person views him/herself from the perspective of an external observer (much like in home movies)" [8, p. 137].

In their exploratory study with Olympic gymnastic team candidates, athletes, who successfully made the team, reported a higher frequency of "internal," rather than "external," images ($r = .51$) on a standard questionnaire. Internal imagery would primarily contain a combination of first-person visual and kinesthetic images (i.e., experiencing the real world through your eyes, ears, movement, etc.), while external imagery would be classified as third-person visual images (i.e., watching a videotape of yourself performing).

Several years later, Lang's "Bio-informational Theory of Emotional Imagery" provided a theoretical model that can be used to explain recent perspective-specific results in terms of image structure [9].

This chapter will identify traditional theoretical explanations for mental practice effects; trace previous research on modality-specific physiological responses during imagery; examine perspective-based learning and performance effects; and make theoretical application toward enhancement of sport performance.

IMAGERY PERSPECTIVE AND SPORT PERFORMANCE

Theoretical Explanations

Previous reviews of literature [1, 3-6] have described several causal theories that attempt to explain the bases for beneficial mental practice effects and suggest different uses for each imagery perspective in sport performance.

Gross Framework or Insight Theory. In order for optimal motor learning to occur, the learner must be able to conceptualize the entirety or "gestalt" (total picture) of the task. Mental rehearsal could help the learner to direct his/her attention to the gross outline of the task. This theory has often been used to explain the prerequisite of previous experience in a skill (either actual or vicarious) that seems to be necessary for positive effects of mental practice to occur. A corollary suggests that improvements are due to behavioral changes resulting from insight or a new perceptual organization of the task. In order to mentally practice effectively, an athlete needs to physically attempt different aspects or watch someone else perform the skill.

Symbolic-Cognitive (-Perceptual) Theory. A learner must learn to selectively attend to important aspects or cues when performing a skill if proficiency is to be gained. It is possible that repetitive mental practice of a skill could help the learner by focusing attention on several "key" cues that constitute important components of successful performance. For example, in tennis serving, the athlete needs to perfect a usable ball toss, "backscratch" position, and wristsnap. Repeated images could reinforce remembrance of these desired cues and prevent forgetting, while allowing subconscious perceptual motor plans (or "schemas") to be constructed in the pre-motor areas of the cortex.

It is postulated that mental practice only facilitates the cognitive aspect of a task such as timing, sequence, and performance strategies [5,6]. In an open loop system, the motor program is determined by a pre-planned movement sequence that determines the motor program without necessitating peripheral feedback [10]. Evidence to support this theory must show that mental rehearsal is as effective or superior to physical practice on performance of tasks identified as primarily cognitive; conversely, on tasks labeled as having largely motor components, mental practice should be inferior to physical practice. According to proponents, tasks can be classified on a hypothetical continuum of highly motor (involving quantities of skeletal muscle) to highly cognitive (involving primarily reasoning, thinking, or verbalization).

Although several reviews support the cognitive function of mental practice [5], this theory has not been adequately tested by employing one task that can be manipulated to test both ends of the continuum in a single experiment. Similarly, scientists cannot comparatively test this theory versus the psychoneuromuscular theory without measuring both performance *and* neuromuscular activity during experimentation. Finally, a potential experiential biasing in testing formats must be eliminated. It may be that since subjects are more familiar with practice in a cognitive rather than a motor (or kinesthetic) mode, evidence is produced that supports the cognitive theory while the motor function does not get a fair test. To date, the majority of evidence produced in laboratory studies [e.g., 10] supports the cognitive theory, although these noted weaknesses have not been logically investigated.

Psychoneuromuscular "Feedback" Theory. As far back as 1855, Carpenter asserted that any idea which dominates the mind finds its expression in the muscles [11]. This "idea-motor principle" postulates that continued concentration upon a certain idea gives it "dominant" power in the mind, that then determines the movement in the muscles ("involuntary instruments of the will"). In other words, if ideas occur that reach a certain level of intensity, then the content of those ideas will be expressed through subsequent muscle activity. This idea-motor principle is the basis of neuromuscular explanations for mental imagery effects.

When a skill is overtly performed, the performer receives visual feedback (knowledge of results and performance) and kinesthetic feedback (body position, muscular tension, tactile feelings) that are necessary for successful task performance, because they allow the performer to constantly evaluate his/her progress. In any trial-and-error learning procedure, the individual receives sensory and perceptual information from the Golgi tendon organs that is "fed-back" to the premotor cortex so corrections or strengthening of the motor program can be made before the next attempt. This feedback principle is well-supported for overt practice and is also surmised to occur with mental practice.

When an individual processes a vivid, well-controlled image of a sport skill, this theory posits that the image produces identical, minute innervation in the muscles actually used in the task (idea-motor principle). For example, if an athlete imagines "curling" a twenty-five-pound dumbbell, then muscular activity should actually occur in the biceps [7, 12, 13]. In this closed loop model, muscular activity is assumed to provide kinesthetic feedback to the cognitive schema in the pre-motor cortex for adjustments on future trials, thus improving skill performance [3]. This theory further suggests that an athlete must be able to develop vivid, controllable visual and kinesthetic imagery in order for muscular innervation and kinesthetic feedback to result.

A recent review rejects the feedback notion and speculates that the neuromuscular innervation during imagery serves to prime the muscles for action by lowering the sensory threshold and facilitating a focused attentional set in the performer (i.e., the muscles are given a "mental warm-up") [5]. Other information processing research in motor learning suggests that the muscular innervation during imagery also does not serve a feedback purpose, but is merely a corollary effect of a central, controlling schema program [10]. A further methodological weakness of supportive evidence is that the data measured to date has been confined to amplitude measures, not frequency or duration, which are necessary to support the "mirror hypothesis."

In the final analysis, it may be impossible to insure that subjects in an imaginary experimental paradigm are not consciously minutely tensing the muscles used in the task and producing localized efference. In order to support the psychoneuromuscular theory, it will be necessary to show that any muscular efference is truly localized to the muscles normally involved in producing the movement. As mentioned previously, all future research should include adequate measurement of motor performance/learning and electrophysiological responses so both theoretical predictions can be compared in a single study.

Recently, a French researcher has attempted to show that the two theories may actually be complementary [14]. According to Savoyant, mental practice may be effective in several cognitive components of the motor task: one component relating to planning and organizing the motor sequence and another component related to motor programming and the control of program execution. It is conceivable that one type of mental imagery (cognitive-symbolic) may be effective in early stages of learning "construction of an image of the action, that is, the definition of the operations and their execution order, the conditions to be taken into account, and the 'logical' aspects of the action," [14, p. 253] and another type of image (neuromuscular feedback) may be most effective in later stages of learning "when the motor action becomes generalized and automatized, when learning without knowledge of results can occur" [14, p. 254]. If applied to the imagery perspective variable, this complementary model suggests that "external" imagery may be most appropriate for cognitive-symbolic effects since it emphasizes a "visual gestalt" of the task, while "internal" imagery may best enhance neuromuscular feedback effects since kinesthetic imagery is a major focus in its processing.

Motivational Effects. It is quite possible that learning and performance differences between treatment and control groups may just reflect differences in levels of motivation between subjects. The positive findings produced to date could just be "Hawthorne" effects, or the result of more attention being paid to one group than another. Coaches may find athletes improving in mental practice and subsequent performance solely because they spend more "quality time" with each individual.

IMAGERY PERSPECTIVE AND SPORT RESEARCH

Muscular Response Findings

The imagery perspective adopted by an athlete during mental practice has been precisely identified as a critical variable in performance enhancement strategies [2, 5-8, 13]. Unknown to Mahoney and Avener in 1977, several earlier studies had also noticed modality-specific results in their subjects when neuromuscular concomitants were measured. Although they did not label these different imagery perspectives as "internal" and "external," it is clear by their published reports that they were dealing with the same variable.

Jacobson's Original Findings. Jacobson's brilliant series of experiments culminated in one that partially supported the ideomotor principle and further specified a relationship between the nature of the imagery modality and the concomitant response [7]. He inserted bipolar needle electrodes into the biceps brachii muscle and a monopolar needle electrode into the recti muscles of the isolateral eye. Amplitude measurements were made by a string galvanometer. When subjects were instructed to "visualize bending the right arm," increased action potential occurred in the ocular muscles but was absent in the biceps. Conversely, when subjects were requested to "imagine bending the right arm," muscular activity appeared in the biceps in almost all trials, while ocular activity occurred only a third of the time. Although only rudimentary electromyographical (EMG) equipment and statistical techniques were utilized, the results suggested that the predominant modality/perspective of the image seemed to be the crucial variable in determining the location of the concomitant physiological response. If Mahoney and Avener's [8] classification of perspective is applied to Jacobson's imagery instructions, then internal imagery produced primarily biceps activity and external imagery generated ocular responses.

Sports and Motor Behavior Research. In an earlier sport science study, Schramm measured EMG activity in eight superficial muscles of students while they performed an imagined dumbbell "curl" [15]. Subjects were requested to concentrate on the "feeling quality" of the muscle contractions (kinesthetic/ internal imagery instructions). Results indicated that neuromuscular activity during mental imagery occurred in all subjects after physical experience in the task had been gained, but not one subject produced activity in all eight muscles sampled.

Shick included an exploratory investigation of muscular and ocular responses in her dissertation examining mental practice effects on volleyball skills [16]. EMG electrodes measured activity at the anterior deltoid and tibialis anterior sites, while electrooculographical (EOG) activity was recorded at the outer canthus and over the center of the eyelid. She reported that most subjects: 1) indicated that they saw the entire person (external perspective) while mentally rehearsing the serve skill, and 2) utilized a first-person visual perspective and kinesthetic (internal) imagery while covertly practicing the volleying skill. Although she was not able to identify any particular EMG and EOG pattern with the small subject groups and lacked quantifiable statistics, a re-examination of one response table for highest-skilled versus lowest-skilled individuals (for six-minute volleying-internal images) suggests that better skill level was associated with greater responses at all electrode sites. Unfortunately, she did not use inferential statistics on each subject's response magnitude for an internal versus external imagery perspective to test if any relationship existed.

More recently, Suinn anecdotally reported, in an uncontrolled case study with an Alpine skier whom he was counseling with "video-motor behavioral rehearsal," that his leg muscle EMG record (recorded on paper) mirrored the terrain of the downhill course he had imagined [17]. He had been instructed to imagine skiing from the same perspective "as if" (internal perspective) he was really there. This unsubstantiated finding conforms to the neuromuscular feedback theory that predicts the generation of identical muscular responses during overt and covert experiences of the same skill.

Similarly, Bird reported bursts of muscular activity occurred at times when they would be expected to occur during actual performance of equestrian events [18]. Strong responses were evoked when riders imagined gliding the horse over jumps, but little response was present when the horses committed a fault.

A more powerful replication by Wehner, Vogt, and Stadler produced the first quantifiable data to support the "mirror hypothesis" [19]. On a contour tracking task where biceps EMG was measured, a similar frequency distribution in the power spectrum occurred for both actual and imagined practice but not for a control group.

Hale reasoned that Jacobson's [7] site-specific findings needed to be replicated with sophisticated EMG analysis and statistical inference by comparing internal and external imagery perspectives under controlled conditions [13]. Using a within-subjects design involving both imagery perspectives of a simple dumbbell curl, he found that internal images (kinesthetically-oriented) produced localized bicep innervations and external imagery (visual orientation) did not. This result further implies that imagery that more realistically involves the individual in visual and kinesthetic experiences is more likely to produce localized neuromuscular outflow than merely visualizing an action.

More recently, several master's theses replicated Hale's finding for internal imagery-mediated muscular concomitants. Harris and Robinson found only EMG responses in the internal imagery of skilled karate participants [20]. They also showed that the muscular concomitants were indeed specific to the body part involved and might also be more strongly produced by veteran performers than by novices. Durall measured EMG activity of the rectus femoris of gymnast-subjects during the imagination of several routines [21]. His significant findings again supported the notion that internal imagery produces concomitant muscular efference in the body parts involved in the action and that the length of time for imagery rehearsal approximates the actual performance duration of the routine.

Jowd used mental practice with a juggling task to examine whether the magnitude of muscular activity concomitance is a function of motor skill level [22]. Although EMG amplitude increased during imagery (a majority naturally used an internal perspective) for all subjects, no significant differences were found between skill levels. Kinesthetic imagery ability on the Movement Imagery Questionnaire and EMG magnitude during imagery were positively related ($r = .78$) for the highly skilled group, suggested that imagery ability may be a more significant variable than motor skill level in mediating muscular responses.

In a replication of Hale's [13] research, Vigus and Williams measured EMG activity at dominant biceps, triceps, and non-dominant triceps during imagery rehearsal in both perspectives of a biceps curl and reported no significant differences, thereby suggesting that neither imagery perspective nor prior experience at imagery or physical practice influence muscle innervation [23]. Two possible methodological weaknesses may help to explain these conflicting results. First, subjects were never given prior relaxation to insure that the pre-imagery baseline was in fact a true, stable tonic baseline, and the imagery instructions were not clearly reported so the script may not have contained sufficient internal imagery perspective cues to produce an EMG response. These apparently conflicting results warrant more sophisticated replication of localized efference at active and nonactive sites.

Perhaps an earlier finding by Ulich may offer a viable explanation for lack of support of the "mirror hypothesis" [24]. He showed that a moderate amount of EMG activity during rehearsal, rather than a low or high amount, may be associated with increases in physical performance. Therefore, it may be hypothesized that the magnitude of muscular concomitance is not the critical indicator of mental practice effects, only part of a total picture that must include measures of duration and frequency. If one part of the brain is sending signals to the muscles to inhibit overt responses during imaging, then one should not expect muscles to show "mirror responses" during imagery versus actual movement because of additional muscle innervation that may prevent actual movement by creating antagonistic muscle tension. Future research must directly show a relationship between muscle activity (presumably during internal imagery) and subsequent task performance in order to fully support a neuromuscular feedback explanation.

Neurophysiological Response Findings

Kohl and Roenker proposed that the neurophysiological mechanisms shared by imagery and actual practice are located high in the central nervous system, while actual practice also includes peripherally-activated mechanisms [25]. In an early study, Davidson and Schwartz found differences in EEG activity patterns while subjects engaged in visual and kinesthetic imagery [26]. In line with internal-external perspective differences, they found significantly greater occipital activation during visual imagery and greater activation of the sensory-motor region during kinesthetic imagery.

Furthermore, a recent review by Decety and Ingvar has concluded that some of the same brain structures are active during actual practice and imagery based on sophisticated neurophysiological recordings [27]. For example, the supplemental motor cortex appears to be involved in both imagined and actual practice [28], but only the motor cortex is active during actual movement. Roland et al. hypothesized that the supplementary motor cortex is responsible for cognitive response planning or maintenance of previously created plans. The motor cortex is believed to be one of the last brain sites to be active before actual response initiation. Therefore, it appears that actual movement activates rolandic areas in addition to the supplemental motor cortex.

To date, no actual testing of brain function has been undertaken using internal/external imagery as an independent variable. Several findings do suggest possible alternative mechanisms. Roland et al. measured regional blood flow and cerebral oxidative metabolism when subjects were asked to imagine *visually* walking along a well-known route in their home town; they were specifically instructed not to imagine their own movements during the walk [29]. Prefrontal cortical areas were active in both hemispheres, in frontal eye fields, and occipital areas. The most pronounced flow occurred in the parietal cortex. Oxidative metabolism increased bilaterally in the subcortical neostriatum and posterior thalamus.

In contrast, Decety and Philippon measured cerebral blood flow when subjects imagined writing numbers with their hand while taking a "first person perspective" and "trying to feel their writing hand" [30]. The prefrontal cortex, supplementary motor area, and cerebellum were significantly active. The inclusion of cerebellar activity in this internal, kinesthetically-oriented perspective may explain why concomitant muscular responses are only measured peripherally with internal images and not with the external, "visual" perspective. Decety and Ingvar further suggest that this cerebellar activity during imagery may act to inhibit efferent outflow [27]. Since pathways through the cerebellum lead through the red nucleus, the reticular formation, and the vestibular nuclei to the spinal cord [31], imagined cognitive processing could innervate the muscles through this route. Subsequent neurophysiological measures must directly measure activation differences between internal and external images.

Imagery Perspective and Sport Performance

As mentioned previously, Mahoney and Avener's original classification of imagery perspectives also suggested that level of performance in sport might also be mediated by these imagery styles [8]. With elite gymnasts, they concluded that a preference for internal imagery use seemed to be associated with success in being selected to the U.S. Olympic team. More recent research has attempted to investigate a possible causal link between imagery perspective and subsequent learning and sport performance.

Descriptive Studies. Subsequent descriptive studies have not clearly replicated Mahoney and Avener's proposed relationship between internal imagery and skill level [8]. Meyers, Cooke, Cullen, and Liles administered a modification of the Mahoney and Avener questionnaire to nine collegiate racquetball champions and correlated these scores with coaches ranking (3 levels of skill) and objective performance records [32]. No differences were found between less and more skilled racquetball players in the frequency of imagery use or in the imagery perspective.

Highlen and Bennett also failed to replicate Mahoney and Avener's findings concerning imagery perspective [33]. Responses from thirty-nine wrestlers attempting to qualify for the 1980 Canadian World Games squad did not correlate with final selection classification for the team.

In another recent replication by Rotella, Gansneder, Ojala, and Billing, forty-seven downhill skiers completed the Mahoney-Avener Inventory and their own Coping and Attentional Inventory [34]. Yearly performance ratings were used to divide the subjects into three ability groups. Imagery questions on the first questionnaire did not correlate highly with ranking; but on the second instrument, more successful skiers indicated that they developed visual images of the course (often including tips of skis and boots—an internal perspective), whereas less successful skiers developed visual images of their entire body skiing down the racecourse (external perspective).

Doyle and Landers administered the revised Mahoney-Avener questionnaire to 184 rifle and pistol shooters [35]. They discovered that elite (international-level) performers used predominantly internal imagery and sub-elite (state and junior champions) shooters prepared for competition with a mixture of internal and external imagery.

Finally, Suinn and Andrews surveyed elite "A" and "B" members of a professional Alpine ski tour [36]. Although there was a suggestion that better skiers' imagery was more vivid and clear, no trends were found on the internal versus external perspective during imagery rehearsal.

The results of these correlational studies are conflicting regarding the importance of imagery perspective for highly skilled athletes. Until larger populations of elite and non-elite participants in a variety of team and individual sports are tested for predominant imagery perspective and some control is obtained over prior performance history, these exploratory investigations must await a reliable conclusion.

Quasi-Experimental Investigations of Imagery Perspective. Several studies have attempted to manipulate a specific imagery perspective utilized during mental practice and assess the treatment effects on athletic performance. Shelton and Mahoney randomly assigned twelve female varsity basketball players from equal-proficiency dyads to internal and external practice groups [37]. For three weeks (15 sessions) after regular practice, each group practiced several minutes of progressive relaxation training and three minutes of one mental imagery perspective. Then, subjects rated the success of their imagery and shot twenty successive free throws in the gym. After mental practice training, the external group was significantly more accurate than athletes in the internal group. Inspection of the means revealed that this difference was due to a non-significant deterioration in performance for the internal subjects, rather than improvement in external athletes. A further analysis of change scores indicated that the performance of less skilled players had changed significantly more than that of highly skilled shooters. Responses on pre- and post-experimental Imagery Exercise Questionnaires (10 sub-scales) were correlated with free throw change scores and reported ability to use auditory images was a significant predictor of a change score ($r = .84$), while degree of active involvement in the scene was marginally related to change score ($r = .52$).

In a published master's thesis, Epstein examined the effects of mental perspective on immediate dart-throwing performance [38]. Seventy-five male and female subjects were assigned to an internal ($n = 30$) or external ($n = 30$) condition or control group ($n = 15$). Treatment groups threw thirty darts to assess baseline ability, then underwent mental rehearsal training and practice (2 minutes), performed mental rehearsal-aided throwing (30 darts), underwent another rehearsal training period (1 minute), and threw thirty more rehearsal-aided darts.

Mental rehearsal perspectives were found to have no significant effect on immediate motor performance. However, according to Epstein, the imagery style question did not correlate with ability for males or females, possibly because it was answered affirmatively by almost every person. Of 300 imagery reports, 39 percent were exclusively internal, 37.7 percent switched from external to internal at a critical point, 12 percent were simultaneously internal and external, 8 percent changed perspective at non-critical points, 3.7 percent were totally external, and 1.7 percent switched from internal to external at a critical point. The notion of stable and encompassing imaginal styles was not supported by the data, which suggests that image perspective may not only be a function of the individual doing the imagining, but also of the scene being imagined and imagery instructions.

More recently, Mumford and Hall examined the effects of three imagery types (internal kinesthetic, internal visual, external visual) on figure performers of sectional and national level figure skaters [39]. Skaters who were given four fifty-minute sessions of imagery types produced subsequent performances that were not rated differently by judges than skaters who watched films related to, but not of, skating figures. Future research must closely control subject mental practice away from the experimental situation and also monitor control cognitions post hoc to insure that treatment manipulations are purely administered.

Clinical Use of Imagery Perspectives. As yet, only one controlled field study has manipulated imagery perspective to test its effect on motor learning and sport performance. But several clinicians have attempted to structure imagery instructions into either an internal or an external emphasis so that close parallels can be tentatively drawn from these published case studies.

Nideffer published rehearsal strategies in words that are very similar to external-internal distinctions [40]. He postulated that continuous, active rehearsal (visual and kinesthetic) is a necessity if beneficial mental practice effects are to follow. But he also suggested that visual rehearsal (external) alone can be conducive to identifying and correcting mistakes in form and analyzing other technical aspects of performance. Furthermore, he proposed that attention should be focused on bodily feelings (kinesthetic cues) during execution, and these feelings should be remembered and mentally rehearsed in order to facilitate selection of discriminant cues necessary for successful performance.

Suinn has offered similar suggestions under his Visuo-Motor Behavior Rehearsal (VMBR) method that have subsequently been scientifically tested [41]. According to Suinn, "This imagery is more than visual. It is also tactile, auditory, emotional, and muscular" [41, p. 512]. He later further differentiates the imagery types by suggesting that imagery *rehearsal* of an action (internal) produces physiological concomitants, while just "thinking about" an action (external) does not. In his review of literature, he describes several case studies of elite athletes and several experimental studies of subjects who have benefitted from VMBR (internal-oriented) rehearsal.

A recent experimental study by Hall and Erffmeyer tested the VMBR method aided by videotaped modeling of performance and imagery perspective [42]. In a methodology similar to Hale's [13] film loop control of the internal manipulation treatment group, subjects viewed a model successfully shooting foul shots from the first-person visual perspective and subsequently imaged their own perfect performance while in a relaxed state. The VMBR-modeling group showed significant improvement in foul-shooting performance over the relaxation and imagery control groups. The authors also mentioned that all VMBR subjects reported feeling kinesthetic sensations in association with visual imagery. As Hale had emphasized earlier, it is necessary to tightly control imagery instructions and perspective through visual aid-facilitated practice and imagery script in order to produce beneficial effects [13].

Until the internal-external differentiation has been strictly tested on both learning and performance in a field and laboratory studies, it is rather speculative to insist that athletes only mentally rehearse from an internal perspective in order to enhance performance. But the initial indirect clinical evidence does suggest that most available techniques already include a predominantly internal emphasis, and the scientific data [42] so far indicate that kinesthetic-oriented rehearsal does lead to performance improvement.

A THEORETICAL EXPLANATION OF THE SPORT RESEARCH FINDINGS

Lang's "Bio-Informational Theory of Emotional Imagery"

Except for the previously noted theories that attempt to explain the general effects of mental practice and imagery on sport performance, very few recent theoretical explanations have been offered in motor behavior that concisely predict the perspective-mediated findings in concomitants and performance that have been reported here. But recently, Lang, a clinical psychologist, has proposed a theory of imagery structure and concomitant emotional-physiological responses which seems to generalize to non-emotional mental practice and accurately explains the specificity of muscular responses produced by the differing imagery perspectives [9]. To date, his data have already partially supported his model when tested for action scenes and motor behavior [9, 43]. It offers some intriguing applications to sport psychology when delineated in terms of internal-external perspectives.

Lang has adopted a cognitive, information-processing analysis of imagery that describes how all knowledge is stored in a single, uniform manner [9]. This model hypothesizes that the brain stores knowledge (processed, abstract information about objects, relationships, and events), not raw appearances. The basic unit of information is the proposition that has been defined as the linkage of two conceptual contents organized into associative information networks. A network contains data about stimuli, responses, and means, and is processed as a unit when a critical number of propositions is accessed.

In his model, an image is defined as "an elaborate description . . . or a functionally organized, finite set of propositions . . . of assertions about relationships, descriptions, interpretations, labels, tags, which prompt percept-like verbal reports, but which are more basically the units of a preparatory set to respond [44, p. 864]. Whenever a network of propositions is processed (in perception or imagery), measurable efferent flow (physiological responses) always occurs. Rather than just emphasizing image content, this theory also focuses on the modality-specific operations of perceptual processing (responses and efference).

Each image structure contains three fundamental classes of statements: stimulus, response, and meaning propositions. Stimulus propositions are descriptors or assertions about stimuli, that is, they describe specific stimulus features of an imagery scene. A sport example would be "a *black, 25-lb.* dumbbell." Response propositions are assertions about behavior, such as verbal responses, overt motor acts, or physiological organ responses, and are modality-specific operations. An athletic example might be "*tensing* a muscle." Meaning propositions function in an analytical and interpretative role in order to define the significance of input and output events, the probabilities of stimulus occurrence, and the consequences of action. A sport-related proposition of this type could be: "I get nervous before competition and my heart begins pounding."

Input and output variables can have a controlling influence on image processing and efference. The three main input variables are:

1. the image cue, i.e., the instruction to imagine something;
2. the image orthesis, an aid to image formation (film, verbal, script, etc.) which may include detailed information about what is to be imagined; and
3. instructions to assume a psychological set of active participation in the imagined events [9, p. 502].

This final variable asks the client to imagine him/herself personally engaged in the context "as if" it was really happening.

The first output variable is the subject's verbal report. These scene descriptions generally follow the input script with spontaneous client deletions and additions shaped by experience and understanding of the task. Subjects can also usually report on the vividness of the experiences. Affective quality and intensity in a wide variety of physiological systems is the last output variable. This somatovisceral arousal can often be measured concomitantly during the imagery session.

Lang's Hypothetical Predictions. Clinical research in the lab and field by Lang and colleagues in the last ten years has shed light on several central hypotheses that form the crux of this bio-informational model.

1. The main efferent hypothesis of the theory has been investigated several times and supported clearly by all published data [9, 43, 45-48]. Simply stated, this prediction states that, during active imagery, the pattern of effector activity is determined by the *response* propositions (kinesthetically-oriented) in the image structure. Stimulus propositions do not influence physiological concomitants. Lang has also shown that fear scenes result in concurrent increases in heart rate and respiration, while action scenes (i.e., sport imagery) are accompanied by enhanced muscular activity; response propositions of one physiological system will produce primarily localized efference in the same physiological organs [43].

2. A corollary to these findings indicates that the response specificity of the individual's physiological system to particular response propositions is mediated by the individual's past experiences [47]. In other words, a veteran athlete might

react more strongly to images of precompetitive anxiety or muscular exertion than a secondary individual because of extensive physical practice and experience with these situations.

3. While many theorists have assumed that vividness is some kind of inherent imagery ability associated with individual differences, Lang has proposed that vividness is determined by the completeness of the evoked propositional structure and pattern of response propositions. By manipulating stimulus and response propositions in different kinds of imagery scripts, Lang and colleagues have strongly supported this notion [9, 43, 45, 47]. Vivid recollections contain long lists of discriminating stimulus elements and the response components can often be measured by psychophysiological instruments.

4. An additional hypothesis by Lang further counters the assumed inherent ability view of image clarity. Lang and his colleagues have repeatedly shown that it is possible to enhance vividness ratings by a training program that systematically reinforces the client's statements of experienced response propositions [9, 43, 45, 48]. When both the imagery script and behavioral training emphasize response propositions, subject reports of vividness and concomitant physiological responses were higher. The findings support the hypothesis that modification of the feedback loop of verbal report (an output variable) can subsequently change the propositional structure of the image. This finding further suggests that biofeedback of physiological concomitants for poor images may offer another technical means for enhancement of clarity.

5. Probably the most speculative and least researched prediction from Lang's theory involves behavior change in a clinical sense. Using emotional images, Lang has asserted that, in order for therapeutic image effectiveness (positive behavior change) to occur, clients must generate affect during imagery which must be subsequently reduced with repeated scene presentation [49, 50]. According to Lang:

> The aim of therapy could be described as the reorganization of the image unit in a way that modifies the affective character of the response elements. . . . Thus, to alter the fear state, response propositions of the fear image must be accessed and changed, bringing about congruence of the components of fear [44, p. 867].

Perhaps the same principle also holds for sport imagery and motor learning, because in order for a task to become learned or corrected, it is necessary to first include correct response propositions in the image structure and subsequently produce concomitant physiological responses.

Several recent sport-specific studies have offered initial support for Lang's theory [51, 52]. In the first study, heart rate response during imagery was significantly greater during action and athletic scenes when compared to a fear scene. In Kaczor's thesis, response VMBR-trained (Suinn [41]) participants did show the desired trends for HR and EMG measures while imagining a juggling scene. The author also suggested that the task manipulation may not have been effective as both participants with and without prior juggling experience, regardless of whether trained in stimulus- or response-oriented VMBR, failed to improve in juggling performance. Kaczor finally recommended that special attention needs to be given to skill learning paradigms, controlled response-laden imagery scripts, relevancy of imagery scripts to participants, and frequent manipulation checks to insure proper imagery processing.

In summary, it seems evident that the inclusion of response information in the image structure is more critical than the perspective adopted by the participant if physiological concomitants are to follow. When Bauer and Craighead independently manipulated focus of imagery (stimulus or response) and perspectives (1st or 3rd person), they only obtained differences in physiological response as a result of the focus of image processing (response focus produced greater activation) [53]. Hale's research with sport movement supports this emphasis on response orientation, not perspective per se [13]. As Cuthbert, Vrana, and Bradley have concluded, it is necessary to have a good conceptual match between information in the image prompt and that stored in memory in order to obtain appropriate physiological concomitants [54]. This match typically occurs when an event is a personally relevant emotional situation or a well-practiced athletic event, or has been experienced in the laboratory.

SPORT IMAGERY APPLICATIONS

Imagery Perspective and Response Propositions

The classification of imagery perspectives into two types by Mahoney and Avener [8] closely parallels Lang's theoretical explanations and presents an opportunity to apply his concepts to sport and motor behavior. In Lang's theory, *external* images would be composed primarily of many stimulus propositions and ocular response propositions because the sense modality is constrained to a third-person *visual* perspective during processing. On the other hand, *internal* images would contain a variety of response propositions involving several modalities because the athlete is experiencing the world "as if" he/she was really there and feeling his/her body react as it actually might. Mental rehearsal for sport performance in this perspective would emphasize the *kinesthetic awareness* and *muscular exertions* of typical motor acts—images might be labeled as first-person visual and kinesthetic.

Previous motor research [7, 13, 17-21, 52] have strongly supported Lang's [9] hypothesis that response propositions are responsible for localized muscular efference during imagery. Internal images (containing mostly kinesthetic response propositions) produce localized muscular innervations, and external imagery (probably ocular response propositions) does not.

Lang's predictions also relate specifically to two of the possible explanations of beneficial mental practice effects. The neuromuscular feedback theory [1] postulates that these muscle innervations during imagery solidify neuromuscular connections (via a "mini-workout"). Similarly, under the "transfer of training" principle, it is hypothesized that the more realistic the practice, the more beneficial the transfer of skill learning to actual competition ("as if" imagery). If these models correctly pinpoint muscular concomitants and realistic response propositions as the two necessary prerequisites in order for beneficial mental practice effects to occur, then Lang's model will have immediate application to non-clinical sport imagery.

So far, little scientific attempt has been made to link Lang's model to sport-specific applications. The following suggestions must be considered purely speculative because of a lack of sport-related research in the lab and on the field. Therefore, caution is advised in blindly applying these principles without first strenuously testing the theoretical components.

Applied Principles for Sport Imagery

1. Physically attempt a skill first in order to develop kinesthetic awareness and inclusion of response propositions in motor imagery. Alternate mental and physical practice in order to replay kinesthetic aspects of prior proper execution to strengthen neuromuscular circuits.

Once the athlete has a clear picture of a skill, then he/she needs to actually attempt it. For example, if he/she is learning a new "back dive," he/she must attempt it several times so he/she can "kinesthetically" experience the body movements and sensations and later cognitively repeat them during the training session. It may be necessary to have learned a task fairly well in order to produce muscular concomitants that might possibly be useful for neuromuscular feedback [14].

The optimal time to mentally rehearse a skill would be *immediately* after he/she has successfully executed it. For example, a gymnast has been practicing a new move in his/her floor exercise routine. After he/she finally accomplishes a successful "move," he/she should stop for a brief time and mentally replay the visual and kinesthetic aspects of the skill. This repetition helps to firmly establish the proper neuromuscular circuits in his/her memory so that future execution of the skill becomes more and more "automatic." If immediate rehearsal is not possible, take several minutes to rehearse during practice breaks or later in the locker room or at home. Learning speed will be increased, and successful performance will become more consistent.

2. Include response propositions in imagery scripts: adopt an internal perspective (emphasizing movement and kinesthetic memories) and

an "as if" psychological set in order for muscular interventions to occur.

For example, "feeling" his/her heart pumping, "experiencing" the muscle exertion and contraction of effort and movement, and bodily "reacting" in his/her mind to the environment the way he/she would in the real situation could process response propositions.

How can one learn to include response propositions and improve his/her kinesthetic imagery? The most obvious way is to pay closer attention to body movements and feelings when performing in practice. First, have them try closing their eyes while they perform. Certainly, this is not feasible in some sports like ski jumping, gymnastics, or running, but could be an important part of practice for some athletes.

For instance, bowlers can practice "pendulum" swinging their bowling ball while standing on the approach with their eyes closed in order to increase their awareness of their swing mechanics. Those athletes who cannot afford to close their eyes might use their free hand to feel the muscles of their leg, arm, shoulder, etc., as they move during execution.

3. Use visual and kinesthetic aids to improve vividness and control. Include film loops, slow-motion playback, helmet camera (for first-person visual perspective), videotapes, and kinesthetic awareness exercises as ways to improve the reality of the image content.

Often when an athlete is learning a new skill and only has a hazy picture of the task components, seeing the skill several times via video-tape will more clearly imprint it into his/her memory. Using visual aids replayed in slow motion can also allow athletes to learn proper technique sooner and obtain a clearer picture of task progression. Imagery can be performed first at "slow motion" speed and then completed with normal pace. This form of practice can also enhance awareness of recurrent errors and aid in correcting execution.

4. Improve vividness by positively reinforcing experienced response propositions (from verbal reports) in a training program for athletes. Biofeedback of muscular concomitants may help to enhance the clarity of kinesthetic imagery.

Imagery scripts that include a variety of movements ("I ran, jumped, threw, etc."), kinesthetic awareness ("My body felt compressed"), feelings of muscular exertion and effort ("I strained," "My biceps tensed," "My feet bounced," etc.), emotional responses ("My heart pounded"), and other active responses can be verbally reinforced to effectively enhance imagery vividness.

5. It may be necessary to include movement-oriented response propositions in scripts which generate motor concomitants in order for performance enhancement to occur.

This principle remains the most speculative prediction of this research, because evidence in sport is lacking. Future investigators will test whether movement-oriented imagery enables individuals to learn motor skills faster.

> 6. External imagery may still be useful in obtaining a clear picture of a new motor skill (the "gestalt" explanation) and to locate recurrent errors in execution.

Live demonstrations and videotapes of the athletes practicing skills can help individuals learning the progression of a new skill and also enable them to easily pinpoint unnoticed, recurrent errors. Vivid, controlled imagery should also aid in these functions.

Sport Uses for Imagery

The use of internal imagery containing muscular response propositions seems particularly well-suited to certain sport situations. Rehearsing moves of particularly effective strategies to insure success in competition would be worthwhile. Athletes could be taught to identify important environmental cues and physically feel themselves reacting successfully. For example, a basketball player could mentally rehearse recognizing a defensive cue, feel him/herself effectively move to execute a driving layup, thereby making various strategies more "automatic" responses during actual competition.

A more direct application from clinical-emotional imagery would involve coping responses. Athletes could mentally practice handling an anxiety-provoking sport situation or overcoming a current mistake in order to improve their success ratio and build confidence for future stressful events. In their images, athletes would begin experiencing the cognitive and physiological manifestations of an anxious situation, practice gaining control by relaxing, positive sub-vocalization, etc., and finish by seeing and *feeling* a successful skill execution. A typical application might be a bowler who experiences disruptive anxiety before his/her turn to bowl in a big tournament.

A similar application would involve error correction. The athlete could rehearse beginning to make an error in execution, and then feel him/herself correcting the movement and performing successfully. Kinesthetic imagery could help performers to compare good and bad attempts and finish with perfect performance. Since performances are rarely perfect, coping with flaws in performance may be especially helpful for all athletes.

Finally, injury rehabilitation is an area where response proposition-laden imagery might speed recovery. If concomitant muscular innervations can be generated solely through vivid mental practice, perhaps the loss of muscle tone, coordination, and timing could be reduced with regular application. In addition, successful, realistic imagery experiences might help the injured athlete overcome any performance mental blocks related to the injury situation.

These situations describe a partial list of sport applications that seem appropriate from Lang's theoretical model. Recently Murphy and Jowdy have listed the following uses of imagery for sport: skill acquisition, skill maintenance, arousal regulation, planning/event management, emotional rescripting, self-image manipulation, and attentional and pain control [6]. Further research is necessary before his model's applications can be confidently judged to be a trustworthy tool in the sport psychologist's repertoire. At present, his theory offers intriguing and rational explanations for widely used mental rehearsal practices common to sport.

CONCLUSION

Since the published report of Mahoney and Avener [8] linking imagery perspective with gymnastic success, several descriptive and experimental studies have examined the internal-external variable. A theoretical model has emerged which viably explains the psychophysiological data of past imagery research [9]. Many practitioners are beginning to construct athletic applications based on this research and its predictions. After a thorough examination of the history of this imagery variable, the following conclusions are warranted:

1. The internal-external orientation in imagery perspective is part of a viable construct with distinct physiological concomitants and possible differential learning effects. The critical element in obtaining effects using imagery manipulation seems to be the processed stimulus or response orientation in the script, rather than a focus on the imagery perspective per se. Various components of the image structure (stimulus and response propositions) must be further examined with motor behavior.
2. Internal imagery (containing primarily response propositions) produces localized muscular efference, and external imagery does not.
3. Based on several prior descriptive and experimental studies, it is unclear whether any causal relationship exists between imagery perspective and sport performance. Concise manipulation of the variable must be undertaken in future experiments in motor learning and performance research in order to reach a conclusion.
4. The neuromuscular feedback explanation of beneficial mental practice effects remains viable. While several investigations contain data that do not support this idea, other research shows support for the localized efference component that is critical to its explanation. Further studies need to study the amplitude, frequency, and duration of efference using sophisticated statistical analyses to more closely examine the "mirror" hypothesis. As elsewhere in science, it may require a rethinking of simplistic explanations into more complex solutions that combine components from each explanation for different levels of learning and performance.

5. Lang's theory offers many testable predictions applicable to imagery perspective and sport research. His predictions about response propositions, vividness, behavioral training, and learning and performance must all be thoroughly tested in sport situations.

Mental practice can be a powerful tool of the sport psychologist in helping athletes to maximize their athletic potential. But, before coaches and athletes undertake a hodgepodge of rehearsal techniques with unproven validity, scientific research is necessary to give practitioners the "how" and "why" learning to beneficial learning and performance effects. To reiterate Corbin's plea, well-controlled research is first necessary in order to determine what "optimal" practice conditions for mental rehearsal are before they can be judiciously applied to sport behavior [1].

REFERENCES

1. C. B. Corbin, *Ergogenic Aids and Muscular Performance*, W. P. Morgan (ed.), Academic Press, New York, 1972.
2. R. S. Weinberg, The Relationship between Mental Preparation Strategies and Motor Performance: A Review and Critique, *Quest, 33*:2, pp. 195-213, 1982.
3. A. Richardson, Mental Practice: A Review and Discussion: Part 1, *Research Quarterly, 38*, pp. 95-107, 1967(a).
4. A. Richardson, Mental Practice: A Review and Discussion: Part 1, *Research Quarterly, 38*, pp. 263-273, 1967(b).
5. D. L. Feltz and D. M. Landers, The Effects of Mental Practice on Motor Skill Learning and Performance: A Meta-analysis, *Journal of Sport Psychology, 5*, pp. 25-57, 1983.
6. S. M. Murphy and D. Jowdy, Imagery and Mental Rehearsal, *Advances in Sport Psychology*, T. Horn (ed.), Human Kinetics, Champaign, Illinois, 1992.
7. E. Jacobson, Electrical Measurements of Neuromuscular States during Mental Activities, *American Journal of Psychology, 96*, pp. 115-121, 1931.
8. M. J. Mahoney and M. Avener, Psychology of The Elite Athlete: An Exploratory Study, *Cognitive Therapy and Research, 1*, pp. 135-141, 1977.
9. P. J. Lang, A Bio-informational Theory of Emotional Imagery, *Psychophysiology, 16*, pp. 495-512, 1979.
10. R. M. Kohl and D. L. Roenker, Mechanism Involvement during Skill Imagery, *Journal of Motor Behavior, 15*, pp. 179-190, 1983.
11. W. B. Carpenter, *Principles of Mental Physiology*, (4th Edition), Appleton, New York, 1894.
12. W. A. Shaw, The Distribution of Muscular Action Potentials During Imagining, *Psychological Record, 2*, pp. 195-216, 1938.
13. B. D. Hale, The Effects of Internal and External Imagery on Muscular and Ocular Concomitants, *Journal of Sports Psychology, 4*, pp. 379-387, 1982.
14. A. Savoyant, Mental Practice: Image and Mental Rehearsal of Motor Action, *Cognitive and Neuropsychological Approaches to Mental Imagery*, M. Denis, J. Englekamp, and J. Richardson (eds.), Martinus Nyhoff, The Hague, pp. 251-257, 1988.
15. V. Schramm, *An Investigation of EMG Responses Obtained during Mental Practice*, unpublished Master's thesis, University of Wisconsin, 1967.

16. J. Shick, *Effects of Mental Practice on Selected Volleyball Skills for Women,* unpublished doctoral dissertation, University of Wisconsin, 1969.
17. R. M. Suinn, Body Thinking: Psychology for Olympic Champs, *Psychology Today, 10*:2, pp. 38-44, 1976.
18. E. I. Bird, EMG Quantification of Mental Rehearsal, *Perceptual and Motor Skills, 59,* pp. 899-906, 1984.
19. T. Wehner, S. Vogt, and M. Stadler, Task Specific EMG-Characteristics during Mental Training, *Psychological Research, 46,* pp. 389-401, 1984.
20. D. V. Harris and W. Robinson, The Effects of Skill Level on EMG Activity during Internal and External Imagery, *Journal of Sport Psychology, 8,* pp. 105-111, 1986.
21. R. T. Durall, *A Comparison between the Time of Mental Practice and the Time of Physical Performance,* unpublished Master's thesis, The Pennsylvania State University, 1985.
22. D. Jowdy, *Muscular Responses during Imagery as a Function of Motor Skill Level,* unpublished Master's thesis, The Pennsylvania State University, 1987.
23. T. L. Vigus and J. Williams, *The Effect of Skill Level and Imagery Experience on EMG Activity and Patterning during Internal and External Imagery,* paper presented at meeting of North American Society for the Psychology and Physical Activity, Vancouver, B.C., 1987.
24. E. Ulich, Some Experiments on the Functions of Mental Practice Training in the Acquisition of Motor Skills, *Ergonomics, 10,* pp. 411-419, 1967.
25. R. Kohl and D. Roenker, Bilateral Transfer as a Function of Mental Imagery, *Journal of Motor Behavior, 12,* pp. 197-206, 1980.
26. R. J. Davidson and G. E. Schwartz, Brain Mechanisms Subserving Self Generated Imagery: Electrophysiological Specificity and Patterning, *Psychophysiology, 114,* pp. 598-602, 1977.
27. J. Decety and D. H. Ingvar, Brain Structures Participating in Mental Stimulation of Motor Behavior: A Neurophysiological Interpretation, *Acta Psychologica, 73,* pp. 13-31, 1990.
28. P. E. Roland, B. Larsen, N. A. Larsen, and C. Shinhoj, Supplementary Motor Area and Other Cortical Areas in Organization of Voluntary Movements in Man, *Journal of Neurophysiology, 43,* pp. 118-136, 1980.
29. P. E. Roland, L. Erikksson, S. Stone-Elander, and L. Widen, Does Mental Activity Change the Oxidative Metabolism of the Brain?, *Journal of Neuroscience, 7,* pp. 2373-2389, 1987.
30. J. Decety and B. Phillipon, rCBF Variations During a Motor and Imagined Graphic Task in Normal Volunteers and Analysis of the Reproducibility with the 133Xe Inhalation Technique, *Journal of Clinical and Experimental Neuropsychology, 10,* p. 328, 1988.
31. D. E. Haines, *Neuroanatomy: An Atlas of Structures, Sections, and Systems,* Urban and Schwartzenberg, Baltimore-Munich, 1991.
32. A. W. Meyers, C. J. Cooke, J. Cullen, and L. Liles, Psychological Aspects of Athletic Competitors: A Replication across Sports, *Cognitive Therapy and Research, 3,* pp. 361-366, 1979.
33. P. Highlen and B. Bennett, Psychological Characteristics of Successful and Nonsuccessful Elite Wrestlers: An Exploratory Study, *Journal of Sport Psychology, 1,* pp. 123-137, 1979.
34. R. J. Rotella, B. Gansneder, D. Ojala, and J. Billing, Cognitions and Coping Strategies of Elite Skiers: An Exploratory Study of Young Developing Athletes, *Journal of Sport Psychology, 2,* pp. 350-354, 1980.

35. L. A. Doyle and D. M. Landers, *Psychological Skills in Elite and Sub-elite Shooters,* unpublished manuscript, 1980.
36. R. M. Suinn and F. A. Andrews, *Psychological Strategies of Professional Competitors,* unpublished manuscript, 1981.
37. T. O. Shelton and M. J. Mahoney, *Mental Practice with Varsity Basketball Players: Parameters of Influence,* paper presented at the convention of the Association for the Advancement of Behavioral Therapy, 1980.
38. M. L. Epstein, The Relationship of Mental Imagery and Mental Rehearsal to Performance on a Motor Task, *Journal of Sport Psychology, 2,* pp. 211-220, 1980.
39. P. Mumford and C. Hall, The Effects of Internal and External Imagery on Performing Figures in Figure Skating, *Canadian Journal of Applied Sport Sciences, 10,* pp. 171-177, 1985.
40. R. M. Nideffer, *The Inner Athlete: Mind Plus Muscle for Winning,* Crowell, New York, 1976.
41. R. M. Suinn, Imagery and Sports, *Imagery: Current Theory, Research, and Application,* A. Sheikh (ed.), Wiley, New York, pp. 507-534, 1983.
42. E. G. Hall and E. S. Erffmeyer, The Effect of VMBR with Videotaped Modeling on Free Throw Accuracy of Intercollegiate Female Basketball Players, *Journal of Sport Psychology, 5,* pp. 343-346, 1983.
43. P. J. Lang, M. J. Kozak, G. A. Miller, D. Levin, and A. McLean, Jr., Emotional Imagery: Conceptual Structure and Pattern of Somatovisceral Response, *Psychophysiology, 17,* pp. 179-192, 1980.
44. P. J. Lang, Fear Imagery: An Information Processing Analysis, *Behavioral Therapy, 8,* pp. 862-866, 1977.
45. G. A. Miller, D. N. Levin, M. J. Kozak, E. W. Cook, III, A. McLean, Jr., J. Carroll, and P. J. Lang, Emotional Imagery: Individual Differences in Imagery Ability and Physiological Responses, *Psychophysiology, 18,* p. 196, 1981.
46. D. Carroll, J. S. Mazillier, and S. Merian, Psychophysiological Changes Accompanying Different Types of Arousing and Relaxing Imagery, *Psychophysiology, 19,* pp. 75-82, 1982.
47. P. J. Lang, D. N. Levin, G. A. Miller, and M. H. Kozak, Fear Behavior, Fear Imagery, and the Psychophysiology of Emotion: The Problem of Affective Response Integration, *Journal of Abnormal Psychology, 92,* pp. 276-306, 1983.
48. D. A. Mermecz and B. G. Melamed, The Assessment of Emotional Imagery Training in Children, *Behavior Therapy, 15,* pp. 156-172, 1984.
49. P. J. Lang, B. G. Melamed, and J. Hart, A Psychophysiological Analysis of Fear Modification Using an Automated Desensitization Procedure, *Journal of Abnormal Psychology, 76,* pp. 299-234, 1970.
50. J. M. Brown, Imagery Coping Strategies in the Treatment of Migraine, *Pain, 18,* pp. 157-167, 1984.
51. J. E. Hecker and L. M. Kaczor, Application of Imagery Theory to Sport Psychology: Some Preliminary Findings, *Journal of Sport Psychology, 10,* pp. 363-373, 1988.
52. L. M. Kaczor, *Bioinformational Theory of Emotional Imagery and Imagery Rehearsal: A Process and Outcome Investigation of Performance Enhancement,* unpublished doctoral dissertation, University of Maine, 1990.
53. R. M. Bauer and W. E. Craighead, Psychophysiological Responses to the Imagination of Fearful ad Neutral Situations: The Effects of Imagery Instructions, *Behavior Therapy, 10,* pp. 389-403, 1979.
54. B. N. Cuthbert, S. R. Vrana, and M. M. Bradley, Imagery: Function and Physiology, *Advances in Psychophysiology* (vol. 4), Jessica Kingley, pp. 1-42, 1991.

CHAPTER 6

Imagery and Motor Performance: What Do We Really Know?

ALAN J. BUDNEY, SHANE M. MURPHY, AND ROBERT L. WOOLFOLK

In competitive athletics, where winning and losing are separated by a fraction of a second or inch, the smallest advantage or disadvantage can determine the outcome. Considering the tremendous investment of time and energy (many hours and years of practice and sacrifice), and the magnitude of the consequences for winning (e.g., millions of dollars), it is no wonder today's athletes search for any edge that might improve performance. Many athletes seek ways to enhance performance via methods other than standard physical practice or training. Ergogenic aids used by athletes have ranged in modality from the physical (technological advances in physical training) to the chemical (anabolic steroids, blood doping) to the psychological (mental skills training). This chapter will address one category of psychological approaches, strategies involving imagery.

Athletes and coaches rank the use of imagery as a valuable sport psychology technique, and imagery procedures are the most frequently used performance enhancement strategies among sport psychologists when consulting with athletes and coaches [1, 2]. Numerous books on psychological skills training that include chapters on imagery have been published during the past ten years attesting to the current popularity of these methods [3].

Athletes and sport psychologists have utilized imagery to influence performance in two primary ways. The first is as mental practice. Mental practice has been used to acquire, sharpen, rehearse, or transfer motor skills. The term "mental practice" has been employed interchangeably with imagery in the motor performance literature, yet mental practice procedures have varied and could involve thinking about, talking one's self through the steps, or imagining some motor movements [4]. Thus, mental practice does not necessarily involve imagery. This chapter will highlight the negative consequences of treating identically all procedures grouped under the rubric mental practice.

The second primary way athletes use imagery is as a preparation or coping strategy to help manage their performance. This use of imagery occurs in close proximity to performance, and usually involves either imagining successful performance or using images to manipulate arousal level or attentional focus. The purpose of "pre-performance" imagery is to achieve an optimal psychological and/or physiological context for maximizing performance.

Other non-performance related methods of imagery application in sport have been described in the literature, and imagery procedures have also been used in combination with other psychological or physical techniques [5]. These applications, however, will receive only limited attention in the final section of this chapter, as our primary purpose is to review the current state of knowledge concerning the relationship between imagery and motor performance.

Considering that imaginal techniques are growing in popularity, it seems appropriate to ask, what do we know about how imagery influences motor performance, and, more importantly, what effects does it have on performance? At least four major theories addressing how imagery affects performance have been proposed in the literature. No consensus exists concerning the merit of these theories. Unfortunately, the research on the effect of imaginal strategies on performance has produced similarly equivocal results.

The purpose of this chapter is to summarize the empirical data concerning the efficacy of imagery as a performance enhancement technique. The chapter will 1) provide a discussion of possible mechanisms of action for imagery in sport, 2) summarize conclusions concerning what is and is not known about the effect of imagery on motor performance, 3) highlight the potential for negative as well as positive influences of imagery on performance, 4) provide a note of caution to athletes and sport psychologists, 5) describe suggestions for future research, and 6) describe the current state of applied issues concerning imagery in sport.

MECHANISMS OF ACTION

We briefly review the primary theories concerning the positive influence of imagery on performance that have received attention in the sport literature. We then summarize the evidence for each, and, based on the tenets of each theory, we highlight the potential for negative effects of imagery on performance. Alternative models explicating the influence of imagery are discussed.

Symbolic Learning Theory

Symbolic learning theories propose that mental practice facilitates motor performance by allowing the subject to rehearse the cognitive components of a task [6]. Accordingly, the more "cognitive" elements required to perform a task, the greater should be the effect of mental rehearsal techniques. This theory has received support in that tasks with primarily cognitive components appear to be facilitated by imaginal practice [7, 8]. Symbolic learning theory, however, does not predict significant facilitation on primary motor and strength tasks, yet a number of studies have found enhancement effects with those kind of tasks. Although one could argue that this theory can account for mental practice facilitating skill acquisition, it offers little explanation for effects on already learned motor skills [9]. Moreover, differentiating between "cognitive" and "motor" components within or between tasks appears artificial and lacks validity.

Psychoneuromuscular Theory

Psychoneuromuscular theories of imagery suggest that imaginal rehearsal activates high level mental nodes priming the corresponding lower level muscle movement nodes, which, in turn, produces identical minute innervations of those muscles activated during overt performance of a given task [10]. The efficacy of imaginal rehearsal of a motor task is purported to result either from the provision of kinesthetic feedback enabling adjustment to be made in the motor behavior [11], or from the facilitation of the rate at which mental nodes representing the desired motor behavior are activated during overt performance [10].

A corollary of psychoneuromuscular theory is that internal imagery (i.e., imagining performance from the vantage point of the imager) is a more effective facilitator of performance than external imagery (i.e., imagining performance from the vantage point of an observer) because muscle innervation should be greater when employing internal imagery. Limited research demonstrates that internal and not external imagery produces localized efference, and that the efference is greater for more skilled subjects [12, 13]. However, level of efference does not correlate with measures of imagery ability or vividness, and skill level is not always a robust predictor of efference [14]. Thus, to date, there exists relatively little support for psychoneuromuscular explanations of imagery's effect on motor performance.

Attention-Arousal Theory

Hypotheses relating arousal and attention posit that imaginal rehearsal functions as a preparatory set that aids the athlete in achieving an optimal arousal level [15, 16]. Optimal arousal serves to facilitate performance by enabling attention to be focused on task-relevant cues. Moreover, it has been proposed that imagery functions as a primary facilitator for tasks of strength, and functions as a secondary facilitator for tasks with more symbolic and cognitive elements [7]. Attention-arousal hypotheses of imagery's effect on performance have received no direct empirical support. However, recent research indicates that task-relevant imagery produces greater improvement than task-irrelevant imagery [17]. Others have found a post-hoc relationship between self-reported attentional focus and performance providing indirect support for attentional focus as a moderator of imagery's effects on performance [18].

Self-Efficacy Theory

Self-efficacy theory has been proposed as an explanation for the effects of imagery on motor performance [19]. Here, imagery is hypothesized to increase an athlete's expectations of success which, in turn, increase the probability of successful motor performance. Research examining the relationship between self-efficacy and motor performance has been equivocal [20]. Both positive and negative findings have been reported concerning the effect of imagery on self-efficacy [21-23]. Although self-efficacy typically correlates with performance, there exists no strong support for imagery-induced enhancement of self-efficacy resulting in enhanced performance.

In summary, we know little about how imagery affects performance. A major problem in the sport literature is that the different uses of imagery have not been examined as discrete phenomena for investigation, but typically have been assessed as a unitary set of procedures [24]. A more fruitful working hypothesis would suggest that the mechanism(s) of action through which imagery affects performance would differ depending on the context in which imagery is employed. For example, one might posit a symbolic-learning mechanism to explain the influence of mental practice on skill acquisition, while attention/arousal or self-efficacy hypotheses might be more appropriate in understanding the effects of pre-performance imagery on performance of a well-learned motor skill.

Moreover, even if the aforementioned mechanisms were valid, it is not clear from the explication of each theory how one could reliably apply imagery procedures to enhance performance. For example, from a symbolic-learning or psychoneuromuscular perspective, it seems essential that an athlete first be able to replicate the maximal or correct physical and/or mental aspects of the motor movement. This would assume first that the athlete is aware of all components of performance, and second can produce an exact imaginal replication of such. To our knowledge, no evidence is available to support such sophisticated imaginal ability, certainly not with any complex motor skill. Thus, it is equally likely that an athlete may imagine inaccurate or "wrong" components of the task, that theoretically would produce performance decrements.

Attention/arousal hypotheses appear to have a greater probability of success in helping guide and understand the use of imagery in sport. From this perspective, imagery putatively helps the athlete obtain a maximal state of readiness, both physiologically and psychologically. Thus, the exact replication of motor movements during imagery is not required to enhance performance. However, as with the other theories, the possibility of imagery negatively affecting performance seems equally likely. For example, images could be distracting or could affect physiologic functioning in a direction detrimental to performance [23, 25]. In a recent survey of elite athletes where 35 percent of athletes reported that imagery had hurt their performance, one athlete reported, "it (imagery) has gotten me so pumped up and excited that I couldn't do anything" [26].

Alternative Models

The summary of existing models of imagery in the sports area reveals many inconsistencies, discrepancies, and divergent findings. Consideration of alternative models may better help guide basic and applied research. As suggested above, individual differences must be taken into account in any model of imagery. Before engaging in the construction of new models, however, sport psychology researchers might first look beyond the field of sport psychology and investigate the relevance of imagery theories developed in other areas of psychology.

Clinical psychology has paid special attention to the development of imagery theories. Clinical theorists have been concerned with explaining how it is that imagery interventions lead to behavior change. Two influential theories from the clinical psychology literature will briefly be examined here. Both models emphasize the importance of psychophysiological responses to imagery as well as the individual's history and how it may influence their response to various types of imagery.

Lang's Bioinformational Theory. A model of imagery originally developed by Peter Lang for the purpose of understanding a great amount of research into phobia and anxiety disorders deals specifically with the psycho-physiology of imagery. Lang's theory utilizes an information-processing model of imagery [27, 28]. The image is believed to contain a motor program containing instructions responding to the image, and it is thus a template for overt responding. It is assumed that modifying either overt behavior or vivid imagery will result in a change in the other. In this sense, this model is somewhat functionally similar to the aforementioned psychoneuromuscular theories. However, Lang's model contains two corollaries that may have important implications for understanding and testing the imagery/motor performance relationship.

First, the model states that a description of an image contains two main types of statements: stimulus propositions and response propositions. Stimulus propositions are statements that describe the content of the scenario to be imagined. Response propositions are statements that describe the imager's response to that scenario. The differences between stimulus and response propositions may be functionally similar to the previously discussed dichotomy, internal versus external imagery. Imagery instructions that contain response propositions elicit far more physiological responses than do imagery instructions that contain only stimulus propositions [29]. Lang's studies of phobic patients have indicated that the greater the magnitude of these physiological responses during imagery, the greater will be the accompanying changes in behavior [30]. This suggests that rehearsal imagery designed to influence sports performance would do well to include many response propositions in the imagery descriptions. Lang and associates findings indicate that imagery instructions containing detailed response propositions are more likely to produce the report of a vivid image and accompanying physiological responses, which, in turn, may make it more likely that the imagery will be effective in altering (positively or negatively) athletic performance. These predictions await empirical verification in the field of sport psychology.

A second important component of Lang's model indicates that an individual's reactions to imagery can affect at least three-response domains (i.e., overt behavior, thoughts, physiological function), all of which may affect performance of a complex motor skill. Individuals exhibit different patterns of reactivity among these systems when exposed to emotional stimuli [28, 29]. Moreover, these three response systems do not always respond in synchrony [29, 31]. Therefore, future research on motor performance must be more concerned with individual differences when using arousing or emotion-laden imagery (which includes most types of imagery employed prior to performance). One might expect great individual variability in the direction and magnitude of effect of imagery on motor performance. A more refined assessment of the imagery and its cognitive, physiological and behavioral concomitants is needed to further understand and predict how imagery affects performance of different individuals.

Ahsen's Triple Code Theory. Another recently developed model of imagery also recognizes the primary importance of psychophysiology in the imagery process, but goes a step further in describing another important aspect of imagery that warrants consideration in any theory of imagery/motor performance—the meaning the image has for the individual. Ahsen's triple code (ISM) model of imagery specifies three essential parts of imagery important to understanding its concomitant effects [32]. The first component is the image (I) itself. Ahsen simply defines an image as a centrally aroused sensation that possesses all the attributes of a sensation but is internal at the same time. The second part is the somatic response (S). That is, as discussed above, the act of imagination results in psychophysiological changes in the body.

The third aspect of imagery, most ignored by other models, is the meaning (M) of the image. According to Ahsen, every image imparts a definite significance or meaning to the individual. Further, every individual brings his or her unique history into the imaginal process, so that the same set of imagery instructions will never produce the same imagery experience for any two individuals. Thus this model recognizes the powerful reality of imagery for the individual, and should remind sport psychologists to pay careful attention to any significant meaning an image may have for their client. The meaning component of Ahsen's model adds to our understanding of the previously described negative effects sometimes produced by imagery techniques.

Ahsen's model suggests at least three important components of imagery research and application that warrant attention. First, the imagery script employed should be described completely in research reports, and the imaginal experience of the subject should be assessed. Second, as suggested by Lang's model, psychophysiological measures should be employed to assess how the imagery affects various physiological systems and their relation to performance. Third, the meaning of the image for each individual should be evaluated to determine whether the image carries "additional baggage" that may distract from optimizing performance.

Clearly, no one model of imagery is sufficiently developed as yet to be deserving of recommendation for use by all sport psychology researchers and clinicians. Aspects of the aforementioned theories warranting more attention are: 1) psychophysiological concomitants of imagery, 2) impact of imagery on attentional processes, and 3) the effect of the meaning of particular images on different individuals. In general, models that attend to understanding individual differences in response to imagery are needed. The use of rigorous imagery models in sport psychology will bring many benefits to researchers. As theory development becomes a more integral part of the research process, the study of imagery in sport psychology might be entering its most productive and exciting stage.

PERFORMANCE ENHANCEMENT LITERATURE

Empirical research investigating the influence of the imagery on motor performance began in the early 1900s, and currently, well over 100 studies have been conducted [7]. This research has focused primarily on mental practice strategies and to a much lesser extent on pre-performance or preparation imagery. Comprehensive reviews of these studies have consistently concluded that the research has yielded equivocal results [7, 11, 33, 34]. At best, one can assert that "mentally practicing a motor skill influences performance somewhat better than no practice at all" [7, p. 41].

In the first major review of the mental imagery/motor performance literature, Richardson examined approximately twenty-five studies [33, 34]. He discussed separately the research on the effects of mental practice on the acquisition, retention, and immediate improvement of a motor skill. From this, a number of general conclusions were asserted. First, the trend of most studies indicated that mental practice procedures are associated with improved performance (11 studies reported significant results, 7 reported positive trends, 3 reported negative results and 1 reported equivocal results). Second, there was some evidence for a positive relationship between task familiarity (experience) and the efficacy of mental practice. Third, mental practice was most effective when alternated with physical practice and when mental practice sessions did not exceed five minutes. Lastly, individual differences on three factors (games ability, selective attentional ability, and the ability to produce vivid and controlled images) received limited correlational support.

A second review of this literature evaluated over fifty studies and came to a slightly more cautious conclusion than did Richardson [11]. Instead of suggesting that mental practice procedures *are* associated with improved performance, Corbin stated that, ". . .there is little doubt that mental practice **can** positively affect skilled performance, especially when practice conditions are 'optimal.' It is equally clear, however, that mental practice is not always an aid to performance . . ." [11, p. 115]. Corbin's findings supported Richardson's earlier assertion that task familiarity may be an important factor related to the efficacy of mental practice. He further suggested that task complexity interacts with experience level to determine effects. Mental practice was most effective with tasks requiring symbolic and/or perceptual skills, and least effective with tasks requiring primarily motor skills. In general, he asserted that the research was inconclusive and certainly did not delineate optimal strategies for the duration or scheduling of mental practice procedures.

The most recent and comprehensive review of the imagery literature used meta-analytic techniques to evaluate sixty studies of both mental practice and preperformance strategies [7]. The only inclusion criterion for a study was the use of mental practice only group with either pretest scores or a control group for comparison. No other methodological standards were employed. Results indicated that, across different tasks and techniques, mental practice improved performance, with a .48 effect size overall. The effect of mental practice on highly "cognitive" tasks (e.g., dial-a-maze, card-sorting, peg-board, maze learning, and symbol digit test) was significantly stronger ($ES = 1.44$) than the effect on motor and strength tasks. Analysis of motor and strength tasks, however, did yield significant albeit smaller effect sizes in the positive direction (motor: $ES = .43$; strength: $ES = .20$). Importantly, the motor and strength tasks are representative of the type of motor performance skills that athletes seek to improve via imagery procedures, whereas the "cognitive" tasks are not.

Other factors, such as task experience, self-paced versus reactive tasks, number and length of practice sessions, immediate versus delayed posttest, type of research design, and published versus unpublished study, were included in the meta-analysis. The mean effect size of the published studies ($ES = .74$) was significantly larger than the unpublished studies ($ES = .32$). The only other significant findings were for length of practice sessions and number of practice trials per session. Although interactional analyses were not feasible because of the large number of factors and unequal n's, the author's suggested that graphic representation of the interaction among type of task, length, and number of trials per session indicated that positive effects for "cognitive" tasks were associated with very few trials and minutes per session. In contrast, positive effects for motor and strength tasks were associated with much longer sessions and many more trials per session.

We further examined this review and found that thirty-three of the 146 effect sizes were in the negative direction suggesting performance decrements associated with mental practice. All of those thirty-three tasks fell into the motor or strength categories. In addition, a number of the 113 other positive effect sizes approached 0.00, indicating that a significant number of subjects' performances must have deteriorated with the use of imagery in those studies as well. Thus, the conclusion of earlier reviews [11, 33, 34] suggesting that mental practice can lead to improvement but does not always do so was supported by the Feltz and Landers' review. Perhaps an additional conclusion acknowledging the potential for negative effects of imagery, particularly among motor and strength tasks, is warranted.

In summary, the three reviews provide cautiously positive evaluations of the efficacy of mental practice, yet the situation remains such that the extant research provides no clear indication of how, when, or where to employ mental strategies effectively, let alone optimally. Suinn asserted appropriately that:

> A major difficulty lies in the diverse methodologies used in the various studies. Tasks have ranged from card sorting . . . to basketball free throws. Studies have sometimes measured skill acquisition . . . and sometimes skill performance. Mental practice sometimes involved thinking about the movements, attempting to experience the feelings associated with the movements . . ., and sometimes simply attending to the "gestalt" of the skill" [4, pp. 510-511].

The value of these reviews is that they highlight important variables that warrant investigation and provide direction for refinement of future research. Moreover, they illustrate the confusion and potential for misunderstanding that is created when a diverse range of procedures are evaluated as one. Separate analyses and reviews of specific mental practice procedures and pre-performance uses of imagery are needed to put order into the field. Below we provide a more focused review.

Pre-performance Imagery

In this section, we review the research on pre-performance imagery. Although these techniques appear to be commonly used in many sports, pre-performance imagery has received less attention in the research literature than mental practice procedures. The majority of studies examined in the reviews discussed above did not employ pre-performance imagery, suggesting that conclusions from those reviews may not apply to this set of imaginal procedures. Below, we examine the research addressing the influence of preperformance imagery on motor skill performance, followed by the research on its effects on motor strength performance.

Motor Skills

An early study of pre-performance imagery on dart-throwing performance demonstrated that positive (success) imagery resulted in improved performance, while negative (failure) imagery did not [35]. The failure to use a control group, however, limited the generality of those results. A second examination of dart-throwing performance found that neither internal or external pre-performance imagery resulted in performance enhancement [36]. An examination of the efficacy of pre-performance imagery on tennis-serve performance found no facilitating effects for imagery for subjects of high and low tennis ability [37]. Studies of basketball free-throw shooting also have not consistently demonstrated enhancement effects with pre-performance imagery procedures, although, some data does support enhancement effects for procedures combining imagery with other pre-performance strategies [38-40]. Pre-performance mastery imagery has been found to increase the number of sit-ups completed in a set time period [17].

In a study of golf ball putting, separate components of pre-performance imagery were examined [41]. A success imagery group employed both positive performance and positive outcome imagery prior to performance, while a failure imagery group used identical positive performance imagery, but employed negative outcome imagery (missing the putt). The success group made significantly more putts than the failure or control groups, and the control group made significantly more putts than the failure imagery group. These findings suggested that pre-performance imagery can serve either to enhance or degrade performance, and that the outcome component of the imagery, not the imaginal rehearsal of the motor behavior, influenced performance.

A follow-up study directly tested the influence of performance versus outcome components of imaginal rehearsal on putting a golf ball [23]. Imaginal rehearsal of the task was crossed with the imaginal depiction of task outcome (success, failure, or no outcome component). Performance of the two groups using failure outcome imagery declined significantly, but the success outcome and no-outcome groups' performances did not improve significantly. These results supported the prior finding that outcome imagery has greater influence on performance than imaginal rehearsal of the motor skill, however, the facilitating effects of positive outcome imagery found in the first study were not replicated. Interestingly, on a post-experimental questionnaire, eight of the seventeen subjects in the success imagery groups indicated that the imagery had a detrimental effect on their performance; fifteen of the seventeen subjects in the failure imagery groups also felt that the imagery had a negative effect.

In summary, the extant research suggests that pre-performance imagery can, but does not consistently, produce improvements in motor skill performance. Pre-performance failure imagery, however, does appear to consistently degrade performance. This finding is consistent with the common belief of athletes that negative thoughts prior to motor performance are detrimental to performance. Moreover, subject reports indicate that even success imagery may negatively affect performance [23]. Lastly, there exists some support to suggest that pre-performance imagery focused on outcome may have a greater influence on performance than imaginal rehearsal of the motor skill.

Strength Tasks

The use of pre-performance imagery to enhance strength performance typically has been referred to as "psyching up." Imaginal rehearsal is not the only psyching up strategy employed by athletes, but it appears to be one of the three most frequently employed [42]. The first examination of pre-performance imagery on strength employed three pre-performance strategies (imagery, preparatory arousal, and attentional focus) with a leg-kick task [43]. The imagery procedure, which involved imagining a successful trial, and the preparatory arousal procedure both produced significantly greater improvement than the attentional focus or two control conditions.

A second study compared the effects of pre-performance imagery, preparatory arousal, and a control-rest group on performance on the same leg-kick task [43]. Results of the first study were not replicated; the imagery group's performance did not differ from the control or the preparatory arousal group. Similar studies examining the effect of imagery on a leg-strength task also have not produced robust enhancement effects [18, 21, 44].

Emotional pre-performance imagery has also been examined as a performance enhancement strategy. This technique employs personalized imagery to induce emotional states that, in turn, putatively produce optimal arousal states for performance. In an initial study, imagery-induced happy moods produced greater performance on a hand-grip strength task than imagery-induced sad moods, but neither differed from a control condition [22].

A second study found that emotional imagery did affect strength performance, but not always in the expected direction [45]. Relaxation, as hypothesized, produced decrements in a hand-grip strength performance task compared to a control condition. Anger and fear imagery, however, did not enhance strength performance. Moreover, strength performance tended to be worse in subjects who reported high levels of anger during anger imagery, and increased minimally in subjects reporting low levels of anger, suggesting that individual differences in the response to the imagery influenced strength performance. A follow-up study replicated those results [25]. In addition, individual differences on anger expression were associated with the direction of the effects of anger imagery on strength performance in that high scores on "anger control" were associated with increases in strength performance, while high scores on "anger out" were associated with decrements in strength performance [46]. Interestingly, in both studies, post-experimental inquiries indicated that subjects were poor judges of the effect of imagery on strength performance. Most subjects believed incorrectly that anger imagery produced their strongest performance.

As with the research examining pre-performance imagery and motor skill performance, the literature addressing imagery as a strength performance enhancer suggests that pre-performance imagery can benefit performance, but that effect is not robust and the potential for negative effects is equally probable. The only replicated finding to date is that relaxation imagery produces decrements in strength performance. On a more optimistic note, the programmatic research on emotive imagery and strength appears to demonstrate that individual responses to the image occur and that it may be possible to predict the direction of those responses. Clearly, more theory-driven, programmatic research is needed to help understand the imagery-performance relationship before sound empirically-based decisions for clinical application can occur.

METHODOLOGICAL ISSUES IN RESEARCH

In this section, we summarize the methodological issues inherent in the imagery/motor performance literature and discuss the implications of those issues for interpreting the data. We then offer suggestions for future research methodology that may increase our understanding of the relationship between imagery and motor performance.

The early literature reviews discussed many weaknesses of the methodology employed in particular studies and of the general approach to the evaluation of mental practice [11, 33, 34]. One primary problem cited was the great variability in mental practice procedures. Under the label of mental practice, subjects employ a wide range of diverse strategies. Imagery scripts differ across studies and usually are poorly described. Moreover, although the research indicates that the ratio of mental to physical practice, the amount of time spent in each, and the latency between the two, each influence the effects of mental practice on performance [8, 47], it is only recently that systematic examinations of those factors have been conducted. Considering the broad range of procedural variation across studies of mental practice, a direct comparison or cumulative evaluation of the research is unlikely to provide a valid assessment of the efficacy of mental practice on performance. As Suinn noted, there is a great need for replicated studies as well as systematic programs of research [4].

Across imagery studies, the failure to control for and to assess the quality of mental practice or pre-performance imagery has plagued the literature. Although only limited data is available, the aforementioned reviews suggest that vividness and control are associated with the efficacy of mental practice. Those conclusions, however, are supported only by one quasi-experimental study, anecdotal impressions, and correlational studies linking more vivid and controlled imagery with the more successful elite athletes [1, 48-50]. Prospective studies that randomly assign subjects based on imagery ability are needed to determine the role of those factors in performance enhancement.

A related methodological issue is the use of manipulation checks. Although it is clear that subjects participating in imagery studies do not always follow the imagery script [13, 14], assessment of the imagery content or quality employed by subjects during experimental trials has not been standard procedure. When imagery has been assessed, typically only vividness and controllability measures have been employed. The discrepant findings reported among studies examining imagery quality and performance effects may be a product of the constricted methods of assessment. The effect of imagery on performance may be associated with other dimensions of the imagery experience, such as its influence on attentional focus, intensity and reality of the image, as well as how it affects the various sensory modalities [24]. Clearly, increased attention to imagery assessment and a multidimensional approach to that assessment is needed.

Concern over the assessment of performance in mental practice studies has also been expressed [4, 7]. Some have argued that, with high level athletes, performance measures may be insensitive to small effects of imaginal procedures (ceiling effects), and suggested measures of consistency or other secondary task measures (e.g., effort expenditure) be used to evaluate the effects of imagery on performance. The putative variability of imagery's effect across skill level may represent one example of how measurement issues can affect interpretation of data. Numerous investigators have suggested that motor tasks provide ideal objective outcome measures for testing the efficacy of psychological interventions. We suggest that outcome measurement is more complex than previously suggested, and, as currently practiced, performance measurement may be a primary contributor to the failure to clearly demonstrate the effects of imagery on motor performance.

Meta-analytic techniques have been used in an attempt to resolve some of the problems of interpretation referred to above. Although useful, criticisms of the use of meta-analytic techniques must be noted [51]. A few potential problems with meta-analysis are: 1) different methods of calculating the effect size can significantly influence the results, 2) studies of variable quality are given equal weight, 3) using more than one effect size from one study biases the results. Moreover, meta-analysis can serve to confirm believers in the efficacy of their intervention without providing any specific evidence, but by offering an overall positive effect size.

The Feltz and Landers meta-analysis reviewed above is not exempt from these criticisms [7]. Furthermore, considering the large variation in the mental practice procedures not codified and included in their meta-analysis, and that statistical evaluation of the interaction effects was not possible (but appears to be critical in this research), their report, like the prior reviews, provides only tentative interpretations of the literature. Also, it should be noted that their inability to find significant effect sizes for many of the individual difference variables should not be interpreted as indicating that these factors are not important in understanding the influence of imagery on performance.

Many of the same methodological problems found in the mental practice literature also exist in the research on pre-performance imagery. For example, strategies such as preparatory arousal, imagery, and attentional focus may overlap such that imagery may be used during attentional focus or preparatory arousal conditions to narrow attention or to achieve arousal, or attentional-focus may be used to either increase arousal or control imagery. Few studies have controlled for or post-experimentally assessed the quality and content of the pre-performance imagery or other pre-performance strategies. Amount of practice has varied, and typically, only minor imagery training or practice has been provided. Moreover, since the instructions for the pre-performance imagery have differed among studies, it is difficult to compare or summarize the results in terms of the efficacy of each pre-performance strategy.

FUTURE RESEARCH ISSUES

The fact that positive imagery has not been conclusively shown to enhance athletic activities by the research conducted to date is not equivalent to demonstrating that it can have no beneficial effects on performance. The effects may be there, but we have simply not investigated the responses under conditions that would clearly reveal them. There are several factors that might account for this.

Idiography versus Nomothesis

Virtually all investigations of imagery have employed aggregated data and averaged effects. In the typical between groups study, imagery techniques are utilized by a treatment group and the mean response shift is compared to the mean change in a control group. The within groups variation involves average responses within the same subject at control versus treatment times. Aggregation of data presents many problems. First and foremost of these is that we are rarely interested in what the average response of a group might be. We really want to know whether imagery can reliably improve performance of a given individual or individuals. If imagery in reality improves performance of person A, has no effect on person B, and impairs the performance of person C, aggregation of their data might indicate that imagery is inert. What we need to know is whether there are individuals for whom imagery can make a positive difference. Potentially more powerful designs with which to detect imagery effects are single- subject designs or matching designs where subjects are matched to an imagery intervention based on subject characteristics putatively related to the efficacy of employing different types or modalities of imagery.

Low External Validity

Many investigations, including some of those from our own laboratory, can be faulted for their external validity. Whenever one wants to manipulate experimental variables precisely in order to achieve high internal validity, some sacrifice of verisimilitude with the world of application outside the laboratory occurs. For example, in many investigations exposure to imagery is exceedingly brief. We have no longitudinal studies that athletes are given intensive imagery training under field conditions over several months or years. Moreover, relatively few studies have been conducted using athletes, let alone elite athletes [52]. Such studies would undoubtedly be difficult to carry out, but it may be that imagery requires extensive and lengthy use before its salubrious effects begin to manifest themselves.

The Complexity of the World

Perhaps imagery has no simple main effect on performance in any individual, but diverse and complicated interactive effects in many individuals. For example, suppose that one individual benefits from imaginal rehearsal combined with positive self-verbalization, while another benefits from some admixture of mental and physical practice interspersed. Imagery might be a necessary but not sufficient condition for performance enhancement. Imagery might "work," but only when combined with other elements. An example of combining imagery with other psychological interventions is visuomotor behavior rehearsal [53]. This procedure combines relaxation training with imagery. Other procedures have also been combined with imagery to enhance performance, and data to support such interventions are encouraging but remain equivocal [52, 54]. The permutations of elements that would be, in combination with imagery, sufficient to improve performance may be manifold and varied, yet difficult to capture in a systematic empirical investigation.

Understanding the Nature of Imagery

The points raised above suggest that asking the question, "does imagery work?," is too imprecise and therefore of little practical value. Alternatively, research assessing the varied effects of specific well-defined imagery procedures may lead to a better understanding of how and for whom imagery works. Measurement of various response modalities such as physiological arousal, emotional arousal, self-efficacy, and attentional focus is essential to delineating the mechanisms by which imagery affects performance. Theory must be more rigorously developed in order to enable researchers to make predictions concerning the effects of imagery on particular individuals under certain conditions.

CURRENT APPLIED ISSUES IN IMAGERY AND SPORT

Imagery research in the sports area has recently seen a resurgence of interest, fueled by attempts to apply research knowledge to the actual improvement of real sports performance. As discussed in the introduction, imagery interventions have become very popular among athletes, coaches, and sport psychologists. This applied interest has created a new generation of research issues that must be addressed. In the next section, we will describe a variety of commonly employed applications of imagery in the sports area. Brief discussions of the research support for each are presented and research questions that subsequently must be addressed are outlined.

Skill Acquisition

Many studies in the imagery literature suggest that learning a new skill can be assisted by imaginal rehearsal of the skill. The more "cognitive" components associated with the performance of the skill, the more assistance to learning is provided by imagery. On the other hand, some researchers have suggested that tasks that emphasize kinesthetic cues may not be mentally rehearsable [55]. While this assertion is challenged by the self-report of many athletes who emphasize the importance of kinesthetic rehearsal, the evidence suggests that tasks which are primarily motoric in nature require a certain level of familiarity with the skill before imagery can be effective.

It has been suggested that there are two principal ways of learning new motor skills [56, 57]. One way is primarily verbal and analytical, the other is intuitive and global. Anyone who has learned a sport skill such as golf swing will recognize that at times attention must be directed to the subcomponents of the total skill for even a poor approximation of the skill to occur (the molecular approach). While other times (perhaps later in acquisition training), the correct skill execution seemed to occur automatically (the molar approach). An interesting research area would be to investigate whether imagery techniques can enhance the transfer of attention from the molecular to the molar level, and thus hasten skill acquisition.

As noted earlier in this chapter, the potential for negative effects must be considered when applying imagery techniques to assist in the development of motor skills. A classic example of the range of possible responses to a particular imagery intervention was cited by Clark [49]. One of his subjects who was asked to imagine making a basketball foul shot, reported that the ball would not bounce in his imagination, but stuck to the floor instead. Thus, until we understand more about the individual variability in responses to even relatively simple images, clinicians and athletes attempting to apply imagery procedures must continuously experiment and evaluate carefully the impact of each image employed in any type of intervention.

Skill Maintenance

The primary imagery technique used by athletes to maintain a skill is mental practice. Despite the wealth of mental practice studies, surprisingly few have looked at long-term retention of the skills studied. Retention tests are much more common in the motor learning area, and should be regularly incorporated in imagery and motor performance research designs. Those few studies that have examined retention have found that if an imagery strategy is used during learning, retention is usually better than that displayed by a no-practice control group [58]. It would be interesting to examine whether a skill, once learned, could be maintained for long periods of time by imagery alone. This issue would be relevant for understanding how injured athletes could optimize their time during rehabilitation. Experimental evidence on this question is sparse.

Planning of Performance

Another popular use of imagery techniques in the applied sport psychology area is to prepare athletes psychologically for upcoming competitions. Support for this technique stems primarily from a retrospective studies and case reports. For example, successful skiers reported developing a visual image of the course after previewing it, and in the time between inspecting the course and reaching the starting gate they concerned themselves with planning effective strategies for skiing the course. Less successful skiers, on the other hand, simply tried to maintain positive thoughts prior to racing [59]. A four-time Olympian who consulted with the second author provided a succinct account of his utilization of this approach:

> It's as if I carry around a set of tapes in my mind. I play them occasionally, rehearsing different race strategies. Usually I imagine the race going the way I want it—I set my pace and stick to it. But I have other tapes as well—situations where someone goes out real fast and I have to catch him, or imagining how I will cope if the weather gets really hot. I even have a 'disaster' tape, where everything goes wrong, and I'm hurting badly, and I imagine myself gutting it out.

As with many imagery interventions, this technique has received scant research attention, but findings regarding the effectiveness of imagery rehearsal in organizing tasks in a conceptual framework suggest that this approach to event planning warrants examination. Clearly, prospective studies testing whether athletes can be taught to apply imagery techniques for planning more effectively, and whether training in the use of this procedure enhances performance are needed.

Stress Management

In this application of imagery to sports performance, athletes rehearse adaptive responses to competitive situations. For example, an athlete might sit down with a sport psychologist and list all the thoughts and feelings she typically experiences in a race situation. Then she will go back and identify those that might interfere with performance, such as "I can't go on," or "I'm not as good as these other competitors." Next, the athlete and sport psychologist devise strategies to replace these negative thoughts or emotions using more appropriate psychological strategies. For example, thought stopping, positive self-talk, and self-affirmations have been suggested as psychological interventions [60]. Finally, the athlete imaginally rehearses a race and sees herself coping successfully via use of the techniques she has practiced. The goal of this intervention is for the athlete to develop and become familiar with a set of effective strategies for coping with stress.

Clinical psychologists recognize these procedures as a typical variant of stress management training. A variety of studies have shown these techniques to be effective in reducing many types of anxiety, from medical and dental anxiety to test anxiety [61, 62]. Studies of stress management applied to sport have been limited, but appear promising [63-65]. More controlled studies of these techniques are needed to evaluate their efficacy as performance enhancement interventions.

Self-Efficacy Enhancement

A typical illustration of the use of imagery to affect self-confidence is provided below. A young athlete sought consultation because she felt she had a problem in defeating certain opponents. Her situation was that she was rapidly improving in her sport, and was meeting stronger opponents in competition. Because they were more highly ranked, she lacked confidence against them. This lack of confidence persisted despite her clearly possessing the skills necessary to defeat them. An intervention strategy was designed in which the athlete practiced imagining herself defeating specific higher-rated opponents, and imagining the consequences of these victories (how others would react, her own emotional responses). Shortly thereafter, she had achieved first-time victories against several of these opponents, and she attributed the success to a new-found confidence generated by her imaginal rehearsal.

Certainly this was not a scientific test of an imagery intervention; any number of uncontrolled factors may have contributed to her success. Nevertheless, many athletes seek help for "confidence problems." The fact that imagery can impact self-confidence has long been recognized by cognitive-behavioral therapists who have developed a number of imaginal strategies that encourage behavior change by asking clients to imagine more successful behaviors than they presently exhibit. These strategies include systematic desensitization, flooding, and coping imagery [66-68]. As discussed earlier, the self-efficacy theory of human behavior change argues that many psychological interventions achieve their effects through modifications of an individual's self-efficacy level [19]. Such modifications can be achieved via both actual experience and through vicarious or even imagined experience [69]. Modeling is a well-established treatment intervention based on this theory, and Cautela has developed an imaginally based variant of this procedure known as covert modeling [70]. Recently, a description of a successful application of covert modeling to deal with lack of confidence in a sport setting appeared in the literature [71].

Although several studies have failed to show a relationship between confidence changes and performance changes during imagery interventions [18, 23], other studies [21] and self-reports from athletes who regularly utilize visualization techniques indicate that confidence changes often accompany imagery rehearsal.

More research examining whether these confidence changes result in improved performance is sorely needed. In addition, controlled studies testing the efficacy of specific imagery interventions for athletes presenting with "confidence problems" may be more appropriate for detecting the effect of imagery interventions on self-efficacy. It may be that performance enhancement effects of imagery interventions targeting self-efficacy, may only be detected in those performers with low self-efficacy at baseline.

Arousal Regulation

Imagery techniques have long been used in clinical psychology to produce or enhance relaxation. This approach has been adopted in sport psychology as a way of calming the anxious athlete prior to competition. For example, it is commonly suggested that athletes practice visualizing whatever provides them with a sense of relaxation [72]. This strategy can be employed when the athlete gets nervous or worried about an upcoming performance in order to restore a sense of calm.

A large body of research has examined the relationship between arousal and performance. The inverted U-hypothesis posits that performance is optimal at some moderate arousal level, and that arousal levels that are too low or too high inhibit performance [73]. More recently, reversal theory and catastrophe theory have added some theoretical depth and complexity to this posited relationship [74]. Oxendine further suggests that different tasks require different levels of optimal arousal [75]. For example, an athlete who is required to lift a heavy weight may need to be at a much higher level of arousal than one who is attempting to shoot at a distant target with an air pistol. Techniques to increase an athlete's arousal have been called "preparatory arousal" techniques, and a body of research exists to indicate that such techniques can enhance performance on certain tasks [18]. The role of imagery in the utilization of these techniques is not clear.

Imagery has been used in research both to increase and decrease arousal (see Pre-performance Imagery section, p. 105). In these studies, imagery-generated moods thought to be inappropriate to the task (sadness, relaxation) resulted in decreased performance [22, 45]. On the other hand, it has been more difficult to demonstrate enhancement effects for imagery-generated task-appropriate arousal. Some research findings suggest that emotive imagery is most effective when used as a coping strategy or when attention is directed toward utilizing the arousal to achieve specific goals [17, 25, 45]. This suggests that pre-performance imagery may achieve its effects through directing attention to the task at hand, not through its effects on mood or arousal level alone. As suggested above, more research examining individual differences in response to these imagery-induced arousal procedures is needed to determine optimal intervention strategies.

A final caveat regarding imagery techniques employed to enhance performance through arousal regulation imagery techniques was gleaned from a clinical experience of the second author. During his work with an elite athlete, he found the following pre-performance image quite helpful for enhancing concentration and assisting the athlete achieve an arousal state associated with optimal performance. The athlete imagined, "a bright ball of energy, glowing golden, floating in front of me, which I inhale and take down to the center of my body. There I feel the energy radiate to all parts of my body, golden and warm, bringing me a peaceful attitude and providing me with the energy I need for my program." Then, when this same image was employed with a group of athletes from the same sport, the following feedback was received. One athlete had imagined the glowing ball "exploding in my stomach, leaving a gaping hole in my body. . . ." Another stated that it "blinded me, so that when I began performing, I could not see where I was going, and I crashed. . . ." A third athlete reported imagining "inhaling a helium-filled balloon, leaving me speaking in a squeaky voice, at which point I began giggling uncontrollably and was unable to perform."

Once again, this report suggests that individual differences in response to imagery should be expected and most likely will have a wide range of effects on motor performance. Clearly, imagery techniques targeting emotional or arousal regulation deserve particularly close evaluation as they can affect motor performance via multiple systems [29, 32]. Research examining these individual differences and multiple response systems may help increase our ability to predict and control the direction of influence of imagery interventions.

To summarize the state of applied interventions using imagery techniques, it is clear that imagery can be used in many ways that go beyond simple practice of sports skills. In many cases, these new applications have been suggested and utilized before research has been conducted into their efficacy. Moreover, the extant research has produced equivocal results regarding the effectiveness of those interventions. Hopefully, continued research efforts will be directed at developing more sophisticated evaluations of imagery intervention techniques, as this area promises to be an exciting and rewarding one for researchers as well as clinicians.

CONCLUSION

What then can we conclude about the effects of imagery on motor performance? Clearly imagery is no panacea. Relatively superficial and brief applications of positive imagery to the acquisition and rehearsal of skills or to the creation of "mind sets" has not yielded consistently the dramatic and substantial effects on performance that one might have expected given the enthusiasm of many athletes, coaches and sport psychologists. While the power of imaginal procedures to enhance performance may be as yet undemonstrated, negative effects of imagery in the form of failure imagery or the use of the "wrong" type of imagery seem to produce rather immediate and meaningful decrements in performance. Perhaps this should not surprise us. For the trained athlete, the ceiling is much closer to mean performance than is the floor. It may very well be that disrupting a well-established response is always easier than enhancing it, by whatever means.

In conclusion, the work described in this chapter strongly indicates that sport psychologists should become more cautious in their application of imagery techniques. Imagery procedures may not always be performance enhancing, or at worst, a benign tool as commonly believed. Strategies that are efficacious for one individual may be ineffective or even deleterious for another. Self-reports of feelings of success or enhanced performance may not consistently correlate with actual performance. Practicing sport psychologists should carefully evaluate the effects produced by their application of imagery strategies. Sport psychology research should continue to examine individual difference models of imagery and focus more attention on potentially inappropriate imagery that may degrade performance.

REFERENCES

1. M. J. Mahoney and M. Avener, Psychology of the Elite Athlete: An Exploratory Study, *Cognitive Therapy and Research, 3,* pp. 135-141, 1977.
2. D. Gould, S. M. Murphy, V. Tammen, and J. May, An Evaluation of U.S. Olympic Sport Psychology Consultant Effectiveness, *The Sport Psychologist, 2,* pp. 111-127, 1991.
3. R. Vealy, Future Directions in Psychological Skills Training, *The Sport Psychology, 5,* pp. 318-336, 1988.
4. R. Suinn, Imagery in Sports, in *Imagery: Current Theory, Research, and Application,* A. A. Sheikh (ed.), Wiley, New York, pp. 507-534, 1983.
5. S. M. Murphy and D. P. Jowdy, Imagery and Mental Practice, in *Advances in Sport Psychology,* T. Horn (ed.), Human Kinetics, Champaign, Illinois, pp. 221-250, 1992.
6. R. S. Sackett, The Influences of Symbolic Rehearsal Upon the Retention of a Maze Habit, *Journal of General Psychology, 10,* pp. 376-395, 1934.
7. D. L. Feltz and D. M. Landers, The Effects of Mental Practice on Motor Skill Learning and Performance: A Meta -Analysis, *Journal of Sport Psychology, 5,* pp. 25-57, 1983.
8. J. S. Hird, D. M. Landers, J. R. Thomas, and J. J. Horan, Physical Practice is Superior to Mental Practice in Enhancing Cognitive and Motor Task Performance, *Journal of Sport and Exercise Psychology, 13,* pp. 281-293, 1991.
9. J. E. Hecker and L. M. Kaczor, Applications of Imagery Theory to Sport Psychology: Some Preliminary Findings, *Journal of Sport Psychology, 10,* pp. 363-373, 1988.
10. D. G. MacKay, The Problem of Rehearsal or Mental Practice, *Journal of Motor Behavior, 13,* pp. 274-285, 1981.
11. C. B. Corbin, Mental Practice, in *Ergogenic Aids and Muscular Performance,* W. P. Morgan (ed.), Academic Press, New York, pp. 94-118, 1972.
12. B. D. Hale, The Effects of Internal and External Imagery on Muscular and Ocular Concomitants, *Journal of Sport Psychology, 4,* pp. 379-387, 1982.
13. D. V. Harris and W. J. Robinson, The Effects of Skill Level on EMG Activity during Internal and External Imagery, *Journal of Sport Psychology, 8,* pp. 105-111, 1986.

14. D. P. Jowdy and D. V. Harris, Muscular Responses during Mental Imagery as a Function of Motor Skill Level, *Journal of Sport and Exercise Psychology, 12*, pp. 191-201, 1990.
15. D. M. Landers, The Arousal-Performance Relationship Revisited, *Research Quarterly for Exercise and Sport, 51*, pp. 77-90, 1980.
16. R. A. Schmidt, *Motor Control and Learning: A Behavioral Emphasis*, Human Kinetics, Champaign, Illinois, 1982.
17. C. Lee, Psyching Up for a Muscular Endurance Task: Effects of Image Content on Performance and Mood State, *Journal of Sport and Exercise Psychology, 12*, pp. 66-73, 1990.
18. R. L. Wilkes and J. J. Summers, Cognitions, Mediating Variables, and Strength Performance, *Journal of Sport Psychology, 6*, pp. 351-359, 1984.
19. A. Bandura, Self-efficacy: Towards a Unifying Theory of Behavioral Change, *Psychological Review, 84*, pp. 191-225, 1977.
20. A. J. Budney and R. L. Woolfolk, *Self-efficacy and Skilled Motor Performance: An Empirical Analysis*, unpublished manuscript, Rutgers University, 1992.
21. D. L. Feltz and C. A. Reissinger, Effects of in vivo Emotive Imagery and Performance Feedback, *Journal of Sport and Exercise Psychology, 12*, pp. 132-143, 1990.
22. D. Kavanagh and S. Hausfeld, Physical Performance and Self-efficacy under Happy and Sad Moods, *Journal of Sport Psychology, 8*, pp. 112-123, 1986.
23. R. L. Woolfolk, S. M. Murphy, D. Gottesfeld, and D. Aitken, Effects of Mental Rehearsal of Task Motor Activity and Mental Depiction of Outcome on Motor Skill Performance, *Journal of Sport Psychology, 7*, pp. 191-197, 1985.
24. S. M. Murphy, Models of Imagery in Sport Psychology: A Review, *Journal of Mental Imagery, 14*, pp. 153-172, 1990.
25. A. J. Budney and R. L. Woolfolk, Using the Wrong Image: An Exploration of the Adverse Effects of Imagery on Performance, *Journal of Mental Imagery, 14*, pp. 75-86, 1990.
26. D. P. Jowdy, S. M. Murphy, and S. Durtschi, *An Assessment of the Use of Imagery by Elite Athletes: Athlete, Coach and Psychologist Perspectives*, unpublished report to the United States Olympic Committee, Colorado Springs, 1989.
27. P. J. Lang, Imagery in Therapy: An Information-processing Analysis of Fear, *Behavior Therapy, 8*, pp. 862-886, 1977.
28. P. J. Lang, A Bio-informational Theory of Emotional Imagery, *Psychophysiology, 16*, pp. 495-512, 1979.
29. P. J. Lang, M. J. Kozcak, G. A. Miller, D. N. Levin, and A. McLean, Emotional Imagery: Conceptual Structure and Pattern of Somato-visceral Response, *Psychophysiology, 17*, pp. 179-192, 1980.
30. P. J. Lang, B. G. Melamed, and J. A. Hart, A Psychophysiological Analysis of Fear Modification using an Automated Desensitization Procedure, *Journal of Abnormal Psychology, 76*, pp. 229-234, 1970.
31. S. Rachman and R. Hodgson, Synchrony and Desynchrony in Fear and Avoidance, *Behavior Therapy and Research, 12*, pp. 311-318, 1974.
32. A. Ahsen, ISM: The Triple Code Model for Imagery and Psychophysiology, *Journal of Mental Imagery, 8*, pp. 15-42, 1984.
33. A. Richardson, Mental Practice: A Review and Discussion, Part I, *Research Quarterly, 38*, pp. 95-107, 1967.
34. A. Richardson, Mental Practice: A Review and Discussion, Part II, *Research Quarterly, 38*, pp. 263-273, 1967.
35. G. E. Powell, Negative and Positive Mental Imagery in Motor Skill Acquisition, *Perceptual and Motor Skills, 37*, pp. 312, 1973.

36. M. L. Epstein, The Relationship of Mental Imagery and Mental Rehearsal to Performance of a Motor Task, *Journal of Sport Psychology, 2,* pp. 211-220, 1980.
37. R. S. Weinberg, D. Gould, A. Jackson, and P. Barnes, Influence of Cognitive Strategies on Tennis Serves of High and Low Ability, *Perceptual and Motor Skills, 50,* pp. 63-66, 1980.
38. A. W. Meyers, R. Schleser, and T. M. Okwamabua, A Cognitive-behavioral Intervention for Improving Basketball Performance, *Research Quarterly for Exercise and Sport, 13,* pp. 344-347, 1982.
39. C. A. Wrisberg and M. H. Anshel, The Effect of Cognitive Strategies on the Free Throw Shooting Performance of Young Athletes, *The Sport Psychologist, 3,* pp. 95-104, 1989.
40. S. G. Ziegler, Comparison of Imagery Styles and Past Experience in Skills Performance, *Perceptual and Motor Skills, 64,* pp. 579-586, 1987.
41. R. L. Woolfolk, W. Parish, and S. M. Murphy, The Effects of Positive and Negative Imagery on Motor Skill Performance, *Cognitive Therapy and Research, 9,* pp. 335-341, 1985.
42. R. S. Weinberg, D. Gould, and A. Jackson, Cognition and Motor Performance, *Cognitive Therapy and Research, 5,* pp. 239-245, 1980.
43. D. Gould, R. S. Weinberg, and A. Jackson, Mental Preparation Strategies, Cognitions and Strength Performance, *Journal of Sport Psychology, 2,* pp. 329-339, 1980.
44. L. L. Tynes and R. M. McFatter, The Efficacy of Psyching Strategies on a Weightlifting Task, *Cognitive Therapy and Research, 11,* pp. 327-336, 1987.
45. S. M. Murphy, R. L. Woolfolk, and A. J. Budney, The Effects of Emotive Imagery on Strength Performance, *Journal of Sport and Exercise Psychology, 10,* pp. 334-345, 1988.
46. C. D. Spielberger, E. H. Johnson, S. Russell, R. J. Crane, G. A. Jacobs, and T. J. Worden, The Experience and Expression of Anger: Construction and Validation of an Anger Expression Scale, in *Anger and Hostility in Cardiovascular and Behavior Disorders,* M. Chesney (ed.), Hemisphere, New York, pp. 5-31, 1985.
47. R. M. Kohl, D. L. Roenker, and P. E. Turner, Clarification of Competent Imagery as a Prerequisite for Effective Skill Imagery, *International Journal of Sport Psychology, 16,* pp. 37-45, 1985.
48. K. Start and A. Richardson, Imagery and Mental Practice, *British Journal of Educational Psychology, 34,* pp. 280-284, 1964.
49. L. Clark, Effect of Mental Practice on the Development of a Certain Motor Skill, *Research Quarterly, 31,* pp. 560-569, 1960.
50. A. W. Meyers, C. J. Cooke, J. Cullen, and L. Liles, Psychological Aspects of Athletic Competitors: A Replication across Sports, *Cognitive Therapy and Research 3,* pp. 361-366, 1979.
51. G. T. Wilson, Clinical Issues and Strategies in the Practice of Behavior Therapy, in *Review of Behavior Therapy: Theory and Practice* (vol. 10), G. T. Wilson, C. M. Franks, P. C. Kendall, and J. P. Foreyt (eds.), Guilford Press, New York, 1987.
52. M. J. Greenspan and D. L. Feltz, Psychological Interventions with Athletes in Competitive Situation: A Review, *The Sport Psychologist, 3,* pp. 219-236, 1989.
53. R. Suinn, Behavior Rehearsal Training for Ski Racers, *Behavior Therapy, 3,* pp. 519-520, 1972.
54. J. P. Whelan, M. J. Mahoney, and A. W. Meyers, Performance Enhancement in Sport: A Cognitive Behavioral Domain, *Behavior Therapy, 22,* pp. 307-327, 1991.

55. C. A. Wrisberg and M. R. Ragsdale, Cognitive Demand and Practice Level: Factors in the Mental Practice of Motor Skills, *Journal of Human Movement Studies, 5,* pp. 201-208, 1979.
56. W. T. Gallwey, *The Inner Game of Tennis,* Random House, New York, 1974.
57. J. Heil, *The Role of Imagery in Sport: As a "Training Tool" and as a "Mode of Thought,"* paper presented at the Sixth World Congress in Sport Psychology, Copenhagen, Denmark, 1985.
58. W. G. Meacci and E. E. Price, Acquisition and Retention of Golf Putting Skill through the Relaxation, Visualization and Body Rehearsal Intervention, *Research Quarterly for Exercise and Sport, 56,* pp. 176-179, 1985.
59. R. J. Rotella, B. Gansneder, D. Ojala, and J. Billing, Cognitions and Coping Strategies of Elite Skiers: An Exploratory Study of Young Developing Athletes, *Journal of Sport Psychology, 2,* pp. 350-354, 1980.
60. K. Porter and F. Foster, *The Mental Athlete: Inner Training for Peak Performance,* William C. Brown, Dubuque, Iowa, 1986.
61. W. H. Miller and R. L. Heinrich, *Personal Stress Management for Medical and Dental Patients,* PSM Press, Los Angeles, 1984.
62. J. Wine, Test Anxiety and Direction of Attention, *Psychological Bulletin, 76,* pp. 92-104, 1971.
63. P. R. E. Crocker, A Follow-up of Cognitive-affective Stress Management Training, *Journal of Sport and Exercise Psychology, 11,* pp. 236-242, 1989.
64. R. D. Mace and D. Carroll, The Control of Anxiety in Sport: Stress Inoculation Training Prior to Abseiling, *International Journal of Sport Psychology, 16,* pp. 165-175, 1985.
65. S. G. Ziegler, J. Klinzing, and K. Williamson, The Effects of Two Stress Management Training Programs on Cardiorespiratory Efficiency, *Journal of Sport Psychology, 4,* pp. 280-289, 1982.
66. J. Wolpe, *Psychotherapy by Reciprocal Inhibition,* Stanford University Press, Stanford, 1958.
67. S. Rachman, *Phobias: Their Nature and Control,* Thomas, Springfield, Illinois, 1968.
68. D. Meichenbaum, *Cognitive-behavior Modification: An Integrative Approach,* Plenum, New York, 1977.
69. A. Bandura, *Psychological Modeling: Conflicting Theories,* Aldine-Atherton, Chicago, 1971.
70. J. R. Cautela and A. J. Kearney, *The Correct Conditioning Handbook,* Springer, New York, 1986.
71. B. S. Rushall, Covert Modeling as a Procedure for Altering an Athlete's Psychological State, *The Sport Psychologist, 2,* pp. 131-140, 1988.
72. D. V. Harris and B. L. Harris, *The Athlete's Guide to Sports Psychology: Mental Skills for Physical People,* Leisure Press, New York, 1984.
73. R. Martens, Arousal and Motor Performance, in *Exercise and Sport Science Review* (vol. 2), J. Wilmore (ed.), Academic Press, New York, 1974.
74. D. Gould and V. Krane, The Arousal-athletic Performance Relationship: Current Status and Future Directions, in *Advances in Sport Psychology,* T. Horn (ed.), Human Kinetics, Champaign, Illinois, pp. 119-142, 1992.
75. J. B. Oxendine, Emotional Arousal and Motor Performance, *Quest, 13,* pp. 23-30, 1970.

CHAPTER 7

Imagery and Motor Skills Acquisition

CRAIG HALL, DARLENE SCHMIDT,
MARIE-CLAUDE DURAND, AND ERIC BUCKOLZ

Athletes in every sport strive for excellence. The best means of achieving this goal has been a primary concern of participants for as long as athletic competitions have existed. During recent years increased attention has been given to the mental side of sport and as a result, various psychological skills training programs have been developed. A common component in these programs is mental imagery.

Mental imagery as a performance enhancing tool has surfaced in both anecdotal and experimental reports as being viable and valuable. Athletes, therefore, should be able to reap the benefits of a well-developed imagery training program. The key is to have such a program. While various programs currently exist, these can undoubtedly be improved upon [1, 2]. Such improvement will only come as we gain a better understanding of how mental imagery functions in sport situations, and what variables are most influential in mediating the effectiveness of imagery use.

The purpose of this chapter is to review the research conducted on the relationship between imagery and motor skill acquisition with the objective being to suggest how imagery training programs might more effectively be constructed. First, the general experimental paradigm employed in mental imagery studies will be outlined and some of the major findings highlighted. Second, some of the variables determining the effectiveness of imagery will be considered including the task to be performed, the instructions or strategies given to participants, the skill level of the performers, and differences in individual imagery abilities. The effects of positive and negative imagery will then be discussed, and finally, suggestions for the development of imagery training programs will be made.

BASIC FINDINGS

Even with just a cursory review of the literature, it is evident that there is what has been referred to as the basic paradigm of mental practice (imagery) studies [3]. Typically, this paradigm has three conditions: 1) a physical practice condition, 2) an imagery condition, and 3) a control condition. Subjects are randomly assigned to one of these conditions after completion of some baseline (pretest) trials on a given motor task. Then the physical practice subjects actually practice the motor task for a set number of trials. The subjects in the imagery condition mentally rehearse the task for the same number of trials that the physical practice subjects actually practice. The control subjects receive no physical or imagery practice, or practice an unrelated task. All subjects are then retested on the task. The findings have been quite consistent across the various studies using this paradigm. Physical practice has a greater effect on performance than imagery practice, which in turn is better than no practice [4-6].

An extension of the above paradigm entails examining the effects of combining imagery and physical practice, as compared to physical or imagery practice alone. The combination group alternates between using physical and imagery practice, 50:50 being the typical ratio employed. In some experiments, subjects systematically alternate between one overt trial and one imaginal trial [7]. In others, a practice session involves alternating between a number of imaginal trials and the same number of physical trials [8]. Sometimes subjects have even been required to alternate these practice techniques between practice sessions [9]. In all these situations it is important to realize that some imagery practice is being substituted for some physical practice (usually 50%).

Early reviews of the literature seemed to suggest that a combination of imagery and physical practice is superior to either imagery or physical practice alone [6, 9]. Recently, this conclusion has been challenged. Feltz, Landers, and Becker used a meta-analysis to examine the data from nineteen studies [10]. They found that the mean change for all practice conditions included in these studies was significantly greater than zero, with physical practice displaying the greatest change effects (0.79), followed by the combined imagery and physical practice groups (0.62) and the control groups (0.22). Hird, Landers, Thomas, and Horan investigated the effects of varying ratios of imagery to physical practice on the performance of a pursuit rotor task and a pegboard task [11]. A trend analysis revealed that as the relative proportion of physical practice increased, performance was enhanced for both tasks. These two studies seem to suggest that combined imagery and physical practice is not more effective than physical practice alone.

Durand, Hall, and Haslam have just completed another review of this issue [12]. After re-examining most of the data currently available, they argue that it may be possible to replace some physical practice with imagery practice without affecting the performance enhancement that normally follows physical practice. They also point out, however, that the replacement of physical practice with imagery practice is not the approach that should, or would normally be used by coaches or teachers. In most situations where imagery is to be employed to facilitate learning and performance, it is a supplement to regular physical practice. That is, an imagery training program is typically incorporated into an athletes overall training program without any reduction in physical practice occurring.

Blair, Hall, and Leyshon realized the need for such a design in applied sports research [13]. She tested skilled and novice players on a task designed to incorporate some of the basic skills required in soccer. Initially, subjects were tested on the task, and then randomly assigned to either an imagery group or a control group. The imagery group received six weeks of imagery practice on the task while the control group spent this time developing a competition strategy for soccer. During this period all subjects also engaged in their regular soccer activities (e.g., team practices). After six weeks the subjects' performance on the task was again tested. The imagery group significantly improved their performance on the task while the control group showed no change. Blair concluded that imagery should be used in conjunction with physical practice to facilitate performance.

FACTORS INFLUENCING THE USE OF IMAGERY

Given that imagery is to be used as a technique for improving the learning and performance of motor skills, there are various factors that can influence how effective imagery will be. Some of the more important ones will be considered here. Other variables that also warrant consideration but are beyond the scope of the present chapter include age, intellectual ability, motivation, and personality characteristics.

Nature of the Task

It is reasonable to assume that the learning and performance of all movement tasks will not benefit equally from imagery rehearsal. Some tasks are likely to lend themselves more to imagery rehearsal than others. It has been shown that different movements can have different imagery values (i.e., a rating of how easily the movement can be imagined) and the easier a movement pattern is to image (higher rating), the better it is remembered [14, 15]. Therefore, when learning a motor task some consideration should be given to how easy the task is to image. If it is somewhat difficult to image, alternative techniques for helping to acquire the skill, such as giving verbal descriptions, might be very useful.

Often the cognitive component involved in performing a motor task has been linked with the benefits of imagery rehearsal. Using a meta-analysis, Feltz and Landers found that the size of the effect produced by imagery was larger for cognitive tasks such as finger maze learning than for tasks such as dart throwing [5]. The latter, in turn, exceeded the effects in tasks in which strength was the major component. The suggestion is that imagery facilitates the performance of cognitive tasks more than those that are predominantly "motor" and/or based on strength. The problem is in attempting to determine the size of the cognitive component in any motor task. What makes finger maze learning more cognitive than dart throwing? Furthermore, the cognitive dimension of a task undoubtedly changes as the skill level of the performer changes. A novice may be thinking about how to do a skill while an expert is concentrating on the strategy and tactics related to performing that skill.

Rather than looking at the cognitive component of skills, the type of task analysis suggested by Paivio could be employed [16]. He argues that one relatively neglected issue is whether the task involves a perceptual target, whether such a target is moving or stationary, and what the performer is doing in relation to the target. Is the performer moving or stationary? Paivio contends that such task differences must have implications for how imagery can be most effectively employed. It is not simply good enough to determine that imagery rehearsal is useful in learning and performing certain types of tasks. We also need to determine how it can be made to work better and in more situations. To do this we require answers to specific task-analytic questions.

Imagery Instructions

Imagery is a complex, multi-dimensional process. Therefore, the imagery instructions given to a performer are extremely important. They must contain sufficient detail to ensure that the performer is imaging the task in the desired manner. For example, it must be clear whether the entire task is to be imaged, or just specific parts. The performance outcome (e.g., the ball going into the goal) may or may not be included as part of the imagery rehearsal. What type of imagery (e.g., visual vs. kinesthetic) to use has to be delineated. The imagery perspective to be employed is also important. If the imagery instructions are vague, two performers could image the same task in very different ways, and possibly realize quite different results.

Paivio believes that imagery has both a cognitive function and a motivational function [16]. Most of the mental practice (imagery) research has examined the cognitive function. As discussed above, subjects can improve their performance on a motor task simply by engaging in the imaginal rehearsal of that task (i.e., imagining themselves correctly performing the task). The motivational function involves imagining the achievement of specific goals such as winning a contest or receiving a medal. While there has been little direct research on the motivational function of imagery, one recent study suggests it can have important implications on the amount and intensity of voluntary practice [17].

One source of indirect research on the motivational function of imagery is those studies that have examined what has been termed "outcome imagery" [18]. For example, Woolfolk, Parrish and Murphy varied the outcome imagery instructions for putting a golf ball [19]. College students were randomly assigned to one of three groups: positive imagery, negative imagery, or control. The imagery instructions for task performance were identical for both the positive and negative groups. With respect to performance outcome instructions, students were asked to form either a positive outcome image, in which the ball was successful in going into the hole, or a negative outcome image, in which the performance outcome was the ball narrowly missing the hole. The control group putted without instructions. Subjects in the positive imagery group improved significantly (30.4%) from their baseline scores over a period of six consecutive testing days. The group using negative imagery showed a significant decline in performance accuracy (21.2%) relative to the control group who showed a slight increase in accuracy (9.9%) over the same period of time. This study is similar to several others showing that imagery that includes a positive or "successful" performance outcome enhances subsequent performance [20, 21].

The majority of imagery studies have emphasized or assumed the use of visual imagery by subjects, but in certain motor skills kinesthetic imagery might be as effective, or even more effective. Kinesthetic imagery is concerned with the feel of a movement. Individuals are instructed to imagine how a movement feels without actually performing the movement. Most subjects that we have tested in our laboratory report being able to separate kinesthetic imagery from visual imagery. Those involved in closed sports (e.g., figure skating, gymnastics) usually report that kinesthetic imagery is very easy to use, and find it just as effective, if not more effective than visual imagery [22]. There has not been to our knowledge, however, any systematic comparison of visual versus kinesthetic imagery instructions.

Assuming that both visual and kinesthetic imagery can facilitate performance, it is probably worthwhile to take the approach employed by Rodgers et al. and use imagery instructions that require individuals to employ some combination of kinesthetic and visual imagery [2]. One study that offers support for this approach was conducted by Ryan and Simons [23]. They investigated the benefits of imagery practice and physical practice in learning to balance on a stabilometer. Subjects in the imagery conditions were asked to complete a questionnaire concerning the amount and quality of any visual or kinesthetic imagery they had experienced. Their basic findings were what would be expected. Physical practice produced greater performance improvements than imagery practice, and subjects who were asked to use imagery were superior to those who were asked not to. More important to the present discussion, they also found that subjects reporting strong visual images showed more improvement than those with weak visual images, and those with strong kinesthetic images were better than those with weak kinesthetic images.

One dimension of imagery instructions that has been considered in some detail is the imagery perspective that subjects are instructed to use. Subjects can use either an external or an internal perspective. The external perspective has subjects view themselves from a third-person perspective; they are instructed to take the position of an observer, as if viewing a videotape of one of their previous performances. The internal perspective entails the performers imagining the performance from within their body. That is, they "view" it through their own eyes. It has been suggested that this perspective has the potential to be more kinesthetic because the performer is rehearsing the task from within the body.

Interest in the imagery perspective adopted by athletes was fostered by a study by Mahoney and Avener [24]. They questioned an elite sample of gymnasts from the American Olympic Team. They found that within this sample the more successful athletes employed an internal perspective while the less successful athletes relied on an external perspective. Using a modified version of Mahoney and Avener's questionnaire, Rotella, Gansneder, Ojala, and Billing examined the imagery perspectives used by elite skiers [25]. Their results also showed that the more successful athletes favored an internal perspective. Barr and Hall recently investigated how elite and non-elite rowers differ in their use of imagery [26]. In support of the previous two studies, they found that elite rowers use an internal imagery perspective more often than novice rowers.

The research reviewed so far suggests that successful elite athletes prefer to use an internal imagery perspective over an external imagery perspective for enhancing performance. There have been a number of studies, however, that have failed to demonstrate this finding. Meyers, Cooke, Cullen, and Liles studied college and elite racquetball players [27]. Their results showed no relationship between imagery perspective and skill level. Highlen and Bennett found similar results in their study of elite wrestlers [28]. Hall et al. conducted a relatively extensive investigation of imagery use by athletes [22]. Athletes from six sports across four skill levels were included in their study. They found that athletes, regardless of skill level, adopted an internal and external imagery perspective with equal frequency.

A number of studies have compared the effects on performance when groups of subjects are instructed to use an internal versus an external imagery perspective. Epstein investigated dart throwing performances of a control group, an internal imagery group, and external imagery group [29]. There proved to be no significant differences among the three groups. Mumford and Hall found similar results in a study involving figure skating [30]. The problem with both of these studies is that the imagery groups did no better than the control groups. McFadden also used a similar experimental design to examine the effects of imagery perspective on goaltending performance in ice hockey [31]. In this study the internal and external imagery groups performed significantly better than the control groups, but the two imagery groups did not differ. These results would seem to suggest that the imagery perspective subjects are instructed to use is irrelevant; however, such a conclusion would probably be premature. Additional research is certainly required.

Given the above findings, we feel that in an imagery training program it is probably best to let the performers decide which imagery perspective to use. Both perspectives can be presented in the instructions and subjects can choose to use either one. Our interviews with athletes indicate that it is not uncommon for a given athlete to switch back and forth between the two perspectives. In an imagery study, for control purposes, it may be desirable to emphasize only one perspective in the imagery instructions. Whether all subjects will adhere to using only this perspective is a concern and should probably be investigated in a post-experimental questionnaire.

Skill Level

Is imagery more beneficial for the novice or the skilled performer? There have been two opposing views on this issue. Some researchers have argued that imagery should be most effective in the initial stage of motor skill learning and thus be of most benefit to the novice performer. This position is based on the premise that the initial stage of learning a skill is primarily cognitive in nature and imagery facilitates the rehearsal of these cognitive components. Support for this position has been offered by Wrisberg and Ragsdale [32]. They introduced mental imagery either early or later in the learning of a motor skill and found that it facilitated performance as a decreasing function of the amount of physical practice the subjects had experienced.

The alternative view contends that imagery should be more effective after the performer has had practice doing the task because this will ensure that a strong internal representation of the skill has been developed. This prior experience permits the performer to form a clear, accurate image of what good task performance is like. Subsequent performance is then directed at mimicking the imaged performance. According to Noel, mere experience at a skill to be imaged is not enough; proficiency is required [33]. In his study, subjects were classified as either high or low in tennis ability. While a significant performance improvement was found in the high ability players who used mental imagery, a deterioration was actually evidenced in the low ability players.

More recently, Blair, Hall, and Leyshon again examined this issue of whether imagery is more effective for novice or skilled performers [13]. Skilled and novice soccer players were tested on a task designed to incorporate some of the basic skills required in soccer. Following initial completion of this task, players in the two skill groups were randomly assigned to either an imagery condition or a control condition. The imagery condition involved six weeks of imagery practice on the task while the control players spent this time developing a competition strategy for soccer. This competition strategy was unrelated to the experimental task; it just pertained to soccer in general. After six weeks, the players' performance on the task was again tested. They found that both skilled and novice players in the imagery condition showed a significant improvement in their performance compared to the control players. They concluded that imagery can positively aid performance at both skill levels.

Given the above results, it is probably appropriate to encourage athletes at all skill levels to use imagery. The manner in which the imagery instructions are constructed for these levels, however, might be quite different. Novices are developing basic skills and so their imagery instructions would emphasize imagining themselves performing these skills correctly. The motivational function of imagery incorporated in these instructions would, therefore, focus on skill improvement (e.g., imagine successfully landing a jump in figure skating). Skilled performers could also be instructed to imagine themselves performing the basic skills correctly, but imagery here might be acting more as a means of reinforcement. Skilled performers are more likely to use imagery for strategy development, confidence building, and controlling arousal levels than novice performers [34]. Consequently, imagery instructions for skilled performers can incorporate these aspects of performance, while for novice performers such imagery may be of minimal value. They are still too concerned with just how to do the basics.

Imagery Ability

Individual differences in imagery ability have been of interest to psychologists for over a century. The main approach has been to try and determine whether it is possible to predict task performance from variations in imagery ability. It seems reasonable to assume that if individuals are instructed to use imagery to help perform a task and they are low in imagery ability, it is likely that imagery will have little or no effect. High imagers, by contrast, should be able to use imagery very effectively. Since motor tasks seem to lend themselves to imagery rehearsal, the imagery ability of the performers should be an important variable to consider.

The movement imagery studies that have considered imagery ability have produced rather inconsistent results. Start and Richardson found no relationship between either vividness or controllability of imagery and the learning and performance of a gymnastics skill [35]. Epstein was also not able to demonstrate any strong relationship between imagery ability and performance accuracy on a dart throwing task [29]. In contrast, Housner and Hoffman have found evidence that in the memory of movement locations high imagers do have an advantage [36, 37].

One key to demonstrating a relationship between imagery ability and motor performance is having a good measure of movement imagery ability. Often the tests that have been employed to classify individuals as high and low imagers have not specifically assessed imagery of movement. To rectify this situation, Hall, Pongrac, and Buckolz developed the Movement Imagery Questionnaire (MIQ) which assesses both visual and kinesthetic movement imagery ability [38]. The use of the MIQ as an imagery ability test for movements has been supported in a number of studies (for a review, see Fishburne and Hall [39]). More importantly, some positive results have been reported showing that high imagery ability, as measured by the MIQ, facilitates the acquisition and memory of movement patterns [40, 41].

Thus far we have been discussing imagery as an ability. It might be more appropriate to think of imagery as a skill varying among individuals that can be improved with practice. Assuming that imagery is a skill, Rodgers et al. investigated the effects of an imagery training program on imagery ability [2]. The study employed two groups of figure skaters, an imagery training group and a verbalization training (control) group. All skaters were assessed for movement imagery ability using the MIQ prior to and following a sixteen-week training period. During the training period the imagery and verbal groups received instructions and guidance in the use of their respective types of mental practice. The imagery training group improved in visual imagery and was beginning to improve in kinesthetic imagery over the training period. The verbal group showed no changes in their visual and kinesthetic MIQ scores. These results suggest that not only is it important to consider the imagery abilities of performers, but to realize that these abilities may change as a consequence of extensive imagery practice.

POSITIVE VERSUS NEGATIVE IMAGERY

A common belief when encouraging athletes to use an imagery training program is that they should be instructed to image a skill exactly the way they wish to perform it. They should image themselves performing accurately and successfully since imaging failure and imaging the skill incorrectly may interfere with its proper acquisition. There is evidence, however, indicating that athletes do sometimes visualize themselves performing incorrectly (e.g., falling on a jump in figure skating) [22]. This is important because several studies suggest that positive or accurate imagery enhances subsequent performance, whereas negative or imperfect imagery results in impaired performance.

One of the first studies to investigate the effects of positive versus negative imagery practice was conducted by Powell [20]. He compared a positive mental imagery group with a negative mental imagery group on the task of dart throwing. Subjects in the positive group were instructed to imagine the dart landing near the center of the target, while those in the negative group imaged a very poor performance outcome (e.g., the dart hitting the edge of the board). Scores were obtained from three blocks of twenty-four actual throws (blocks 1, 3, and 5) which were interspersed with two blocks of imagery throws (blocks 2 and 4), either positive or negative. Subjects in the positive group improved their performance scores from block 1 to block 5 by an average of 28 percent, whereas the performance of the subjects in the negative group actually deteriorated by an average of −3 percent. Powell concluded that "what a subject imagines during mental practice is liable to affect differentially later performance" [20, p. 312].

Woolfolk, Parrish, and Murphy randomly assigned college students to one of three experimental groups: positive imagery, negative imagery, or control [19]. The motor task they were asked to perform was putting a golf ball. For the two imagery groups, the imagery instructions for task performance were the same (they were to imagine themselves correctly putting the ball), but the outcome imagery instructions differed. The positive group was instructed to imagine the ball going into the hole while the negative group imagined the ball narrowly missing the hole. The control group putted without any imagery instructions. The results of the study supported Powell's finding that pre-performance imagery can have varying effects on subsequent performance. Subjects in the positive group improved significantly (30.4%) from their baseline scores over a period of six consecutive testing days. The group using negative imagery showed a significant decline in performance accuracy (21.2%) relative to the control group, who showed a slight increase in accuracy (9.9%) over the same period of time.

Woolfolk, Murphy, Gottesfeld, and Aitken extended this line of research by examining the presence or absence of task performance imagery with different types of performance outcome imagery, either positive, negative or no outcome [21]. The subjects were sixty-six male undergraduate students and the performance task was once again putting a golf ball. Contrary to their previous study, positive outcome imagery failed to significantly enhance subsequent performance. The researchers suggested this may have been due to some differences in methodology. Results for negative imagery were consistent with their previous finding; negative imagery produced a significant performance deterioration. It was suggested that negative imagery may be more detrimental to performance than positive imagery is in enhancing it. In addition, they argued that imaging the outcome component of a task prior to performing that task has a greater influence on actual performance than imaging the task performance.

The above studies indicate that incorrect or negative images of performance outcome can have a damaging effect on actual motor performance. As noted earlier, however, athletes report sometimes imaging themselves performing incorrectly. Should this be strongly discouraged? Perhaps not. It may depend on what athletes do with these negative images. If they image themselves making a correction to these negative images after they occur, beneficial results may be realized. This would be similar to actual physical practice when they make changes to their performances, these changes often being based on feedback they receive from their coach. Furthermore, the negative images athletes experience do not occur frequently [22]. Therefore, negative imagery is probably not a major concern, especially if it is turned into a positive outcome (i.e., meaningful corrections to the images are made). Of course, this is not to suggest that imagery instructions should normally emphasize anything other than the imagery of a correct and successful task performance.

IMPLICATIONS FOR IMAGERY TRAINING PROGRAMS

The literature on mental skills training programs is growing rapidly. There are numerous books and articles on how athletes should mentally prepare for competition [42-46]. Virtually all of these programs include the use of mental imagery. Is imagery being employed as effectively as possible in all these programs? We believe it is not. When developing an imagery training program or a mental skills training program that includes imagery, it would seem important to consider some of the issues discussed above.

First, the nature of the sport is important. Most sports are multi-dimensional and some aspects may lend themselves to imagery practice more than others. Start with those that are relatively easy to image and then move to those more difficult. Another consideration is the athletes that are involved. The more successful mental skills training programs seem to cater to individual differences among the athletes rather than gearing the program to the entire team [47-50]. Given this approach, the imagery ability and the skill level of each athlete, if unknown, should be assessed before an imagery training program is initiated. Those athletes low in imagery ability should start by imaging skills they can already do well, and later move to imaging skills they find difficult or are just learning. High imagers may immediately image new and challenging skills. An athlete's skill level will indicate whether their imagery should primarily focus on basic skills, or whether it should also include the strategies and tactics of the sport.

The next consideration should be the imagery instructions given to the athletes. Athletes should be encouraged to try both imagery perspectives and to use kinesthetic as well as visual imagery. The instructions should emphasize positive imagery, and this imagery should include both the performance of the skill (e.g., imagine the proper way to stroke a golf ball) and the performance outcome (e.g., see the ball go into the hole). Inform athletes that experiencing some negative imagery is not unusual, but they should always imagine themselves making the appropriate corrections (i.e., changing the negative imagery to positive imagery).

A final concern when developing an imagery training program is deciding how long it should be. An examination of various mental skills training programs suggests the successful ones were often conducted over a complete season, the total length depending on the sport [48, 50]. If an extensive program is conducted, two changes in an athletes' imagery can probably be expected over the course of the program. One is they will improve in their imagery ability and this, in turn, should permit them to use their imagery in more creative ways and for more purposes. The other change is that athletes may give more emphasis to the motivational function of imagery, especially if the imagery training program coincides with their competitive season. That is, they will be more likely to imagine themselves being in control and being successful (e.g., winning) as the major competitions approach. An effective imagery training program should capitalize on these changes and ensure they are incorporated in other aspects of an athletes' mental preparation, such as in precompetition and competition strategies.

REFERENCES

1. R. M. Fenker, Jr. and J. G. Lambiotte, A Performance Enhancement Program for a College Football Team: One Incredible Season, *The Sport Psychologist, 1,* pp. 224-236, 1987.
2. W. Rodgers, C. Hall, and E. Buckolz, The Effect of an Imagery Training Program on Imagery Ability, Imagery Use, and Figure Skating Performance, *Journal of Applied Sport Psychology, 3,* pp. 109-125, 1991.
3. M. Denis, Visual Imagery and the Use of Mental Practice in the Development of Motor Skills, *Canadian Journal of Applied Sport Sciences, 10,* pp. 4S-16S, 1985.
4. C. B. Corbin, Mental Practice, in *Ergogenic Aids and Muscular Performance,* W. P. Morgan (ed.), Academic Press, New York, 1972.
5. D. L. Feltz and D. M. Landers, The Effects of Mental Practice on Motor Skill Learning and Performance; A Meta-Analysis, *Journal of Sport Psychology, 5,* pp. 25-57, 1983.
6. A. Richardson, Mental Practice: A Review and Discussion, Part I, *Research Quarterly, 38,* pp. 95-107, 1967.
7. S. G. Zeigler, A Comparison of Imagery Styles and Past Experience in Skill Performance, *Perceptual and Motor Skills, 64,* pp. 579-586, 1987.
8. E. R. McBride and A. L. Rothstein, Mental and Physical Practice and the Learning and Retention of Open and Closed Skills, *Perceptual and Motor Skills, 49,* pp. 359-365, 1979.
9. R. S. Weinberg, The Relationship between Mental Preparation Strategies and Motor Performance: A Review and Critique, *Quest, 33,* pp. 195-213, 1982.
10. D. L. Feltz, D. M. Landers, and B. J. Becker, A Revised Meta-Analysis of the Mental Practice Literature on Motor Skill Learning, in *Enhancing Human Performance: Issues, Theories and Techniques,* D. Druckman and J. Swets (eds.), National Academy Press, Washington, 1988.
11. J. S. Hird, D. M. Landers, J. R. Thomas, and J. J. Horan, Physical Practice is Superior to Mental Practice in Enhancing Cognitive and Motor Task Performance, *Journal of Sport and Exercise Psychology, 8,* pp. 281-293, 1991.
12. M. Durand, C. Hall, and I. Haslam, *The Effects of Combining Mental and Physical Practice on Motor Skill Acquisition: Review of the Literature and Critical Appraisal,* manuscript submitted for publication, 1993.
13. A. M. Blair, X. Hall, and X. Leyshon, Imagery Effects on the Performance of Skilled and Novice Soccer Players, *Journal of Sport Sciences, 11,* pp. 95-101, 1993.
14. C. R. Hall, Imagery for Movement, *Journal of Human Movement Studies, 6,* pp. 252-264, 1980.
15. C. Hall and E. Buckolz, Recognition Memory for Movement Patterns and Their Corresponding Pictures, *Journal of Mental Imagery, 5,* pp. 97-104, 1981.
16. A. Paivio, Cognitive and Motivational Functions of Imagery in Human Performance, *Canadian Journal of Applied Sport Sciences, 10,* pp. 22S-28S, 1985.
17. C. Hall, J. Toews, and W. Rodgers, Les Aspects Motivationnels de L'imagerie en Activites Motrices, *Revue des Sciences et Techniques des Activités Physiques et Sportives, 11,* pp. 27-32, 1990.
18. L. G. Lippman, Positive versus Negative Phrasing in Mental Practice, *The Journal of General Psychology, 117,* pp. 255-265, 1989.
19. R. L. Woolfolk, M. W. Parrish, and S. M. Murphy, The Effects of Positive and Negative Imagery on Motor Skill Performance, *Cognitive Therapy and Research, 9,* pp. 335-341, 1985.
20. G. E. Powell, Negative and Positive Mental Practice in Motor Skill Acquisition, *Perceptual and Motor Skills, 37,* p. 312, 1973.

21. R. L. Woolfolk, S. M. Murphy, D. Gottesfeld, and D. Aitken, Effects of Mental Rehearsal of Motor Task Activity and Mental Depiction of Task Outcome on Motor Skill Performance, *Journal of Sport Psychology, 7,* pp. 191-197, 1985.

22. C. Hall, W. Rodgers, and K. Barr, The Use of Imagery by Athletes in Selected Sports, *The Sport Psychologist, 4,* pp. 1-10, 1990.

23. E. D. Ryan and J. Simons, Efficacy of Mental Imagery in Enhancing Mental Rehearsal of Motor Skills, *Journal of Sport Psychology, 4,* pp. 41-51, 1982.

24. M. J. Mahoney and M. Avener, Psychology of the Elite Athlete: An Exploratory Study, *Cognitive Therapy and Research, 1,* pp. 135-141, 1977.

25. R. J. Rotella, B. Gansneder, D. Ojala, and J. Billing, Cognitions and Coping Strategies of Elite Skiers: An Exploratory Study of Young Developing Athletes, *Journal of Sport Psychology, 2,* pp. 350-354, 1980.

26. K. Barr and C. Hall, The Use of Imagery by Rowers, *International Journal of Sport Psychology, 23,* pp. 243-261, 1992.

27. A. W. Meyers, C. J. Cook, J. Cullen, and L. Liles, Psychological Aspects of Athletic Competitors: A Replication Across Sports, *Cognitive Therapy and Research, 3,* pp. 361-366, 1979.

28. P. Highlen and B. Bennett, Psychological Characteristics of Successful and Non-successful Elite Wrestlers: An Exploratory Study, *Journal of Sport Psychology, 1,* pp. 123-137, 1979.

29. M. L. Epstein, The Relationship of Mental Imagery and Mental Rehearsal to Performance of a Motor Task, *Journal of Sport Psychology, 2,* pp. 211-220, 1980.

30. B. Mumford and C. Hall, The Effects of Internal and External Imagery on Performing Figures in Figure Skating, *Canadian Journal of Applied Sport Sciences, 10,* pp. 171-177, 1985.

31. R. S. McFadden, *An Investigation of the Relative Effectiveness of Two Types of Imagery Rehearsal Applied to Enhance Skilled Athletic Performance,* unpublished doctoral dissertation, University or Toronto, 1982.

32. C. A. Wrisberg and M. R. Ragsdale, Cognitive Demand and Practice Level: Factors in the Mental Rehearsal of Motor Skills, *Journal of Human Movement Studies, 5,* pp. 201-208, 1979.

33. R. C. Noel, The Effect of Visuo-motor Behavioral Rehearsal on Tennis Performance, *Journal of Sport Psychology, 2,* pp. 221-226, 1980.

34. J. Salmon, C. Hall, and I. Haslam, The Use of Imagery by Soccer Players, *Journal of Applied Sport Psychology,* in press.

35. K. B. Start and A. Richardson, Imagery and Mental Practice, *British Journal of Educational Psychology, 34,* pp. 280-284, 1964.

36. L. Housner and S. J. Hoffman, Imagery and Short-Term Motor Memory, in *Psychology of Motor Behavior and Sport,* G. C. Roberts and K. M. Newell (eds.), Human Kinetic, Champaign, Illinois, 1978.

37. L. Housner and S. J. Hoffman, Imagery Ability in Recall of Distance and Location, *Journal of Motor Behavior, 13,* pp. 207-223, 1981.

38. C. Hall, J. Pongrac, and E. Buckolz, The Measurement of Imagery Ability, *Human Movement Science, 4,* pp. 107-118, 1985.

39. G. Fishburne and C. Hall, Imagery Ability and Movement, in *Proceedings of the Alberta Teacher Educators in Physical Education Society Meeting,* M. Lashuk (ed.), University of Calgary, Calgary, 1988.

40. S. Goss, C. Hall, E. Buckolz, and G. Fishburne, Imagery Ability and the Application and Retention of Movements, *Memory and Cognition, 14,* pp. 469-477, 1986.

41. C. Hall, E. Buckolz, and G. Fishburne, Searching for a Relationship between Imagery Ability and Memory of Movements, *Journal of Human Movement Studies, 17,* pp. 89-100, 1989.
42. T. Orlick, *Psyching for Sport: Mental Training for Athletes,* Human Kinetics, Champaign, Illinois, 1986.
43. K. Porter and J. Foster, *The Mental Game Plan: Inner Training for Peak Performance,* Wm. C. Brown, Dubuque, 1986.
44. H. H. Schomer, Mental Strategy Training Programme for Marathon Runners, *International Journal of Sport Psychology, 18,* pp. 133-151, 1986.
45. R. M. Suinn, *Seven Steps to Peak Performance: The Mental Training Program for Athletes,* Hans Huber, Toronto, 1986.
46. R. S. Vealey, Future Directions in Psychological Skills Training, *The Sport Psychologist, 2,* pp. 318-336, 1988.
47. S. H. Boutcher and R. J. Rotella, A Psychological Skills Education Program for Closed-skill Performance Enhancement, *The Sport Psychologist, 1,* pp. 127-137, 1987.
48. H. A. Dorfman, Reflections on Providing Personal and Performance Enhancement Consulting Services in Professional Baseball, *The Sport Psychologist, 4,* pp. 341-346, 1990.
49. S. Gordon, A Mental Skills Training Program for the Western Australian State Cricket Team, *The Sport Psychologist, 4,* pp. 222-230, 1990.
50. K. Ravizza, Sportpsych Consultation Issues in Professional Baseball, *The Sport Psychologist, 4,* pp. 330-340, 1990.

CHAPTER 8

Optimal Arousal, Stress and Imagery

HARVEY L. RISHE, ERIC W. KRENZ,
CRAIG McQUEEN, AND VICKIE D. KRENZ

Since the classic work of Seyle, the area of optimal arousal and stress has been the focus of considerable attention. In the field of athletic competition, the demands placed on time, energy and financial resources produce considerable pressure to become the best competitor possible. Since the rewards and recognition allotted to superior athletic performance can be tremendous, many athletes will use every tool available to have the advantage in competition.

Though the physiological aspects of performance were acknowledged, very little value was placed on the mental preparation of athletes for competition. Traditional athletic training programs emphasized the physical execution of motor skills and relied on fiery pep talks to instill optimal precompetitive arousal.

At present, athletic performance has become very precise and refined. As athletes continue to reach higher skill levels, the greater the need to control all factors that influence competition. Considerable research has been invested on the mental preparation of athletes for optimal arousal. Thus, a multitude of psychological strategies have evolved that are aimed at optimizing competitive performance.

STRESS AND ITS EFFECT ON OPTIMAL AROUSAL

Stress can have a direct effect on arousal for athletic performance. When confronted with the additional mental and emotional strains of competition athletes experience varying levels of stress and anxiety. However, this complex interaction between stress and arousal of athletic performance has defied definition. While sophisticated models have been developed in an attempt to describe this relationship, stress is at best defined as a perceptual phenomena, that results from a conflict between an individual's cognitive appraisal of a set of circumstances and the demands placed on him/her [1].

According to Cox, stress is a perceptual conflict between demand and the ability to cope [1]. When an imbalance occurs between a perceived demand and the actual demand, and the perceived capabilities and the actual capabilities of an individual, stress results. This imbalance between subjective perception and reality produces both emotional and stress responses, that in turn, lead to psychological and physiological responses. The physiological response provides feedback to the actual and perceived demands, while the psychological response produces a cognitive and a behavioral response. The process is completed when the cognitive response feeds back to the cognitive appraisal of the situation and the behavioral response affects the actual and perceived demand. In other words, this perceptual phenomena is cyclic and can serve to escalate an individual's psychological and physiological reactions to stress.

For example, a collegiate athlete may perceive an upcoming tennis match to be of major importance not only to his/her ranking, but also to their position on the team and their self-worth. However, the coach may only place minor value on that particular meet. Furthermore, the athlete may perceive his/her opponent as being a better competitor and minimize their own capabilities, while in actuality they have beaten this person on several occasions. Due to the incongruencies between the subjective perceptions of the athlete and reality, stress can have a tremendous effect on the outcome of the match.

The further effects of stress on optimal arousal can be seen in an apparent change in the athlete's routine prior to the impending meet. While practices may be more extensive and demanding, it is not unusual for an athlete to experience changes in appetite and sleep patterns, become nauseous and have feelings of apprehension and irritability. All of this, in turn, feeds back to the athlete's subjective perceptions of the upcoming match and capability.

Though Hull's "Drive Theory" has been used to describe the complex relationship between optimal arousal and stress [2], subjective perceptions can produce unnecessarily excessive levels of stress that can have a direct effect on the successful execution of a motor task. Based on a linear association between these variables, it is proposed that as stress levels increase, there will be a positive increase in arousal. However, the weakness in this theory is the assumption that stress will only positively affect arousal and does not sufficiently explain the detrimental effects of excessive levels on performance. Therefore, the "Invert-U" hypothesis has gained considerable popularity. Yerks and Dodson hypothesized that the relationship between stress and performance as curvilinear [3]. That is, low levels of stress can produce low arousal and result in poor performance. As stress levels increase to an optimal level, arousal will increase to an optimal level and enhance performance.

Though it is difficult to empirically document this phenomena, several studies have supported the detrimental effect of stress on performance. Sarason reported a direct relationship between anxiety and poor performance in complex motor skills [4]. Martens reported that as stress and state anxiety (or arousal) increased to an optimal point, performance was enhanced. However, increases in state anxiety beyond this point had a detrimental effect on performance [5]. Similarly, research by Castaneda, McCandless, and Palermo [6], Sarason and Palola [7], Ryan [8], Carron [9], Hollingsworth [10], Gerson and Deshaies [11], Krenz, Edwards, and Henschen [12], and Bar-Eli [13] have also added support to this process.

When confronted with the additional mental and emotional stress of competition, athletes experience varying amounts of stress and anxiety. Though occasionally heightened levels of stress and anxiety may enhance athletic performance, increased levels of arousal usually tend to have a detrimental effect on optimal performance [14]. Though the intensity of competitive stress may vary, individual perceptions of the stress and coping mechanisms have a significant impact on the outcome of athletic performance [15-18].

Due to this negative effect on performance, many researchers have investigated the role of stress and anxiety in the performance of various complex tasks. Weinberg and Genuchi studied the relationship between competitive trait anxiety, state anxiety and golf performance [19]. Based on state anxiety and performance, it was concluded that sports requiring fine motor control and precision can be greatly hindered by increased levels of arousal. The negative effect of stress on performance on motor tasks is further supported by Gould, Horn, and Spreeman [20], Krenz, Grodin, and Edwards [21], and Burton [22].

Further research on the detrimental effects of these variables in athletic performance has produced a wide variety of psychological interventions designed to help athletes control their negative reactions to the competitive environment. According to Santomier, how individuals cope with stressors is a critical factor in their perception of competition as a threatening ordeal [23]. These are defined as palliative coping and instrumental coping. Palliative coping is a cognitive evaluation designed to provide temporary relief from the emotional impact of stressors. Though this does not alter the stressor, it allows an individual to "regroup" in order to reduce emotional arousal. Instrumental coping, on the other hand, involves the development of skills that directly relate to the nature and characteristics of the stressor.

Though often overlooked, adequate preparation and the development of specific skills are the major determinants of perceived stressful situation. Therefore, it is important that athletic preparation for sport-specific demands include an understanding of the nature of stress and its relationship to sport.

IMAGERY FOR ATHLETIC COMPETITION

Since the effects of stress can have a detrimental effect on performance, the use of psychological strategies have been employed to enhance athletic skills for performance. Mental imagery is visualizing a task or performance skill and is particularly helpful in learning new motor skills. It involves picturing the skill being executed either by the athlete or a model. Mental rehearsal takes imagery one step further, in that it requires visualizing the task as it is performed and concentrating on the minute details necessary for its successful execution in a repetitious manner.

Several studies have used imagery techniques for the acquisition of athletic skills. Clark investigated the effect of mental practice and imagery skills on the development of foul shooting [24]. Within the experimental conditions, it was concluded that the use of mental rehearsal techniques were nearly as effective for learning certain motor skills as was physical practice. Numerous investigations have documented the beneficial effects of imagery techniques development of athletic skills [25-27].

Among the mental techniques that have been used in precompetition preparation, mental imagery has been used successfully to enhance athletic performance [28-32]. Pulos employed mental imagery to prepare athletes for competition [33]. Krenz and Jencks used imagery techniques with a variety of athletes and reported positive results [34]. Similarly, Lodato, and Kosky reported improved athletic performance using visual imagery in such athletic motor skills as tennis ground strokes, football place kicking and basketball foul shooting [35]. Further uses of imagery for athletic performance include gymnastics [36], karate [37], basketball [38], tennis [39], soccer [40], ice hockey [41], and golf [42].

The use of relaxation techniques are extremely important to mentally prepare the athlete for effective use of imagery for performance. While hypnosis and progressive relaxation training techniques have been used to introduce altered states where imagery can be utilized [43-48], the authors prefer to use an autogenic training modality. Due to its emphasis on natural physiological functions, this technique has been useful in combining the benefits of imagery with sensory awareness.

Based on Schultz's "Standard Autogenic Training" [49-54] that combines self-hypnotic suggestions and physical exercise, Krenz [55-56] developed Modified Autogenic Training (MAT) to reduce the framework required for mastery of autogenic training exercises. MAT is a deep relaxation method that is body-related and progresses with teaching instruction over a six-week period. It is intended to relax the body, but keep the mind active and aware so that special instructions can be inserted. This model attempts to synthesize the strengths of many of the accepted hypnotic and relaxation techniques, reducing their deficits and increasing their effective use for managing unexpected incidences during competition.

MAT uses the six Standard Autogenic Training exercises: 1) heaviness of limbs, 2) warmth of limbs, 3) heartbeat, 4) respiration, 5) warmth of solar plexus and 6) coolness of forehead. Coupled with these exercises is the breathing response developed by Jencks and Krenz [57]. Then the number of repetitions of the exercises needed to produce the desired psychophysiological effects is sequentially decreased each day.

Since MAT is a self-practice technique, there are no dependencies upon either a therapist or taped session. MAT is designed to teach the athlete to control natural psychological and physiological reactions to stressful stimuli, rather than simply reacting to stress. MAT is a self-taught method, allowing athletes to use altered states of consciousness with posthypnotic suggestions to learn mental imagery and practice, problem solving and self-coaching.

MAT produces an altered state of consciousness by relaxing the body, while the mind is active and alert so that suggestions can be introduced for optimal performance. These suggestions, called "constructive daydreaming," are introduced into the program during the third week of training. This term, constructive daydreaming, is used so that mental imagery and mental rehearsal is conceptually understood by the athlete and can be used immediately without special training by all athletes. They are short, positive suggestions that focus on various psychological techniques to improve performance and prepare athletes for competition. These techniques utilize the five senses (i.e., visual, auditory, kinesthetic, olfactory, and taste) to produce a solid sensory awareness. Mental imagery and rehearsal are used to help athletes focus their attention on the task at hand, by picturing themselves performing the task perfectly and then transferring that image to a mental videotape, which can be played over and over again. These association techniques are used to help athletes creatively use mental imagery "as if" they were looking through their own eyes and provide an experiential basis for further imagery training.

A further extension of the use of mental imagery and rehearsal in this program is dissociation techniques. Athletes are given the instruction to picture a "split screen," showing on one side the task being performed perfectly by another athlete and, on the other side, themselves performing the same task. They can then make comparisons between a perfect performance and their own, and make adjustments to the chosen model.

Similar dissociation techniques are used to help the athlete experience how a perfect execution of the task feels. It is suggested to athletes, to observe someone performing a task four to five times perfectly. Then, the athletes are to imagine themselves stepping inside the model's body while they again perform the task four to five more times, remaining sensory-aware of the minute feelings and movements of the task as it is executed. Then, they imagine themselves stepping outside of the model's body and the model to step inside the athlete's to perform the task. Again, the athletes are told to be sensory-aware of each detail of the task. Finally, the model steps out and watches the athletes perform the task on their own, giving suggestions on what the athletes can do to improve their performance.

Mental imagery and rehearsal techniques are especially useful when combined with problem solving and motivation suggestions. The suggestions used in this program are given to the athletes to look at the task at hand and act as their own coach, correcting any mistakes they see. Coupled with mental imagery and problem-solving techniques, athletes can be instructed to devise strategies for a positive mental attitude.

For example, a gymnast falls off the balance beam during practice or competition. Before returning to the beam, the gymnast takes one to three exhalations and mentally pictures the task as it is performed perfectly. Then, the gymnast can return to the beam with a positive image of the task.

Mental imagery techniques have also been useful in preparing athletes for competition in unfamiliar surroundings. Suggestions can be used to familiarize athletes with the potential setting by picturing the surroundings, crowd, noises, distractions, etc., while performing. This is especially beneficial if athletes have, for example, performed in Madison Square Garden once or twice and are looking forward to a critical meet there in the immediate future. Athletes can visualize the setting as complete as possible and mentally rehearse there for the impending event. For athletes who have no knowledge or experience with competing in Madison Square Gardens, for example, visual aids such as pictures or videos of previous competitions there can aid in creating an image of the environment.

CASE STUDIES

The case studies presented are from various sports. All of the athletes have participated in the MAT program with the use of suggestions for seven weeks.

Case Study One

These subjects are female gymnasts from a private Utah gymnastics club. Their ages range from seven to eighteen years of age. Prior to beginning the MAT program, subjects reported excessive levels of arousal during practice, as well as prior to and during competition. Also, it was reported that the subjects were unable to concentrate and were highly distractible during practice and competition.

After completing the MAT program, subjects reported that they felt more in control of their excessive arousal levels and were able to focus their attention to the task at hand. They were more aware of how hard they could push themselves without fear of injury. By using mental imagery techniques, the subjects reported that they were able to learn new tricks and routines quickly. If they fell, they would use the "positive mind set" to regain their concentration and continue on with the task.

The coaching staff have also reported a positive improvement in the athletes. By taking time at the beginning of the practice session for the athletes to practice this program, the quality of the practice sessions have greatly improved. The coaches reported that the athletes are able to calm down and make a transition from school to the practice sessions.

Use of the mental training techniques has had a positive effect on the performance of this club at meets. During the past year, this club took first place in the state meet in Class I, II and III by approximately 5.5 points in each division. This is quite a feat for one club, especially by such a wide margin. Furthermore, two of the athletes were advanced from regions to national for Class I gymnasts and two athletes have advanced to Western Zone, with four going to elite zone.

Case Study Two

The second case study consisted of a sixteen-year-old male tennis player who was diagnosed as hyperkinetic at age ten and has been on Ritalin since. Prior to the MAT program, the subject reported that he was about to be thrown out of organized age-group sports because of excessive emotional outbursts on the court. He also reported that he had not won a major match in over six years. His parents reported that he has a behavioral problem at home and at school.

Two weeks following the competition of the MAT program, the subject won the state doubles championship and a major regional singles tournament. He reported that he felt that he had greater control over his reactions to stress and anxiety and was able to focus his attention to the task at hand. Also, it should be noted that the subject's school grades went up one full letter grade (from a D+ to a C+) and that his parents and teachers felt that his behavior had improved. At present, this athlete is now competing at the junior college level and is ranked first on his team.

Interestingly, this athlete's younger sister (15 years of age) also participated in the MAT program and is currently ranked second in the state. Both of these athletes are High School All-Americans. It is quite unusual for two All-American athletes to be from one family.

Case Study Three

The third case study consisted of two figures skaters from a Utah figure skating club. Prior to participating in the MAT program both reported trouble concentrating and unable to control their level of arousal. After completing the program, both skaters reported that their concentration had improved and that they felt that they were more in control of their performance. One athlete reported that she "dreams" (mental imagery) to improve her performance by watching either herself or someone else perform the "trick" over and over. Like gymnastics, being able to imagine herself performing is important due to the number of injuries that result from falls on the ice. Furthermore, ice time is quite costly and being able to use the mental imagery and rehearsal techniques helps reduce this expense.

Both athletes have shown significant improvement during the past year. One of the athletes went on to compete in the Junior Worlds in Sarajevo. The other athlete placed in the Junior Women's National competition and finished fifth in the Novice division in 1985, sixth at Pacific Junior Ladies competition in 1986.

Case Study Four

This case study consists of three high school men's and women's swimming clubs, which included approximately 110 athletes. All three teams stated that they wanted to not only improve their performance, but more importantly become more consistent in their times. Prior to participation in the program the coaches reported that their meet performances were inconsistent and widely varied throughout the season. They considered their athletes to be distractible and unable to concentrate on their techniques. Furthermore, it took twenty to thirty minutes to get the athletes settled into practice sessions.

Following the completion of the program, the teams took a five minute time-out to practice relaxation exercises and mental imagery techniques as a group. It was reported by both the athletes and coaches that by taking this small amount of time, practice sessions became more effective. It was reported that the athletes seemed to get along better and work more as a team. One coach reported that his team had become supportive of each other and were cheering their team mates on at meets.

Since consistent performance was one of the goals for these teams, mental imagery focuses on improving swimming technique. During the course of the season, athletes' performance improved early in the season and new Personal Records (PR's) were set consistently throughout the season. One of the coaches stated that it was as if the athletes reached their peak early in the season but continued to set new PR's.

At the conclusion of the swimming season, all three teams placed in the state results. Of the three teams, one of the men's teams took second place and one of the women's teams finished in first position in water polo. One athlete finished first in state in diving. Finally, all three teams finished very high in state competition. In men's competition, the high schools finished in first, third and fourth place, while the women placed first, second and fourth. All coaches reported that this had been the most competitive season that they've had.

Case Study Five

This final case study consisted of three men and six women divers from a collegiate swimming team. All divers stated that they wanted to improve their performances. Furthermore, they reported a fear of particular dives and wanted to overcome their anxiety. Several of the divers said that they had trouble concentrating on their dives.

During the MAT, mental imagery techniques were individualized to help the divers overcome their fear of certain dives. Since they would become anxious about the dive and would start to think negative thoughts about its execution, mental imagery was used to rehearse the different components of the dive. Then, the athletes were instructed to imagine the dive as whole to make sure all of the components fit together and they were hitting their dive.

At the conclusion of the season, three of the men's diving team qualified for Western Athletic Conference Championships. On the low board, one diver finished fourth and another finished eighth. On the high board, they placed first and sixth. In the Zone meet, this team placed a fifth on the high board.

The women's team also finished their season with improved performances. In the High Country Athletic Conference Championships, the team placed first, fifth, sixth, seventh, eighth, and ninth on the low board. On the high board, they finished first, fifth, seventh, eighth, eleventh, and thirteenth. In Zone, the divers finished first and second. Nationals also showed improvement for the women divers. In the outdoor competition, one of the divers placed fifth on low board and one placed third on high. Indoor competition produced a third on the low and a second on the high.

All of the athletes reported that the program had helped them improve their performance. They stated that they felt more in control of their dives and were able to concentrate on their performance. Furthermore, the coach reported that he was very pleased with the results of their season. He felt that this had been their most successful season ever.

CONCLUSION

Research on the complex interrelationship between the physiological and psychological aspects of athletic performance supports that stress can have a significant effect on optimal arousal, this in turn may influence performance outcome. Though traditional athletic training regimens have focused on the physiological refinements for optimal arousal and successful performance, mental imagery may enhance performance.

When athletes are confronted with precompetitive and competitive stress, they react negatively and perform below their optimal level. Mental imagery is a technique that can be used in a variety of athletic situations and has been beneficial in improving competitive performance. Due to its vast creative potential, mental imagery can be customized to meet the individual needs of athletes. Coupled with such mental training techniques such as MAT, mental imagery can be beneficial in reducing negative psychophysiological reactions to stress and anxiety and thereby help athletes achieve their optimal level of arousal.

REFERENCES

1. Cox, *Stress,* Macmillan Press, London, 1960.
2. C. L. Hull, *Principles of Behavior,* Appleton-Century-Crofts, New York, 1943.
3. R. M. Yerkes and J. D. Dodson, The Relation of Strength of Stimulus to Repaidity of Habit-Formation, *Journal of Comparative Neurology and Psychology, 18,* pp. 459-482, 1906.
4. I. G. Sarason, The Effects of Anxiety and Threat on the Solution of a Difficult Task, *Journal of Abnormal and Social Psychology, 62,* pp. 165-168, 1961.

5. R. Martens, Anxiety and Motor Behavior: A Review, *Journal of Motor Behavior, 3,* pp. 151-179, 1971.
6. A. Castaneda, B. McCandless, and D. Palermo, Complex Learning and Performance as a Function of Anxiety in Children and Task Difficulty, *Child Development, 27,* pp. 327-332, 1956.
7. I. G. Sarason and E. Palola, The Relationship of Test and General Anxiety, Difficulty of Task and Experimental Instructions to Task Performance, *Journal of Experimental Psychology, 59,* pp. 186-191, 1960.
8. E. D. Ryan, Effects of Stress on Motor Performance and Learning, *The Research Quarterly, 33:*1, pp. 111-119, 1962.
9. A. V. Carron, Motor Performance under Stress, *The Research Quarterly, 39:*3, pp. 463-469, 1968.
10. B. Hollingsworth, Effects of Performance Goals and Anxiety on Learning a Gross Motor Task, *The Research Quarterly, 46:*2, pp. 162-168, 1975.
11. R. Gerson and P. Deshaies, Competitive Trait Anxiety and Performance as Predictors of Pre-competitive State Anxiety, *International Journal of Sport Psychology, 9:*1, pp. 16-29, 1978.
12. E. Krenz, S. Edwards, and K. Henschen, *The Inverted-U Hypothesis: Anxiety vs. Motor Performance,* presented at the Southwestern Regional Convention of the American Alliance for Health, Physical Education, Recreation, and Dance, Honolulu, 1982.
13. M. Bar-Eli, Arousal Performance Relationship: A Transactional View on Performance Jags, *Journal of Sport Psychology, 16:*3, pp. 193-209, 1985.
14. R. Martens, *Sport Competition Anxiety Test,* Human Kinetics, Champaign, Illinois, 1977.
15. M. J. Mahoney and M. Avener, Psychology of the Elite Athlete: An Exploratory Study, *Cognitive Therapy and Research, 1:*2, pp. 135-141, 1977.
16. A. C. Fisher and E. F. Zwart, Psychological Analysis of Athletes' Anxiety Responses, *Journal of Sport Psychology, 4,* pp. 139-158, 1982.
17. C. Lee, Self-Efficacy as a Predictor of Performance in Competitive Gymnastics, *Journal of Sport Psychology, 4,* pp. 405-409, 1982.
18. L. Hardy, Psychological Stress, Performance and Injury in Sport, *British Medical Journal, 48:*3, pp. 615-619, 1992.
19. R. S. Weinberg and M. Genuchi, Relationship Between Competitive Trait Anxiety, State Anxiety, and Golf Performance: A Field Study, *Journal of Sport Psychology, 2,* pp. 148-154, 1980.
20. D. Gould, T. Horn, and J. Spreeman, Competitive Anxiety in Junior Elite Wrestlers, *Journal of Sport Psychology, 5,* pp. 58-71, 1983.
21. E. W. Krenz, R. Grodin, and S. W. Edwards, Effects of Hypnosis on State Anxiety and Stress in Male and Female Intercollegiate Athletes, in *Modern Trends in Hypnosis,* D. Waxman, P. Mistra, M. Gibson, and M. A. Basker (eds.), Plenum, New York, 1985.
22. D. Burton, Do Anxious Swimmers Swim Slower? Reexamining the Elusive Anxiety-Performance Relationship, *Journal of Sport and Exercise Psychology, 10:*1, pp. 45-61, 1988.
23. J. Santomier, The Sport-Stress Connection, *Theory Into Practice, 22:*1, pp. 57-63, 1983.
24. L. V. Clark, Effect of Mental Practice on the Development of a Certain Motor Skill, *The Research Quarterly, 31:*4, pp. 560-569, 1960.
25. M. J. Mahoney, Theoretical Analysis of Aggressive Golf Putts, *Research Quarterly for Exercise and Sport, 53,* pp. 165-171, 1982.
26. D. L. Feltz and D. M. Landers, The Effects of Mental Practice on Motor Skill Learning and Performance: A Meta-analysis, *Journal of Sports Psychology, 5,* pp. 25-57, 1983.

27. E. E. Price and T. Braun, Waking the Sleep Giant, *Athletic Journal, 63,* pp. 42-44, 1983.

28. C. Deschaumes-Molinaro, A. Dittmar, and E. Vernet-Maury, Relationship Between Mental Imagery and Sporting Performance, *Behavioural Brain Research, 45*:1, pp. 29-36, 1991.

29. R. Madigan, R. D. Frey, and T. S. Matlock, Cognitive Strategies of University Athletes, *Canadian Journal of Sport Science, 17*:2, pp. 135-140, 1992.

30. B. L. Howe, Imagery and Sport Performance, *Sports Medicine, 11*:1, pp. 1-5, 1991.

31. G. H. Van-Gyn, H. A. Wenger, and C. A. Gaul, Imagery as a Method of Enhancing Transfer from Training to Performance, *Journal of Sport and Exercise Psychology, 12*:4, pp. 366-375, 1990.

32. J. P. Whelan, M. J. Mahoney, and A. W. Meyers, Performance Enhancement in Sport: A Cognitive Behavioral Domain, *Behavior Therapy, 23*:3, pp. 307-327, 1991.

33. L. Pulos, *Hypnosis and Think Training with Athletes,* paper presented at the 12th Annual Scientific Meeting, American Society of Clinical Hypnosis, San Francisco, 1969.

34. E. W. Krenz and B. Jencks, *Research and Utilization of Hypnosis in Sports,* presented at the American Society of Clinical Hypnosis 23rd Annual Scientific Convention, Minneapolis, November 1980.

35. F. J. Lodato and E. M. Kosky, *Hypnosis and Visual Imagery as a Means of Improving Concentration of Athletes,* presented at the American Society for Clinical Hypnosis Annual Scientific Program, Denver, Colorado, 1982.

36. J. Massimo, Relaxation/Activation: Self-Imagery Training, *IG Technical Supplement,* No. 1, October 13-14, 1979.

37. R. S. Weinberg, T. G. Seabourne, and A. Jackson, Effects of Visuo-Motor Behavior Rehearsal, Relaxation, and Imagery on Karate Performance, *Journal of Sport Psychology, 3,* pp. 228-238, 1981.

38. B. J. Kolonay, *The Effects of Visuo-Motor Behavioral Rehearsal on Athletic Performance,* unpublished Master's thesis, Hunter College, The City University of New York, 1977.

39. R. C. Noel, The Effect of Visuo-Motor Behavior Rehearsal on Tennis Performance, *Journal of Sport Psychology, 2,* pp. 221-226, 1980.

40. S. Davies and J. D. West, A Theoretical Paradigm for Performance Enhancement: The Multimodal Approach, *Sport Psychology, 5*:2, pp. 167-174, 1991.

41. H. Davis, Cognitive Style and Nonsport Imagery in Elite Ice Hockey Performance, *Perceptual and Motor Skills, 71*:3, pt. 1, pp. 795-801, 1990.

42. N. McCaffrey and T. Orlick, Mental Factors Related to Excellence Among Top Professional Golfers, *International Journal of Sport Psychology, 20*:4, pp. 256-278, 1989.

43. W. L. Howard and J. P. Reardon, Changes in the Self Concept and Athletic Performance of Weight Lifters Through a Cognitive Hypnotic Approach: An Empirical Study, *American Journal of Clinical Hypnosis, 28*:4, pp. 248-257, 1986.

44. D. M. Onestak, The Effects of Progressive Relaxation, Mental Practice, and Hypnosis on Athletic Performance: A Review, *Journal of Sport Behavior, 14*:4, pp. 247-282, 1991.

45. H. E. Stanton, Using Rapid Change Techniques to Improve Sporting Performance, *Australian Journal of Clinical and Experimental Hypnosis, 17*:2, pp. 153-161, 1989.

46. E. M. Schreiber, Using Hypnosis to Improve Performance of College Basketball Players, *Perceptual and Motor Skills, 72*:2, pp. 536-538, 1991.

47. E. G. Hall and C. J. Hardy, Ready, Aim, Fire . . . Relaxation Strategies for Enhancing Pistol Marksmanship, *Perceptual and Motor Skills, 72*:3, pt. 1, pp. 775-786, 1991.

48. L. C. Cancio, Stress and Trance in Freefall Parachuting: A Pilot Study, *American Journal of Clinical Hypnosis, 33*:4, pp. 225-234, 1991.
49. J. H. Schultz, *Das Autogene Training,* Verlag, Leipzig, 1932.
50. S. E. Thomas, Hypnosis in Athletes, *Hypnosis, 1,* pp. 11-14, 1955.
51. H. Lindemann, *Alone at Sea,* Random House, New York, 1958.
52. J. H. Schultz and W. Luthe, *Autogenic Training: A Psychophysiologic Approach in Psychotherapy,* Grune and Stratton, New York, 1959.
53. G. Naruse, Hypnotic Treatment of Stage Fright in Champion Athletes, *Psychologia, 7*:324, p. 199, 1964.
54. B. Jencks, Relaxation and Invigoration for Skiers, *Journal of the United States Ski Coaches Association, 3*:2, pp. 9-15, 1979.
55. E. W. Krenz, *Gaining Control: Turning Stress into an Asset with Modified Autogenic Training,* I.I.P. Associates, Salt Lake City, Utah, 1983.
56. E. W. Krenz, Improving Competitive Performance with Hypnotic Suggestions and Modified Autogenic Training: Case Reports, *American Journal of Clinical Hypnosis, 27*:1, pp. 58-63, 1984.
57. B. Jencks and E. W. Krenz, Hypnosis in Sports, in *Comprehensive Clinical Hypnosis,* A. H. Smith and W. C. Wester (eds.), Lippincott, Philadelphia, 1984.

CHAPTER 9
Channeling Addictive Energy into Healthy Training
JOANN DAHLKOETTER

For most athletes, exercising serves an adaptive function, providing a sense of self-confidence, a feeling of control over one's life, and the chance to test limits and reach new goals. The adaptive function of exercising becomes problematic only when goals become unrealistically high, a desensitization to the body appears while unknowingly overtraining, and a denial of the onset of potentially serious injury dominates psychological makeup.

In general, athletes tend to think of exercising as a positive outlet for handling stress. Vigorous physical exercise produces increased endorphin activity, which serves as a potent reinforcer by lowering one's sensation of pain, and elevating mood. Sense of self-discipline and confidence is further enhanced as the rituals of training (e.g., workout schedules, races, log books), become part of daily life. In fact, exercising is such an effective way of handling so many needs, that for some athletes it may become a consuming activity that preempts all other interests. Having a single-minded commitment to physical improvement is by no means harmful in itself. However, one may become so attached to exercising that it becomes the sole means for coping with life. When overtraining takes its toll, the hazards of obligatory exercising begin to appear.

THE PROFILE

The compulsive athlete shows classic Type A behavior: high achieving, stoically independent, tense, and emotionally unexpressive. While these characteristics may lead to productivity and success in many work situations, they can also drive an individual into stress, overtraining, and injury in the physical arena. If an athlete's training patterns fit the following description, he/she may be unknowingly setting himself/herself up for injury and disappointment.

* He/she uses training goals as a way to continually prove himself/herself, but is rarely satisfied, even when his/her goals are reached.

- He/she avoids developing a broad-based lifestyle, with social support, a variety of interests, and a firm sense of self.
- He/she clings to his/her exercising as the only coping mechanism.

Compulsive athletes are often so caught up in their fast-paced lifestyle that they have difficulty developing the sensitivity to notice the early signs of overtraining. When the impending injury screams for attention, the athlete becomes even more anxious, and inflexible in the training schedule.

When an athlete becomes repeatedly injured because of a rigid, repetitive schedule, it is time to slow down, take a good look at what has happened, and find out what needs to be changed. This type of cycle affects not only one's physical status, but also one's self-confidence level and entire lifestyle. Whether the injuries are temporary or chronic will depend not only on the rigidity of the athlete's patterns, but also on the manner in which the athlete handles them.

HABITUAL TRAINING

Certain recurrent behaviors may contribute directly to a cycle of injury or illness. To prevent this pattern we need to first understand the behavior cycle. Here are some of the danger signs:

1. Obsession — The athlete feels he/she must do the daily workout regardless of the weather, state of health, or enjoyment level. It is a duty—a personal obligation.
2. Lack of full concentration — The athlete has so much anger and stress tied up inside that he/she can't relax while training. He/she has trouble letting go of thoughts about his/her external world, loses body sensitivity, judgment becomes inaccurate, and may overlook certain danger signals (e.g., not noticing subtle knee pain, overlooking an oncoming pothole in the road).
3. Negative thought traps — Negative thoughts lead to negative emotions; this leads to muscular strain, which increases the chance of injury.
4. Avoidance — Becoming overly anxious about meeting a goal may lead to subconsciously wanting out. An injured athlete does not have to face the pressures of the real race.
5. Overwork — The athlete is driven to train and compete constantly to reassure himself/herself that he/she is getting stronger. Never taking time off from training leads to mental and physical fatigue. If you do not schedule in rest time regularly, your body will break down and do it for you. Many athletes are afraid to rest before a race, or in between hard days of training because they have trouble changing gears. They cannot relax and trust that their bodies will remember what to do.

6. Mr. Tough Guy — The athlete continues to train through pain that worsens throughout the workout. He/she fights it and considers it almost as a challenge to see how much pain can be endured.

THE GRIEF PROCESS OF INJURY

The injury cycle is something which many athletes have to come to terms with. The joints and tendons can only handle so much stress from an unforgiving training environment. Once an injury does force athletes to stop exercising, they may experience a tremendous letdown. They can no longer feel the high energy from daily training, the feeling of accomplishment from achieving goals, and the social praise from fellow athletes. He/she loses that period of time to be alone, the built-in system of appetite control, the feeling of being light and fit, and the chance to release stress from his/her work and family life. Injury disrupts one's capabilities in a wide variety of areas. The result is that activities that used to require minimal effort now may seem much more difficult to accomplish.

The stages in the injury cycle are quite similar to what happens when someone close to you is dying or has passed away. There are several stages (listed below) that follow a distinct pattern. The process of moving through the stages can take three days, or three years, or a lifetime, depending on the flexibility of the athlete's thinking, how much he cares about himself, and his desire to change.

The following example illustrates the stages that commonly occur in the injury cycle.

1. Initial Problem — Something goes wrong in your training or your personal life.
2. Denial — You feel specific pain and ignore it. You say, "It's just fatigue, it'll go away tomorrow. I'll train through the pain and work it out." Sometimes you might not even sense pain at all if your mind is somewhere else, if you're heavily involved in a workout, or if you're conversing while training with a partner.
3. Anger: Fighting the Body Signals — You acknowledge the pain after three days, but keep training because you "have to get the mileage in." You need exercise and you have no other sport to substitute. You feel angry that your training schedule may need to be adjusted, and you fear losing your sense of accomplishment from training. Common self-statements include: "If I don't train I'll eat too much." "I'll lose all the training I've gained over the past year in one day." "I can't change my schedule, the team will think I'm a quitter." "My mate is counting on me to perform well this weekend; he/she has helped me through my training for so long." "I can handle the pain, I'm not a pansy."
4. Fear of the Unknown — You don't know the source or extent of the injury, and you're afraid to find out.

5. Mental Fatigue — Your motivation is worn down because you know deep inside that you can't continue training; the symptoms are only getting worse. Your training is not fun anymore, it is only an obligation. You continue training, but your heart is not in it.

6. Withdrawal Syndrome — You find out the extent of your addiction to sports. You finally stop training because the pain is so profound that "giving up" is the only alternative you have left.

7. Overreaction — You stop writing in your log book and announce to all your athletic friends: "Count me out; I'm injured."

8. Substitution Behaviors — You begin to overeat and adopt a sedentary lifestyle, making self-defeating statements to punish yourself (e.g., "This injury will never get better").

9. Depression — You start isolating yourself from social contacts, doing poorly at work, distancing yourself from important relationships, and disrupting your personal growth process.

10. Resignation — You finally resign yourself to being injured. You see a doctor and obtain a diagnosis and treatment. But you don't adequately follow the treatment program. The primary treatment is, of course, rest, an anathema to the compulsive athlete.

11. Acceptance — You accept the injury and comply with the treatment regimen. You can then finally begin the rebuilding process. You're still very impatient, and want the healing to progress quickly. Rather than relaxing, and enjoying the vacation from training, you continue to use your injured body and slow down the healing process.

12. Reinjury — After a long treatment period you feel that you can finally resume training, but you've been so starved for exercise, that you start out too soon, and increase the time and intensity of training too quickly. You never reach the point of full recovery, and the injured area becomes inflamed again. You repeat the same cycle.

This injury cycle often becomes an integral part of obligatory exercising. The rigid, fast-paced lifestyle of the compulsive athlete precludes a rapid recovery because they are caught in a closed cycle of behavior patterns. However, even with stressful exercising pattern or injury cycle, regardless of its seriousness, some positive change to improve one's health and coping skills is possible.

BREAKING OUT OF THE INJURY CYCLE

Recovery from the injury cycle involves taking a good look at one's attitudes, behavior, and priorities. There has to be a willingness to confront and if necessary, modify one's own lifestyle and training patterns. When an athlete is stuck in any injury cycle, he almost certainly needs to rethink his priorities in life.

Changes that seem painful or awkward at first, will later be the key to long-term success in athletics, and in many lifetime goals.

I would like to introduce a program that has worked well for a variety of athletes. This system is designed to take any injured athlete and remove him/her from the injury cycle as rapidly and safely as possible. The program applies to athletes at any level, regardless of the type of injury.

The basic assumption of this program is that every injury has both a mental and a physical component. We cannot consider our physical state without also looking at our mental and emotional health. Each part influences the other, and so becoming physically injured is often a reflection of some stress or conflict in other areas of our lives. A physical problem then is a signal that it's time to examine your feelings and thoughts to find the source of tension. You can then bring the mental and physical, social and emotional parts all into balance.

Our bodies carry out an ongoing dialogue with our minds. When the mind is under pressure, the body will send the brain signals of fatigue, pain, sickness, or disease. The body is quite truthful and direct; the key is in teaching the mind to listen. The body indicates exactly what it needs to remain healthy. When you avoid these messages, you shut off the body-mind communication system. You overtrain when you should be resting, and the body ultimately breaks down in order to obtain the rest it needs.

Injury and health are both cyclical processes. Because both cycles are self-perpetuating processes, moving from one to the other becomes very difficult. For example, when you are doing well in a sport, your energy level is always high from the last good workout. You feel powerful, your movements are smooth and precise, your concentration becomes sharper than ever. Your successes seem to continually build upon each other.

The same process works for an injury. Once something goes wrong in your life, your body responds with tension and fatigue. You worry about potential body strain, and your anxiety causes further body tension. For example, if one leg becomes injured, you may attempt to compensate for it by overusing the other. However, this increases the risk of a second injury, which is frequently worse than the first one. The inevitable discouragement and depression from further injury translates into improper sleep and poor eating habits, possibly leading to an illness.

THE RECOVERY PROGRAM

The heart of the recovery program is the idea that athletes are the primary determinant of the course of their health or injury. This does not mean to imply that the individual is the total cause of his/her problems, or that illness is a simple problem to resolve. All areas of life are complex, with a variety of contributing factors. External stress from one's family, job, travel, or nutritional level can exert a combined influence on one's state of health. For example, the mental fatigue from a long car ride may make it hard to become motivated to do a tough workout. Internal stress can come from one's own thoughts, feelings, images, or actions. For instance, if an athlete trains while thinking about how stressful things are at work, they will probably have trouble training with much intensity and concentration.

How the athletes perceive and interact with their environment is also crucial to the recovery program. The athlete can use positive internal energy to regulate the amount of control the external environment has over him/her. Changing one's external environment to better compliment personal needs can be quite useful (e.g., take a long lunch hour in order to allow time for a full warm-up, a quality run, a cool-down, and stretching). Athletes can also modify what they say to themselves, how they feel, and what they do with their personal schedule. The point is that we always have a choice of modifying either our external or internal environment. We may not have total control of all the events in our lives, but we can make a good portion of them work in our favor. With the ideas outlined below, the athlete can become the primary decision maker for the state of his/her injury or health.

Before presenting a program for safely recovering from the injury cycle, there are certain prerequisites that will allow the athlete the best chance of making durable improvements.

1. Be able to take full responsibility for your injury. In order to turn your injury cycle around, and make the lasting changes that will prevent further problems, you must recognize that you have total control over your thoughts, feelings, and actions. Although there are certainly some external circumstances over which you have little influence, the primary responsibility for altering your own environment rests with you. One of the best ways to acquire this ability is to get out of the habit of making excuses when things don't turn out the way you would like. Making excuses diverts the control from you to an external source. If you do poorly in a run, you can always blame your shoes, the weather, the course, or a hundred other factors. The responsible athletes can take even the worse situation, and turn their feelings of frustration into an opportunity for learning. In almost every instance, there is some element that you can control.

2. Be open to learning from past mistakes and discovering personal weaknesses that are blocking your progress. You can't begin to tackle a problem until you can conceptualize it. To expedite the process of self-understanding, you need to have an attitude of humility and openness. Asking questions such as "What am I refusing to look at in myself?" and, "Why am I choosing to injure myself?", may leave you open to some painful answers, but this method will be a source of valuable information to aid you in the healing process. Many times just the act of acknowledging and accepting a problem

may be enough to bring about spontaneous change without any further energy on your part.

3. Expand your idea of what you are willing to change in your lifestyle and habits. As discussed earlier, you cannot separate a physical injury from your mental state of being. If an injury is at all reflective of what is going on in the rest of your life, then changing your attitude, taking up a new interest, and paying more attention to personal relationships, can only improve your physical outlook. Broaden your basis for judging personal achievement. Find avenues to meet your needs other than through exercising.

4. Make a personal contribution toward your recovery. Sports medicine has come a long way toward conquering illness, but the doctor's success is dependent upon the cooperation of the patient. The more personally invested you are in your own recovery, the more likely you will turn your goals into visible results. Athletes can speed their recovery rates by as much as 50 percent if they feel that they are doing something significant toward the healing process.

5. Cultivate a strong desire to recover quickly. Develop an image of yourself in a healing cycle. Suspend judgment for a while, and open yourself to the possibility that you will get well. Declare yourself no longer injured, but in a state of healing. Once you've switched gears mentally, altering your behavior patterns will come much easier.

A PROGRAM DESIGNED FOR SUCCESS

This recovery program will help the athlete and the coach or sports psychologist set up a plan that focuses not only on physical needs, but will deal with the mental, behavioral, and social stresses that may have led to physical strain. The following section outlines a program with specific instruction to the athlete for prevention and treatment of the compulsive injury cycle.

The first concern, as an athlete, is with the healing of your injury, and the maintenance of your fitness level during the recovery period. Once you discern the medical problem and arrive at a treatment plan, you can then begin to map out your total program. Most likely, the treatment will involve a rest period from training, or at least a reduction in workout frequency or intensity. Since exercising fills so many needs and keeps your motivation level high, it's important to keep this system working by substituting another sport into your training regimen. A dependency on one sport can lead to overtraining, but if you have a second sport that you enjoy, you can use it to keep your energy and fitness level high while healing, and resume training at a reasonable level once you've recovered. Ideally, you will want to continue training in the second sport to supplement training in your primary area. This will add interest and variety to your overall program and will be quite helpful in preventing future injuries.

MENTAL TRAINING

Your second concern is in dealing with the mental aspects of injury, and a change in lifestyle. Mental training is a useful tool for healing both your mind and body, because it is aimed at the issues which stand in the way of healthy training: your own mental pictures, thoughts, and self-esteem. If you are willing to evaluate and alter your inner beliefs, you can then get to the problem source, and change your perception of what happened in the past. The key is to develop a more constructive attitude about injury. Instead of regarding a physical problem as an unavoidable stroke of bad luck, consider it a signal for change and an opportunity to learn something about yourself.

You can look at your attitudes and thoughts with greater clarity and intensity through a process known as mental imagery. This is a technique of using your imagination to create a mental picture of what you want in your life. You generate an image of a particular goal, focus on it regularly, and think about it positively until it manifests itself in your life. Imagery is more than just painting pictures or positive thinking. It involves seeing yourself actually doing the things that it takes to meet your goal. While this technique takes only ten to fifteen minutes per day, it can become a powerful catalyst for a comprehensive type of healing.

Here is an exercise that you might try to become familiar with this process. Move into a comfortable position while seated or lying down, and take a few deep breaths. Let your breathing take you into a deep state of relaxation. When you feel very calm and peaceful, let an image come into your mind that concerns your injury. It could be a memory of the moment when injury set in, and you decided it was time to quit training. Or you may imagine the pain of working out on an injured leg. You may hear negative statements that you make to yourself when you are not mentally prepared for a run. Feel free to use any of your five senses, and move toward whatever image is most captivating. Once an image comes to mind, try to focus your total attention on that scene or feeling or object, making it as clear and vivid as possible. At this point, you have two choices: you can either be a passive observer and watch the scene developing as though viewing a film on a TV screen, or you can become a film director, and edit the scene as it progresses. In the first instance, you can gain new insights to your own thoughts and behavior by taking a deeper look at what your body and mind are doing. Your past training errors and life stresses may become clearer and the solutions may become more apparent. You may then want to use the second technique of editing your imagery film. If your image is, for instance, a disappointing memory, you can allow yourself to feel differently now, and respond in ways that you could not respond then.

Since injuries, and all their associated feelings, are often quite complex, you might want to turn your injury episode into something more simple and concrete. In this way, the painful feelings and sensations can be dealt with on a more objective level. For instance, try imagining that the cartilage of your injured knee is a nest of tangled yarn that you slowly unravel in your mind's eye. Turn the throbbing pain of a shin splint into a hot bed of coals that you then cool with a vase of water. You may generate a wide variety of ideas, and you can use them all in mental imagery session. The particular images that you use are not that important. What matters is that you realize your power to create and work with images at any moment you need them, and to translate those images into productive, visible outcomes.

SOCIAL SUPPORT

A third concern that you may have, as an injured athlete, is that of social stress, and social support. An injury is one of the most difficult things an athlete must deal with, and social support may be a tremendous aid for you at this time. Socializing with other athletes may be frustrating during your injury period. Being around training partners tends to continually remind you that you are injured and cannot partake in their activity. You may want to seek out new friendships while training in your alternative sport. If you are new to this particular sport, other athletes can help you get involved.

One last need that you have is for time alone. This is especially important for anyone involved in endurance sports. You need to spend the time alone that training no longer provides in order to relieve stress, and renew your energy level. You can do this by going for walks, reading, doing relaxation and mental imagery exercises, going on vacations, or doing anything you enjoy that changes the pace of your everyday life. Spending time with yourself can bring new sources of personal reward and stimulation.

SELF-MONITORING

Evaluation and Log Book

After you have begun to integrate these techniques into your life, you will want to develop a close and lasting relationship with your log book. This can become your record keeping system not only for physical workouts, but for mental training as well. You might need to develop a new type of log book specifically for your injury period. Write down everything you are doing in your recovery program, including physical therapy, mental imagery, and building a social support network. You may also want to begin a journal of your thoughts and images, so that you can take note of small progressive changes in many areas of your life.

Once you begin opening up communication lines between your body and mind, and you realize that injury involves a rethinking of your entire lifestyle, then you are well on your way to a lasting recovery.

CHAPTER 10

The Use of Imagery in the Rehabilitation of Injured Athletes

LANCE B. GREEN

"The mind's direction is more important than its progress."
—Laurence B. Green, 1985

A recent study conducted by Wiese, Weiss, and Yukelson reported that athletic trainers support the use of psychological strategies when dealing with injury rehabilitation of athletes [1]. Listening to coaches and trainers, intrinsic motivation on the part of the athlete, and social support were identified as key strategies and skills in the recovery process. The use of imagery was not perceived as important relative to the other techniques.

Wiese et al. indicated that the trainers' reluctance to advocate use of imagery may have resulted from their not feeling qualified to use imagery techniques and/or not believing in the techniques' efficacy [1]. It may be important to educate health professionals involved with the rehabilitation of injured athletes about the "why and how to" of imagery techniques.

PERSPECTIVES ON MIND-BODY INTEGRATION

In most cases, athletes are left with a rehabilitation program housed in the traditional confines of a medical model that does not include a mind-body orientation. That the athlete may have the capacity to expedite his or her own recovery by using cognitive strategies such as imagery, does not seem to be recognized to the degree that it should. The purpose of the treatise is to provide an educational text that 1) cites existing literature supporting a mind-body paradigm for rehabilitation from philosophical, historical, psychophysiological, and psychomotor perspectives, 2) demonstrates the application of imagery techniques within the chronology of an athletic injury, and 3) describes the performance-related criteria to which an athlete can compare his or her progress during rehabilitation.

Philosophical Perspectives

In paraphrasing the works of Watts [2] and McCluggage [3], a philosophical perspective concerning human existence, functioning, and rehabilitation is offered that attempts to blend the thinking of Western and Eastern cultures. Watts admonishes the typically Western approach of scientists to use biology and physiology to measure and classify the world according to their own particular uses, as opposed to the way it exists in its totality. Likewise, those who would use an exclusively psychological approach would be considered equally as deficient in their assessment of the components of human existence and healing. Not coincidentally, Watts offers the analogy of sight as a means of explaining the type of thinking needed to assess human existence. He establishes the difference between central and peripheral vision.

> Central vision is used for accurate work like reading; it is like the light cast by a spotlight; it represents linear thinking or conscious, one-at-a-time thinking. The complexity in understanding our bodies is not so much in our bodies as in the task of trying to understand them by using this type of thinking. It is like trying to make out the features of a large room with no other light than a single bright ray. Peripheral vision can take in very many things at a time; this process enables us to regulate the complexity of our bodies without thinking at all; it is like the light cast by a floodlight [2, pp. 8-12].

McCluggage recognizes that many think in terms that draw a separation between mind and body, as if they were opposites to be dealt with exclusive of one another. However, she offers that these two entities are "interdependent of one another and that they exist together synergistically" [3, p. 26]. She maintains that the interplay between mind and body is not only constant, but constantly changing. At one point in time, there may be an imbalance toward the intellectual. At another time, the imbalance may indicate a need for less intellectuality and more physicality. Underlying both premises offered by Watts and McCluggage is a need to understand and treat human existence in a holistic manner that utilizes linear thinking but does not rely on it.

Historical Perspectives

McMahon and Sheikh have described the historical place and subsequent demise of imagination in the realm of medicine and philosophic interpretation of human existence [4]. They note that during premodern times and the late European Renaissance, imagination and its impact on psychosomatic consequences was viewed within a holistic framework and was the dominant force in interpreting human behavior.

Shamanic healing procedures dating back to the primitive societies of the Polynesian Kahunas included a process of four steps: 1) awareness of thoughts, 2) establishing goals, 3) changing, and 4) directing energy [5]. Their use of "deliberate imagination" is pervasive throughout the healing process [6, p. 474].

Religions such as Judaism, Christianity, and Islam have historical references to visualization and have relied on imagery to assist partisans in achieving spiritual goals, e.g., the Jewish Kabbalistic mystics [7], Christian communion services described in I Corinthians 11:23-25, and Sufi meditative techniques [8]. In addition, Indian yogis have utilized visualization for centuries within their practices of trantic medicine [9], mandalas [10], and mantras [6].

In Western medicine during the Grecian era, imagery was used to diagnose and treat disease [11]. Imagination was also used within the Renaissance period as physicians viewed health as a holistic function of spiritual, physical, and mental balance [12].

However, in the late seventeenth century, this gave way to the Cartesian notion of dualism that used a reductionist perspective in depicting the exclusivity of the mind in explaining existence (a notion that met with considerable opposition from his contemporaries!). "By the middle of the eighteenth century, mechanism was instated where holism formerly had held sway. All bodily functions were accounted for by mechanical principles" [4, p. 11].

While scholars of the eighteenth century did their best to reinstate a holistic perspective, their attempts failed, and dualism assumed its position of authority. Not until the 1870's did imagery reappear as a viable component in the theoretical chain between psychology and physiology [13]. This subsequently led to the classic work of Jacobsen who, in the 1930's, reinvented the wheel when he established a connection between the neuromuscular system and mental imagery [14].

Psychophysiological Perspectives

Substantial evidence exists concerning the credibility of using a mind-body approach in explaining human existence and the intricacies of the healing process. "The results of controlled research corroborate the clinical evidence that imagery has a curative effect and refute the misguided 'scientific' assumption that *mental* imagery cannot have any effect on the physical body" [6, p. 493]. By viewing the human being as a package that contains a constant interchange between mental and physiological functions, one recognizes the interdependence of one's actions. Historically, patients' beliefs about the efficacy of the treatment they received and their own input into the process have been at the forefront of Chinese and Navajo practices [15-16].

Indeed, Gardner spoke of the multiple intelligences each individual possesses to varying degrees [17]. One of these is the "body-kinesthetic intelligence . . . the ability to use one's body in highly differentiated and skilled ways," including "being trained to respond to the expressive powers of the mind" [17, p. 206]. At the cornerstone of this position, however, lies the principle of homeostasis advanced by Cannon that establishes the interaction between one's brain and body in an effort to maintain internal stability [18]. Green, Green, and Walters adhered to what they called the psychophysiological principle, that suggests that for every physiological change that occurs in the body, there is an appropriate change in the mental-emotional state [19]. They also suggested that the converse of this phenomenon is equally true. Others have established that imagery triggers similar neurophysiological functions, as does actual experience [20-22].

Surgent suggested that a mind-body connection facilitates the healing process. He indicated that:

> Your immune system doesn't work alone . . . your mind also has a voice in what goes on. There is a communication network between your brain and your immune system, like telephone lines between a general and his field commanders. . . . Feelings, attitudes, and beliefs are organized in your brain and communicated to your immune system by chemical messengers. These can have an effect on the healing process which can be either positive or negative [23, pp. 4-5].

This claim has been substantiated through findings reported by Hall, who revealed an increased immune response when he tested the effects of hypnosis and imagery on lymphocyte function [24]. The most recent support for the interplay between the use of imagery and immune-system responses has been reported by Achterberg [25], AuBuchon [26], and Post-White [27]. They have provided evidence describing the positive effects the immune system experiences when triggered by imagery. In addition, specific health-related processes have been shown to be influenced by an individual's capacity for imaging, e.g., vaso-constriction and vasodilation [28-31], heart rate deceleration and acceleration [32-38], suppressed and enhanced immunoreaction [39-40].

Literature pertaining to psychoneuroimmunology has further established the plausibility of the mind-body paradigm during rehabilitation. Achterberg, Matthews-Simonton, and Simonton [41], as well as Fiore [24], have reported that certain psychological characteristics of patients influenced recovery from cancer. Simonton, Matthews-Simonton, and Creighton [43] provided evidence supporting the use of imagery in cancer treatment. Others have reported positive effects of the use of imagery during rehabilitation from various illnesses and injuries: psoriasis [44]; stress management [45]; ulcers, paraplegia, fractures, hip disarticulations, and intra-abdominal lesions [46].

In addition, numerous studies have indicated that the use of imagery produces physiological responses such as salivation [47], increase in pupillary size [48], increased heart rate [49], changes in electromyograms [50], increases in blood-glucose, inhibition of gastrointestinal activity, and changes in skin temperature [51]. Taken to its logical end, then, when one takes physiological measurements, one is in fact taking corresponding psychological indicators simultaneously. The results reported may depend entirely on what category of measurement is being taken and the perspective from which the investigator originates (e.g., psychology, physiology, psychophysiology).

The specialization in professional orientation prevalent in today's scientific community may be merely part of the lasting ripple effect created by Cartesian's medical model and may do nothing but perpetuate an all-too-narrow perspective from which to draw conclusions concerning the human condition. The thoughts of Diderot, from the middle nineteenth century, may be applicable today. He spoke of scholars' intentions at that time to reinstate holism as an appropriate perspective for medicine so that it "may be advanced to the point of where it was two thousand years ago" [4, p. 12].

Psychomotor Perspectives

From a sport psychology perspective, there is at the very least a logical leap from the relationship between imagery and sport performance to the impact of imagery on the healing process of injuries. That the use of mental rehearsal facilitates the execution of certain motor skills under certain conditions is well documented (for reviews, see Corbin [52]; Feltz and Landers [53]).

In addition, Hecker and Kaczor have summarized existing theoretical models that have been advanced to explain the processes involved with mental imagery and its influence on athletic performance (e.g., motor skill development) [54]. These include 1) the symbolic learning theory, which posits that symbolic rehearsal advances the development of skills requiring cognitive processes [55]; 2) the psychoneuromuscular theory associated with Jacobsen's [14] work, which identified muscular innervations during imagery similar to those occurring during actual performance; 3) the attention-arousal set, which integrates cognitive and physiological aspects of rehearsal in order to distinguish between relevant and irrelevant cues [53, 56]; and 4) Lang's bioinformational theory, in which imagery processes the stimulus characteristics of an imagined scenario and the physiological/behavioral responses that accompany them [57]; and, 5) the mind-brain identity theory originally advanced by Feigl [58] that includes a self-regulatory hypothesis proposing that the imaged innervation of brain structures with voluntary qualities serve innately with perceptually induced innervations to regulate autonomic responses [59].

Other models, such as Greene's [60] multilevel hierarchical control of motor programs and Pribram's [61] two-process model of imagery, have been applied to the development of motor programs and further describe the interdependence of mind and body. Greene maintained that a motor movement is the result of a mind-body system composed of many levels. The higher levels initiate a "ballpark" motor response to environmental input, that is then refined by lower levels of neuromuscular processing. The end result is the appropriate motor movement that meets the requirements of the task.

Pribram's two-process model of imagery includes neuropsychological processes identified as the TOTE and TOTEM systems [61]. The TOTE system refers to the exchange of feedback and feedforward mechanisms between the environment and the organism in order to produce movement. The TOTEM system is an application of these processes in that images conduct TOTE operations on each other but exclusively within the mental environment.

It seems viable to suggest, therefore, that the same models used to explain psychophysiological and psychomotor processes used in athletic performance can be applied when describing the place of imagery in the rehabilitation associated with the healing of athletic injuries (e.g., the reestablishing of fine and gross motor movements, the reestablishing of psychoneurological pathways). However, as Hecker and Kaczor have indicated, when each of these theories is taken alone, it proves to be inadequate in explaining the complex, mind-body process of imagery [54]. Therefore, a more encompassing approach must be advanced, such as the systems theory suggested by Schwartz [62].

Schwartz maintained that systems theory "has the potential to provide a meta-theoretical framework for integrating the biological, physiological, and social consequences of imagery on health and illness" [62, p. 35]. In describing the synthesis attained by implementing systems theory, he elaborated on the meta-principles of systems theory:

> A system is an entity (a whole) which is composed of a set of parts (which are subsystems). These parts interact. Out of the parts interaction emerge unique properties that characterize the new entity or system as a whole. These emergent properties represent more than the simple, independent sum of the properties of the parts studied in isolation. It is hypothesized that the emergent properties appear only when the parts are allowed to interact [62, p. 39].

Thus, independent theories that appear to be in competition can be integrated into a comprehensive perspective that is both logical and substantiated by scientific evidence. This may provide the necessary body of knowledge through which the education of health professionals (i.e., athletic trainers) may be enhanced. The use of psychophysiological techniques such as imagery may increase once the educational barriers are weakened. Hopefully, this will lead to the use of psychological techniques that go beyond the traditional skills of communication and motivation.

What follows is an example of how the mind-body perspective might be applied in the development of a rehabilitation program for injured athletes. It is offered with the understanding that it is not all-encompassing. However, it should provide a starting point from which sport medicine teams can develop programs of rehabilitation from a mind-body perspective.

THE CHRONOLOGY OF AN INJURY

The following is a chronology of athletic injuries adapted from Nideffer's scheme [63]. Although his scheme included factors related to the onset of the injury and to the athlete's coping and recovery, this chronology addresses three periods of time associated with injuries: preinjury, attention to the athlete immediately following injury, and the rehabilitation program leading to the athlete's recovery and reintegration into the competitive situation. Each will be described with the intended purpose of demonstrating the application of imagery techniques within the context of an integrated mind-body approach to rehabilitation.

Preinjury

Any athlete is subject to periods in his or her life when injury is more likely to occur. In keeping with Selye's classic work in the area of stress, these periods are characterized by stressors that cause distress, rather than eustress (an exhilarating and positive force) or stress (that energy necessary for daily existence and the body's search for homeostasis) [64]. These periods of distress may be categorized as either *general life* or *athletic* stressors.

General life stressors may include the transition to college life for first-year students, the homesickness experienced by athletes of all levels, or the feelings of sorrow and anguish that accompany the death of someone close. Athletic stressors might include trouble with a coach, teammate, or fans; loss of playing status; or the athletic event itself [65-68]. The resultant injury may be a function of the fatigue associated with dealing with these situations or of the divisive effect they have on the athlete's concentration [66]. Inasmuch as an athlete may experience these or other circumstances that have an adverse effect on his or her normal life pattern, injury is often the result.

As a form of preventive medicine to lessen the impact of stressors and, thus, reduce the potential for injury, imagery techniques that enhance relaxation and perspective on specific situations of stress may be developed and implemented throughout the season as circumstances mandate. An imagery technique used for relaxation, centering, and self-control is entitled "My Favorite Place." For example, imagine yourself in the place you most like to go when you want to be alone, comfortable, and secure. As you enter this place, find a place to sit. Once seated, continue to breathe in a controlled fashion. Now look in front of you . . . identify a specific object . . . look at it very closely . . . what does it look like? How big or small is it? What color is it? What is its texture? How far away from you is it? . . . Now turn your head to the left . . . identify a specific object . . . look at it very closely . . . what does it look like? How big or small is it? . . . What color is it? What is its texture? . . . Rough? Smooth? . . . How far away from you is it? . . . Now, in your mind's eye, without turning around, identify an object behind you. You know this place so well, there is no need to turn around. What does this object look like? How big or small is it? What color is it? What is its texture? Rough? Smooth? How far away from you is it? . . . Continue to breathe comfortably. Listen to the sound of your inhale . . . the pause before your exhale . . . Listen to the sound of your exhale . . . and the pause before your next breath. . . . Now look to your right . . . identify a specific object . . . look at it very closely . . . what does it look like? How big or small is it? What color is it? What is its texture? . . . How far away from you is it? . . . continue to breathe comfortably . . . now get a sense of being in the center of your objects . . . get a feel of how far away each is from you . . . tune in to the feelings of being in control . . . centered . . . secure . . . comfortable . . . when you are ready, count your breaths from one to ten . . . then backward toward one . . . when you are ready, open your eyes.

An imagery experiential can also be developed that places the athlete's immediate needs within a long-term context that enhances perspective and produces a relaxed state of mind. For example, an athlete may have an immediate need to cope with stress related to homesickness. Imagery could be implemented by introducing a relaxed state, possibly with some form of Jacobsen's progressive relaxation [14]. This may be followed by guided imagery to help the athlete gain perspective on the situation. This has also been described by Samuels and Samuels as developing the ability "to see . . . to look at an object from different mental points of view, as well as from different vantage points" [69, p. 115].

For example, imagine yourself as a first-year student entering college. As soon as the Thanksgiving break arrives, you can't wait to get on the first plane home. Same for the December/January break. Same for the summer break. . . . Now you are a sophomore. When Thanksgiving comes, you definitely want to go home, but you'll miss some of your college friends. Same for the December/January break. Same for the summer break. . . Now, you're a junior. You've established your "place" on campus. You have developed close relationships with male and female friends. As Thanksgiving break approaches, you weigh the pros and cons of going home against staying on campus. You decide to go home as usual. The same thoughts happen, but not as strongly, when December rolls around. But with summer, you make plans to travel with your friends and tell your parents you'll see them when you finish your trip. . . . Now you're a senior. Your apartment or room seems more like home to you than your parents' home. Because Thanksgiving and the December break are family occasions, your parents want you home more than you want to go. But, still, you go. Then it's summertime and your parents are calling you to come home, instead of you calling them. What does it feel like to be self-reliant, self-sufficient?

Attention Immediately Subsequent to Injury

Once the injury occurs, standard first-aid procedures should be followed so that further complications are not created unnecessarily. Someone associated with the program (e.g., trainer, coach, sport psychologist, parent) should accompany the athlete to the physician, and the athlete should be given at least "the illusion of hope" at the outset [63].

Once the athlete has seen a physician, information concerning the injury should be discussed by the attending medical personnel, the athlete, the team trainer/physician, and the coach. This should include specifics about the anatomy and physiology of the injured area. By using anatomical models and photographs, the abstraction of the injury is translated into more tangible and recognizable terms. The injury might be explained in lay terms that facilitate an image—for example, "the rubber bands (ligaments) need to grow back onto the bone." This knowledge is critical in that it can be applied to the rehabilitative imagery employed later on [23].

Rehabilitation of the Injury

The structure of the rehabilitation program (an instant preplay of the program) should be discussed by all parties directly involved as the sports medicine team (e.g., trainers, coaches, athletes). This may include the expected time frame associated with recovery, as well as the general parameters of the physical and mental program to be used during rehabilitation. The expectations of the individuals involved—appointments with trainers, coaches, and sport psychologists; attendance at practice and games; and the criteria to be used to determine when the athlete is ready to return to practice and competition—should also be identified. *Who* will make the final decision (e.g., the athlete, the coach, the physician) as to the athlete's readiness may also be discussed as part of the criteria [70].

Of considerable importance are the factors relating to the athlete's adherence to the rehabilitation. These should be identified and discussed with the athlete. Successful rehabilitation is characterized by specific adherence behaviors. Wiese et al. have identified the following: willingness to listen to the trainer, maintaining a positive attitude, and intrinsic motivation [1]. Characteristics described by Duda, Smart, and Tappe include the athlete's belief in the efficacy of the treatment, the presence of a social support system, and the athlete's orientation toward task-related goals in his or her sport [71]. Imagery experientials in which the athlete envisions the overt behaviors associated with these factors may become an integral part of daily treatments in the training room.

An example of such an application of imagery may be created by adapting the work of Lazarus, who has developed procedures that depict an individual taking psychological risks [72]. Once the behaviors associated with carrying out specific instructions from the trainer, personifying a positive attitude, demonstrating intrinsic motivation, and task-related goal setting are imagined, the athlete is encouraged to go out and perform them.

Finally, Lynch [67] and Rotella and Heyman [68] applied Kübler-Ross's [73] work concerning the emotional recovery from a loved one's death to the athletic setting and the recovering athlete. They suggested that athletes may experience similar patterns of emotional reaction during their rehabilitation. This might include denial, anger, bargaining, depression, and acceptance. Were an athlete given insight into the process of recovery through imagery depicting each stage, he or she may be able to facilitate the transition from one stage to the next.

For example, an experiential entitled "Time Projection or Time Tripping" [72, pp. 131-137] may facilitate the development of an athlete's awareness of potential emotional reactions throughout rehabilitation. By projecting himself or herself back and forward in time and by describing the emotions associated with different stages of rehabilitation from these retrospective and futuristic perspectives, the athlete is encouraged to recognize various stages of recovery. For example, the athlete may recognize that he or she may become depressed during the rehabilitation but may also recognize that depression may be part of the process eventually leading to recovery.

In summary, the following four examples have been described to demonstrate how imagery might be applied to the first two phases of the chronology of an injury: for the preinjury phase—relaxation and perspective imagery as preventative medicine; for the time immediately following injury—an instant preplay of the rehabilitation program, attitude and belief imagery, and imagery depicting emotional stages of transition during recovery.

THE MIND-BODY REHABILITATION PROCESS

The rehabilitation program for an athlete should be devised by a sports medicine team composed of the attending physician, athlete, trainers, coach, and sport psychologist. The program should reflect a mind-body approach to the process of recovery [74-75]. It should address the appropriate mind-set for the recovering athlete as well as the physical dimensions of rehabilitation.

Creating the Mind-Set for Recovery

A character named Socrates from Dan Millman's book *The Way of the Peaceful Warrior* describes the part the mind plays in creating one's way of being [76]. He suggest that

> 'Mind' is one of those slippery terms like 'love.' The proper definition depends on your state of consciousness. We refer to the brain's abstract processes as 'the intellect' . . . The brain and the mind are not the same. The brain is real; the mind isn't. The brain can be a tool. It can recall phone numbers, solve math puzzles, or create poetry. In this way, it works for the rest of the body, like a tractor. But when you can't stop thinking of that math problem or phone number, or when troubling thoughts and memories arise without your intent, it's not your brain working, but your mind wandering. Then the mind controls you; then the tractor has run wild [76, p. 62].

In essence, an athlete in rehabilitation must accomplish the same task of getting rid of a mind full of negative and counterproductive wanderings. Only then might the brain be able to do its work. These counterproductive wanderings may include certain fears associated with being injured: fear of reinjury, fear of the pain associated with the original injury and/or the pain experienced during rehabilitation, fear of not returning to previous levels of ability, fear of the loss of status.

Ievleva and Orlick reported that recovery time for injured athletes was faster for those who did not engage in injury-replay imagery [77]. Thus, athletes must use their intellect to guide the neuropsychological processes of the brain in such a manner as to facilitate recovery.

Developing Possible Selves

Upon injury, athletes are faced with what Cantor and Kihlstrom referred to as a life task [78]. They are immediately confronted with a problem that must be resolved before normal existence can continue. Injured athletes must make a conscious effort to redirect their attention from playing the game to playing a new game called rehab. They must adopt a mind-set that focuses all of their energies toward recovery. The immediate life task, then, becomes one of rehabilitation. This new game requires a conscious shift of attention and has as its ultimate goal their return to competition.

In addressing the goal setting associated with the rehabilitation process, sport psychologists might consider applying the theoretical framework of Markus and Ruvolo [79]. This framework depicts the development of "possible selves" and addresses the potential for "personalized representations of goals" [79, p. 211]. Markus and Ruvolo discussed goal setting in terms of "constructing a possible self in which one is different from the now self and in which one realizes the goals" [79, p. 211]. Thus, a progression of possible selves assists in developing the working self-concept [80-81].

What is critical is the athlete's ability to formulate and maintain the possible selves that lead toward the desired goal. They must be able to repress possible selves that are inconsistent with the task of recovery (e.g., possible selves depicting injury-replay or negative attitudes). The desired possible selves might depict the athletes as having a positive outlook, using descriptive self-talk, or setting performance-related goals. As several authors have suggested, the athletes should engage in affirmation imagery that portrays them fulfilling short-term goals [77, 82]. To the extent that they are able to accomplish these tasks, their behavior will be "focused, energized, and organized by this possible self" [79, p. 214].

For example, imagery scenarios could be patterned after Maxwell Maltz's work concerning the self-image. Ishii described provocative experientials that focus on developing positive, assertive, and successful self-images as well as attitudes pertaining to happiness and a willpower [83]. One experiential places the client in an empty theater. The client is asked to imagine a movie unfolding in which he or she handles a problem successfully. Another technique requires the client to visualize an uneraseable chalkboard that he or she lists past successes.

The task of the sport psychologist, then, becomes the creation of a series of "programmed visualizations" [69, p. 229] that reflect the rehabilitative tasks and outcomes established by the sports medicine team. That possible selves may depict performance goals as well as outcome goals presents the sport psychologist with the task of identifying specific scenarios depicting each. In fact, Bandura maintained that performance and outcome selves should be separated [84, 85].

Korn agreed that there should be a progression from product to process goals [46]. That is, as an initial step, athletes should imagine themselves as completely recovered and able to do all the things they were capable of doing prior to the injury. Once they have become reasonably proficient at this form of product-oriented image, they may progress to more specific, process-oriented images. These process-oriented possible selves should reflect instrumental selves. That is, they should represent a sequence of possible selves that depicts the athlete in the process of performing specific motor skills, each leading to a self that is one step closer to total recovery. In essence, the instrumental possible selves are intended to result in a summation effect, that finally matches or surpasses the initial product-oriented image.

For example, a female basketball player undergoing rehabilitation for a knee injury used the following series of possible selves over nine months of rehabilitation:

- Possible Self 1 — "Knee at 90 degrees" and "I want to be a success story." For example: getting out of bed and out of the hospital, establishing image of desired outcome.
- Possible Self 2 — "Strut your stuff." For example: getting off crutches, watching other people walk, establishing own gait.
- Possible Self 3 — "Hurt to get better." For example: progression of physical therapy including weight training, electric stimulation, stationary bike, stair master.
- Possible Self 4 — "Spring forward." For example: running at 75 percent, jumping exercises, increasing work load.
- Possible Self 5 — "Let's play." For example: pick-up games.
- Possible Self 6 — "Dribble, drive, and dive!" For example: playing with no fear of failure.
- Possible Self 7 — "No brace." For example: the final stage due to school policy of mandatory use of brace following such an injury.

Other Uses of Imagery

The processes of guided and nondirected imagery in the form of relaxation techniques, motor skill rehearsals, and rehabilitative experientials can be utilized by the athlete [23]. Rehabilitative imagery has been shown to have significant effects on recovery time [77]. As described earlier during the chronology of an injury, information gathered from the physician concerning the anatomy and physiology of the injury facilitates the use of rehabilitative imagery. Day has developed an educational discourse on the immune system that uses cartoon imagery and immune cell caricatures to explain the function of each cell involved in the rehabilitation process [86]. Korn described a technique of rehabilitation imagery that consists of:

> envisioning the wounds as filling from the inside out rather than just being covered over at the surface. The filling material was cement and the repair process was analogous to the method of repair of a hole in a concrete walkway [46, p. 28].

In addition, similar techniques have been developed by the author in conjunction with athletes that utilize images associated with Disney characters and video games such as "Tetris."

Specific mind-sets that might be addressed through the use of imagery may include the following: maintaining a positive outlook, stress control, the use of positive and descriptive self-talk, sustaining belief in the rehabilitation process. Performance-related imagery may take the form of mental rehearsal while attending practices and competitions in that the athletes imagine themselves playing. In addition, imagery has been shown to be effective in coping with pain [43, 46, 69, 87, 88].

Rotella and Heyman have recommended the use of videotapes of past performances [68]. This technique may serve to reinforce the symbolic learning and psychoneuromuscular processes. Imagery may also be used to facilitate closure of the rehabilitation process once the athlete has returned to competition.

Physical Rehabilitation

The use of targeted performance criteria facilitates the athlete's return to preinjury performance levels on specific tasks associated with his or her sport. These criteria may also serve as the impetus for creating specific instrumental and performance-related possible selves. The groundwork for this, however, must be laid at the onset of training prior to the season and, most certainly, prior to injury.

As the season progresses, baseline data should be gathered on specific tasks associated with the athlete's training (e.g., maximum weight, sets, and repetitions for weightlifting routines; range of motion measurements for flexibility; physiologic parameters such as heart rate, time of recovery, and max VO2 for endurance; recorded times on specific distances for speed). These data provide the target criteria to which an athlete can compare his or her progress during rehabilitation.

In addition, a functional progression of specific sport skills that represent "being back" to the athlete should be identified. For example, baseball pitchers who have been out with elbow injuries may wish to use a particular pitch (e.g., breaking off a hard slider) to gauge effectiveness upon return. Tennis players may engage in the side shuffle used on the baseline as an indicator that they have recovered from the pain associated with shin splints.

These tasks, in addition to other methods of progressive-resistance exercises and cross-training, form the foundation for physical rehabilitation with tangible indicators of recovery. Of course, these are undertaken in proper sequence relative to the initial training-room duties prescribed by the physician and trainer (e.g., whirlpool, electrical stimulation, ice therapy).

SUMMARY

Wiese et al. have reported that many athletic trainers agree with the need for further education in the area of psychology and, in particular, for methods that can be applied in the athletic setting [1]. The purpose of this treatise has been to provide an educational text that 1) supports a mind-body paradigm for rehabilitation, 2) demonstrates the application of imagery within the chronology of an injury, and 3) describes performance-related criteria used in physical rehabilitation. The chronology includes that period of time preceding the injury, the attention given to the athlete immediately following the injury, and the subsequent rehabilitation program leading to the athlete's return to practice and competition. It has been suggested that imagery may be applied during the preinjury stage as a tool for preventive maintenance. During the actual rehabilitation program, the purpose of imagery is 1) to facilitate the healing process, 2) to promote the development of a positive and relaxed outlook toward recovery, 3) to create the mind-set required for optimum performance, and 4) to bring closure to the injury experience.

REFERENCES

1. D. M. Wiese, M. R. Weiss, and D. P. Yukelson, Sport Psychology in the Training Room: A Survey of Athletic Trainers, *The Sport Psychologist, 5,* pp. 15-24, 1991.
2. A. W. Watts, *The Way of Zen,* Vintage Books, New York, pp. 8-12, 1957.
3. D. McCluggage, *The Centered Skier,* Warner Books, New York, p. 26, 1977.
4. C. E. McMahon and A. Sheikh, Imagination in Disease and Healing Processes: A Historical Perspective, in *Anthology of Imagery Techniques,* A. A Sheikh (ed.), American Imagery Institute, Milwaukee, Wisconsin, pp. 1-36, 1986.
5. D. L. King, Imagery Theory of Conditioning, in *Imagery: Current Theory, Research, and Application,* A. A. Sheikh (ed.), Wiley, New York, pp. 156-186, 1983.
6. A. A. Sheikh, R. G. Kunzendorf, and K. S. Sheikh, Healing Images: From Ancient Wisdom to Modern Science, in *Eastern and Western Approaches to Healing: Ancient Wisdom and Modern Knowledge,* A. A. Sheikh and K. S. Sheikh (eds.), Wiley, New York, pp. 470-515, 1989.
7. G. Scholem, *Jewish Mysticism,* Schoken, New York, 1961.
8. H. Corbin, *Creative Imagination in the Sufism of Ibn 'Arabi,* R. Manheim (trans.), Routledge & Kegan Paul, London, 1970.
9. T. Clifford, *Tibetan Buddhist Medicine and Psychiatry,* Samuel Weiser, New York, 1984.
10. A. Moorkerjee, *Tantra Art,* Ravi Kumar, Paris, 1971.
11. J. Achterberg, *Imagery in Healing,* Shambhala, Boston, 1985.
12. F. Hartman, *Paracelsus: Life and Prophecies,* Rudolf Steiner, Blauvelt, New York, 1973.
13. A. Bain, *The Senses and the Intellect,* D. Appleton & Co., New York, 1872.
14. E. Jacobsen, *Progressive Relaxation,* University of Chicago Press, Chicago, 1938.

15. M. Porkert, Chinese Medicine: A Tradition of Healing Science, in *Ways of Health: Holistic Approaches to Ancient and Contemporary Medicine,* D. S. Sobel (ed.), Harcourt, Brace, & Jovanovich, New York, pp. 117-146, 1979.
16. D. F. Sandner, *Navaho Symbols of Healing,* Harcourt, Brace, & Jovanovich, New York, 1979.
17. H. Gardner, *Frames of Mind: The Theory of Multiple Intelligences,* Basic Books, New York, 1985.
18. W. B. Cannon, *The Wisdom of the Body,* Norton, New York, 1932.
19. E. E. Green, A. M. Green, and E. D. Walters, Biofeedback for Mind/Body Self-regulation: Healing and Creativity, in *Mind/Body Integration: Essential Readings in Biofeedback,* E. Peper, S. Ancoli, and M. Quinn (eds.), Plenum Press, New York, 1979.
20. C. Leuba, Images as Conditioned Sensation, *Journal of Experimental Psychology, 26,* pp. 345-351, 1940.
21. C. W. Perky, An Experimental Study of Imagination, *American Journal of Psychology, 21,* pp. 422-452, 1910.
22. A. Richardson, *Mental Imagery,* Routledge & Kegan Paul, London, 1969.
23. F. S. Surgent, Using Your Mind to Beat Injuries, *Running & FitNews, 9:1,* pp. 4-5, January 1991.
24. H. R. Hall, Hypnosis and the Immune System: A Review with Implications for Cancer and the Psychology of Healing, *American Journal of Clinical Hypnosis, 25:3,* pp. 92-103, 1983.
25. J. Achterberg, *Enhancing the Immune Function Through Imagery,* paper presented to the Fourth World Conference on Imagery, Minneapolis, Minnesota, May 1991.
26. B. AuBuchon, *The Effects of Positive Mental Imagery on Hope, Coping, Anxiety, Dyspnea, and Pulmonary Function in Persons with Chronic Obstructive Pulmonary Disease: Tests of a Nursing Intervention and a Theoretical Model,* paper presented to the Fourth World Conference on Imagery, Minneapolis, Minnesota, May 1991.
27. J. Post-White, *The Effects of Mental Imagery on Emotions, Immune Function and Cancer Outcome,* paper presented to the Fourth World Conference on Imagery, Minneapolis, Minnesota, May 1991.
28. M. Dugan and C. Sheridan, Effects of Instructed Imagery on Temperature of Hands, *Perceptual and Motor Skills, 42,* p. 14, 1976.
29. R. G. Kunzendorf, Individual Differences in Imagery and Autonomic Control, *Journal of Mental Imagery, 5,* pp. 47-60, 1981.
30. R. G. Kunzendorf, Centrifugal Effects of Eidetic Imaging on Flash Electroretinograms and Autonomic Responses, *Journal of Mental Imagery, 8,* pp. 67-76, 1984.
31. Y. Ohkuma, Effects of Evoking Imagery on the Control of Peripheral Skin Temperature, *Japanese Journal of Psychology, 54,* pp. 88-94, 1985.
32. J. M. Arabian, Imagery and Pavlovian Heart Rate Decelerative Conditioning, *Psychophysiology, 19,* pp. 286-293, 1982.
32. J. M. Arabian and J. J. Furedy, Individual Differences in Imagery Ability and Pavlovian Heart Rate Decelerative Conditioning, *Psychophysiology, 20,* pp. 325-331, 1983.
34. G. E. Jones and H. J. Johnson, Physiological Responding During Self-Generated Imagery of Contextually Complete Stimuli, *Psychophysiology, 15,* pp. 439-446, 1978.
35. G. E. Jones and H. J. Johnson, Heart Rate and Somatic Concomitants of Mental Imagery, *Psychophysiology, 17,* pp. 339-347, 1980.
36. T. R. McCanne and R. S. Iennarella, Cognitive and Somatic Events Associated with Discriminative Changes in Heart Rate, *Psychophysiology, 17,* pp. 18-28, 1980.
37. R. J. Roberts and T. C. Weerts, Cardiovascular Responding During Anger and Fear Imagery, *Psychological Reports, 50,* pp. 219-230, 1982.

38. J. D. Shea, Effects of Absorption and Instructions on Heart Rate Control, *Journal of Mental Imagery, 9,* pp. 87-100, 1985.
39. M. S. Rider, J. W. Floyd, and J. Kirkpatrick, The Effect of Music, Imagery, and Relaxation on Adrenal Corticosteroids and the Reentrainment of Circadian Rhythms, *Journal of Music Therapy, 22,* pp. 46-58, 1985.
40. J. Schneider, C. W. Smith, C. Minning, S. Whitcher, and J. Hermanson, *Psychological Factors Influencing Immune System Function in Normal Subjects: A Summary of Research Findings and Implications for the Use of Guided Imagery,* paper presented to the Tenth Annual Conference of the American Association for the Study of Mental Imagery, New Haven, Connecticut, June 1988.
41. J. Achterberg, S. Matthews-Simonton, and O. C. Simonton, Psychology of the Exceptional Cancer Patient: A Description of Patients Who Outlive Predicted Life Expectancies, *Psychotherapy: Theory, Research, and Practice, 14,* pp. 416-422, 1977.
42. N. A. Fiore, The Inner Healer: Imagery for Coping with Cancer and Its Therapy, *Journal of Mental Imagery, 12*:2, pp. 79-82, 1988.
43. O. C. Simonton, S. Matthews-Simonton, and J. Creighton, *Getting Well Again,* St. Martin's Press, New York, 1978.
44. L. Gaston, J. Crombez, and G. Dupuis, An Imagery and Meditation Technique in the Treatment of Psoriasis: A Case Study Using an A-B-A Design, *Journal of Mental Imagery, 13*:1, pp. 31-38, 1989.
45. G. L. Hanley and D. Chinn, Stress Management: An Integration of Multidimensional Arousal and Imagery Theories with Case Study, *Journal of Mental Imagery, 13*:2, pp. 107-118, 1989.
46. E. R. Korn, The Use of Altered States of Consciousness and Imagery in Physical and Pain Rehabilitation, *Journal of Mental Imagery, 17*:1, pp. 25-34, 1983.
47. T. X. Barber, H. M. Chauncey, and R. A. Winer, The Effect of Hypnotic and Nonhypnotic Suggestions on Parotid Gland Response to Gustatory Stimuli, *Psychosomatic Medicine, 26,* pp. 374-380, 1964.
48. H. M. Simpson and A. Pavio, Changes in Pupil Size During an Imagery Task Without Motor Involvement, *Psychonomic Science, 5,* pp 405-406, 1966.
49. J. May and H. Johnson, Psychological Activity to Internally Elicited Arousal and Inhibitory Thoughts, *Journal of Abnormal Psychology, 82,* pp. 239-245, 1973.
50. A. A. Sheikh and C. S. Jordan, Clinical Uses of Mental Imagery, in *Imagery: Current Theory, Research, and Applications,* A. A. Sheikh (ed.), Wiley, New York, 1983.
51. T. X. Barber, Hypnosis, Suggestions and Psychosomatic Phenomena, A New Look From the Standpoint of Recent Experimental Studies, *The American Journal of Clinical Hypnosis, 21,* pp. 13-27, 1978.
52. C. Corbin, Mental Practice, in *Ergogenic Aids and Muscular Performance,* W. Morgan (ed.), Academic Press, New York, pp. 93-118, 1972.
53. D. L. Feltz and D. M. Landers, The Effects of Mental Practice on Motor Skill Learning and Performance: A Meta-analysis, *Journal of Sport Psychology, 5,* pp. 25-27, 1983.
54. J. E. Hecker and L. M. Kaczor, Application of Imagery Theory to Sport Psychology: Some Preliminary Findings, *Journal of Sport & Exercise Psychology, 10,* pp. 363-373, 1988.
55. R. S. Sackett, The Relationship Between the Amount of Symbolic Rehearsal and Retention of a Maze Habit, *Journal of General Psychology, 13,* pp. 113-128, 1935.
56. R. S. Vealey, *Imagery Training for Performance Enhancement,* paper presented to the Sports Psychology Institute, Portland, Maine, June 1987.
57. P. J. Lang, A Bio-informational Theory of Emotional Imagery, *Psychophysiology, 16,* pp. 495-512, 1979.

58. H. Feigl, The 'Mental' and the 'Physical', *Minnesota Studies in the Philosophy of Science, 2,* pp. 370-497, 1958.
59. A. A. Sheikh and R. G. Kunzendorf, Imagery, Physiology, and Psychosomatic Illness, *International Review of Mental Imagery, 1,* pp. 95-138, 1984.
60. P. H. Greene, Problems of Organization of Motor Systems, *Progress in Theoretical Biology,* (vol. 2), R. Rosen and F. M. Snell (eds.), Academic Press, New York, pp. 304-333, 1972.
61. K. Pribram, *Languages of the Brain,* Prentice-Hall, Englewood Cliffs, New Jersey, 1971.
62. G. E. Schwartz, Psychophysiology of Imagery and Healing: A Systems Perspective, in *Imagination and Healing,* A. A. Sheikh (ed.), Baywood, Amityville, New York, pp. 38-50, 1984.
63. R. Nideffer, *Psychological Aspects of Injury,* paper presented to the National Conference on Sport Psychology, Arlington, Virginia, October 1987.
64. H. Selye, *Stress Without Distress,* J. B. Lippincott, Philadelphia, Pennsylvania, 1974.
65. S. T. Bramwell, T. H. Holmes, M. Masuda, and N. N. Wagner, Psychosocial Factors in Athletic Injuries: Development and Application of the Social and Athletic Readjustment Rating Scale (SARRS), *Journal of Human Stress, 1*:2, pp. 6-20, 1975.
66. G. Kerr and H. Minden, Psychological Factors Related to the Occurrence of Athletic Injuries, *Journal of Sport & Exercise Psychology, 10,* pp. 167-173, 1988.
67. G. P. Lynch, Athletic Injuries and the Practicing Sport Psychologist: Practical Guidelines for Assisting Athletes, *The Sport Psychologist, 2,* pp. 161-167, 1988.
68. R. J. Rotella and S. R. Heyman, Stress, Injury, and the Psychological Rehabilitation of Athletes, in *Applied Sport Psychology: Personal Growth to Peak Performance,* J. M. Williams (ed.), Mayfield, Palo Alto, California, pp. 343-364, 1986.
69. S. Samuels and N. Samuels, *Seeing with the Mind's Eye,* Random House, New York, 1975.
70. C. Thomas, *Locus of Authority, Coercion, and Critical Distance in the Decision to Play an Injured Player,* paper presented to the Philosophic Society for the Study of Sport, Ft. Wayne, Indiana, October 1990.
71. J. L. Duda, A. E. Smart, and M. K. Tappe, Predictors of Adherence in the Rehabilitation of Athletic Injuries: An Application of Personal Investment Theory, *Journal of Sport & Exercise Psychology, 11,* pp. 367-381, 1989.
72. A. Lazarus, *The Mind's Eye: The Power of Imagery for Personal Enrichment,* The Guilford Press, New York, 1984.
73. E. Kübler-Ross, *On Death and Dying,* Macmillan, New York, 1969.
74. J. S. Gordon, D. T. Jaffe, and D. E. Bresler, *Mind, Body, and Health: Toward an Integral Medicine,* Human Sciences Press, New York, 1984.
75. E. Peper, S. Ancoli, and M. Quinn, *Mind/Body Integration: Essential Readings in Biofeedback,* Plenum Press, New York, 1979.
76. D. Millman, *The Way of the Peaceful Warrior,* H. J. Kramer, Tiburon, California, 1984.
77. L. Ievleva and T. Orlick, Mental Links to Enhanced Healing: An Exploratory Study, *The Sport Psychologist, 5,* pp. 25-40, 1991.
78. N. Cantor and J. Kihlstrom, *Personality and Social Intelligence,* Prentice-Hall, Englewood Cliffs, New Jersey, 1987.
79. H. Markus and A. Ruvolo, Possible Selves: Personalized Representations of Goals, in *Goal Concepts in Personality and Social Psychology,* L. A. Pervin (ed.), Erlbaum, Hillsdale, New Jersey, pp. 211-241, 1989.
80. H. Markus and Z. Kunda, Stability and Malleability of the Self-concept, *Journal of Personality and Social Psychology, 51,* pp. 858-866, 1986.

81. H. Markus and P. Nurius, Possible Selves, *American Psychologist, 41,* pp. 954-969, 1986.
82. E. R. Korn and K. Johnson, *Visualization: The Uses of Imagery in the Health Professions,* Dow Jones-Irwin, Homewood, Illinois, 1983.
83. M. M. Ishii, Imagery Techniques in the Works of Maxwell Maltz, in *Anthology of Imagery Techniques,* A. A. Sheikh (ed.), American Imagery Institute, Milwaukee, Wisconsin, pp. 313-323, 1986.
84. A. Bandura, *Social Foundations of Thought and Action: A Social Cognitive Theory,* Prentice-Hall, Englewood cliffs, New Jersey, 1986.
85. A. Bandura, Self-regulation of Motivation and Action Through Goal Systems, in *Cognitive Perspectives on Emotion and Motivation,* V. Hamilton, G. H. Bower, and N. H. Frijda (eds.), Kluwer Academic, Dordrecht, Netherlands, pp. 36-61, 1988.
86. C. H. Day, *The Immune System Handbook,* Potentials Within, North York, Ontario, 1991.
87. J. Achterberg, C. Kenner, and G. F. Lawlis, Severe Burn Injury: A Comparison of Relaxation, Imagery and Biofeedback for Pain Management, *Journal of Mental Imagery, 12*:1, pp. 71-88, 1988.
88. N. P. Spanos and P. A. O'Hara, Imaginal Dispositions and Situation-specific Expectations in Strategy-induced Pain Reductions, *Imagination, Cognition and Personality, 9*:2, pp. 147-156, 1990.

This chapter is a revised version of a previously published paper: "The Use of Imagery in the Rehabilitation of Injured Athletes" by L. B. Green, 1992, *The Sport Psychologist,* (Vol. 6, No. 4), pp. 416-428. Copyright 1992 by Human Kinetics Publisher, Inc. Included here with permission.

CHAPTER 11

Optimal Sports
Performance Imagery

EMMETT MILLER

A complete exercise in image rehearsal for peak performance in a sporting event consists of several distinct phases. Although some of these phases may
be left out on some occasions, certain others, such as the "Deep Relaxation Phase"
and "Return to Waking Consciousness" phase should always be present to some
degree. In addition, each represents a specific skill and serves as a training in this
skill and an affirmation of its importance.

Each of these phases is indicated below. Footnotes indicate recommended
reading material or cassettes associated with this particular skill. In many cases the
wording itself has been directly borrowed from the indicated audio cassette.

A deeply moving, stimulating, personal, sensory rich experience is the most
effective. The positive emotion and enthusiasm developed through such an
experience provides the inner fuel that drives the cortical and neuromuscular
machinery toward the desired goal (image ideal). To this end, the use of music,
nature sounds and a pleasant, skilled voice for the narration is of enormous value.
The training tapes mentioned in footnotes can also serve as excellent models for
developing your own specific imagery experience.

GOOD SETTING AND COMMITMENT

The following experience is designed to guide you in the use of the
"Master Skill," image rehearsal.[1] Before you begin the deep relaxation process,
bring to mind a specific upcoming event where you want to perform at your peak.
Develop in your mind a clear idea of the outcome you want to produce, and the
knowledge of how, specifically you will know when you have achieved that
outcome. You need to have a clear awareness of the kind of performance and
behaviors—physical, intellectual, and emotional—you would like from yourself.

---

[1] *Opening Your Inner "I"/Software for Your Mind* (text), Celestial Arts, 1987. Available from
Source Cassettes.

Become aware of how important it is to you to be successful in this event, and of how valuable it is to focus your total concentration on it at this moment in time. Make a commitment to yourself to set aside all other issues in your life for a few minutes and choose to give this inner training experience the amount of attention it deserves, now, within, make a commitment to yourself to devote the next few minutes totally to developing the kind of mental discipline and the kind of mental image rehearsal that creates winners.

Centering

Let yourself be seated in a comfortable position, or if you prefer, you can lie down. Choose a point out in the distance to focus your eyes on and keep your eyes fixed on that point as if it is a goal that you want to be certain to keep in focus. *(PAUSE)*

Now take a long, slow, deep breath in, filling your abdomen and your chest completely full . . . and as you let this breath out, let yourself become aware that at this moment in time there's no other place you have to go . . . nothing else you have to do and no problem you have to solve. . . *(PAUSE 20-60 SECONDS)*

Think to yourself: My each and every thought during this period of time is focused on a single goal—my excellence . . . I have decided that I want to be not just good, not just very good, but *outstanding* . . . My body can do it, my muscles can do it, my nervous system is capable of it . . . My responsibility is to train my mind. . . . Good.

Focusing

The first step in mental training is *focus*. A winner wins because he or she focuses on a goal that he or she desires. You may have noticed that the point your eyes have been looking at has been slipping in and out of focus. That's O.K., since what you really want to focus on now is what I'm saying. And as you let your mind follow the sound of my voice and listen to my words, you may let that outside point slip completely out of focus . . . like when you're daydreaming, staring off into space. . . . Good.

Now take a slow deep breath in, and as you let this breath out, let your eyelids close . . . and as you do let your eyes roll upwards behind your closed eyelids. Imagine that you can see written on the back of your forehead the word "Relax" . . . and as you see the word "Relax," let your entire body begin to let go . . . take another deep breath in and as you let this breath out, imagine you're a balloon letting out all the air . . . letting go completely . . . then stop breathing, and let the air breathe for you . . . just as it does when you're asleep at night . . . the air breathes in filling your chest and abdomen while you simply observe. Breathing . . . and focused on the breath entering and leaving.

Deep Relaxation

The second step in mental training is to remove all distractions . . . to stop all unnecessary mental activity so that the entire focus of your brain, muscles, and nervous system will be on what you want it to focus on . . . Your breathing will continue all by itself.

The best way to let go of distractions is by relaxing. Distractions are present in the body as tension in muscles . . . distractions are present in the emotions as anxieties, frustrations, anger, and fear . . . and in the mind as unnecessary thoughts that pull your attention away from your true goal.

Take a moment and feel the weight of your body sinking deeply into the surface beneath you. Imagine that as your body becomes more and more still it is being slowly filled with a thick clear oil and you are becoming heavier and heavier . . . and let yourself enjoy this feeling of fullness . . . as though your body . . . becoming heavier . . . is gently sinking . . . as though you're sinking, in slow motion, into a soft, welcoming feather bed.

Feel your feet growing heavier and heavier . . . your legs growing heavier . . . your arms and hands growing heavier and heavier . . . a heavy leaden feeling flowing throughout all of your body . . . a heavy, warm, dense, and yet comfortable feeling filling your entire body from head to toe . . . and letting your body lie quietly with this feeling.

Excellent. Now, in a few moments I'm going to count from one to ten . . . and as I do, I'm going to ask you to let your body become lighter . . . and to let the feeling of heaviness be replaced with the feeling of lightness and fluidity.

In your mind's eye, imagine there are openings on either side of your waist around toward your back. With each breath out, imagine the thick, heavy oily substance flowing out of your body. Imagine it flowing outward onto the floor . . . and being absorbed into the floor. One . . . imagine the floor becoming dark with it, as though the floor is a giant blotter or a sponge underneath you . . . two . . . the sponge is absorbing all the heaviness . . . three . . . imagine the heaviness sinking deeper and deeper through the floor and into the earth . . . four . . . feel it draining from all parts of your body . . . feel it draining from your abdomen as your breathing becomes easier . . . and rising and falling of your abdomen feels lighter and lighter . . . five . . . and now draining your buttocks and your thighs . . . feeling them empty . . . as though they're becoming hollow and empty . . . draining your knees and calves . . . six . . . feeling it draining from your toes and your feet . . . from your heels . . . from the entire lower part of your body . . . emptying . . . seven . . . and feel your body getting lighter and lighter . . . your feet and calves, knees, thighs and pelvis emptying and becoming lighter . . . eight . . . and imagine yourself floating up . . . that you are floating up higher and higher with each breath . . . nine . . . and as all the oil flows completely out of your body, you float up lighter and lighter . . . completely relaxed . . . ten.[2]

And as you gently float up higher and higher imagine you can look down below and see the earth . . .perhaps you are floating above a lake . . . maybe over a forest . . . maybe over a beautiful meadow . . . or even over the seashore . . . anyplace you would like to be. Feel yourself floating in this place and enjoying the feeling and the sights down below you.

And anytime any unnecessary thoughts come along just imagine that your nostrils are like two little exhaust pipes, and that with your next breath out you breathe the unnecessary thought out of your mind, and that the next breath in breathes in fresh clean air . . . that it breathes relaxation into your mind . . . and throughout all the rest of your body. And if that thought or any other unnecessary thought comes along again, repeat this process . .[3] *(PAUSE)*

Accessing Performance Resources

Good . . . now you are mentally focused and free of distractions. My voice will now guide you to visualize real excellence in your sport. Each thing you picture will be perfect. Not only will you see it happening . . . you will feel it happening, you will hear the sounds around you . . . Every part of you will participate.

Now let yourself float, in your imagination, back . . . back . . . to a time in the past when you performed optimally . . . to an important success. If possible, choose a time when you achieved a personal best in athletics . . . or if you wish, you can choose a time when you felt that thrill of success in any other area of your life . . . in art . . . school . . . business . . . and to recreate this scene in your mind's eye.

Visualize it vividly and clearly . . . see the colors . . . the shapes . . . hear the sounds . . . and feel the sensations of being there. Actually step into this scene and feel within that wonderful feeling of self confidence . . . of success . . . and of personal satisfaction. Feel it strongly within . . . *(PAUSE)*

And as you continue to enjoy this image and this feeling, feel the air breathing you. Feel the rising of your chest and abdomen as the air enters . . . and the feeling of letting go as the air leaves . . . and feel the pause that comes after the air leaves and before the next breath comes in . . . *(PAUSE)*

---

[2] Imagery adapted from Part A of Cassette #228 *High Performance Sports,* available from Source Cassettes, P.O. Box W, Stanford, CA 94305/ 1-800-52-TAPES. Most of this entire imagery exercise are represented on this two cassette series.

[3] Imagery adapted from Cassette #14 *I AM: Awakening Self Acceptance,* available from Source Cassettes.

And at the end of this pause feel that little spark of energy that starts the next breath in. Notice that the spark comes from deep inside you . . . that you don't have to *make* it happen . . . it happens all by itself. And as you enjoy this pleasant feeling of mastery, satisfaction and success in your inner image, notice that this feeling is much like the spark of energy that begins each new breath. You don't have to make it happen . . . it comes all by itself . . . if you let it. Feel your inner sense of energy growing greater and greater with each new breath in. *(PAUSE)*

Mental Image Rehearsal

And now begin to orient yourself ahead toward the future. In your minds eye visualize an ideal image of yourself in your athletic event . . . performing the way you would like to perform. Start from the beginning and see your performance in each phase of this activity.

And as you picture yourself performing at your peak, see it as clearly as you can, hear the sounds in the environment and feel the inner excitement of watching yourself do really well . . . the same way you would feel looking at a videotape of an excellent performance from the past. . . . *(PAUSE)* . . .

What specific challenges confront you in this particular event? Envision yourself handling them smoothly, efficiently, and effectively. Visualize your body relaxed . . . yet strong. Emotionally you are aware, flexible, and balanced . . . your emotions enthusiastically support your efforts. Your muscles are like coiled springs . . . your movements are fluid and coordinated . . . inside you feel stimulated and enjoyably excited . . . your mind is crystal clear. Enjoy watching this . . . *(PAUSE)*

Take a deep breath in . . . and as you let this breath out, rewind this scene back to the beginning . . . and step into your body. Make it present. Feel yourself there. Look around . . . see the world around you. It's right at the beginning of your event. Feel your body, what you're wearing, anything you may be carrying, the feel of the earth beneath you . . . the posture of your body.

Within, feel your emotion . . . sense your passion . . . your caring . . . your power . . . sense your courage, clarity, and purpose . . . sense your mission . . . clearly and vividly. Now live through this event in slow motion . . . feeling yourself perform just the way you've planned . . . and achieving the results you wanted at each phase . . . feeling successful at every step of the way. You are performing perfectly . . . flawlessly . . . as never before . . . performing at your peak . . . bringing your best to life . . . with a kind of perfection that is truly *worthy* of you.[4] *(PAUSE)*

---

[4] Imagery adapted from Side B of Cassette #53 *The Ten-Minute Stress Manager*, "Ten-Minute Peak Performance Self Program" available from Source Cassettes.

Feel your inner desire and creative tension spurring you into action . . . into powerful, decisive, yet sensitive action . . . you are efficiently solving problems . . . moving smoothly and gracefully . . . gliding on the surge of energy like a surfer. As each spark of energy starts each new breath in, it pumps more power and enthusiasm through the muscles of your body . . . *(PAUSE)*

Encoding the Spirit of Victory

(With Enthusiasm) Feel within that same quality of success, confidence, and satisfaction you felt in your past victory . . . only much stronger this time. Taking yourself through each phase of your performance . . . feeling the muscles of your body . . . tensing . . . relaxing . . . surging with strength and vitality . . . *(PAUSE).* And now, entering the final phase, feel yourself breaking through the last obstacles, meeting these challenges successfully . . . and emerging feeling victorious.[5] You know you have won the victory you set out to win, but you don't stop yet. You keep going and you complete a beautiful follow through. Graceful . . . smooth . . . flowing . . . honest . . . real . . . and really enjoying the experience . . . fully and totally. You met the challenge and you were victorious . . . you were successful . . . let yourself feel the success . . . feel the joy . . . feel the happiness. The better you can let yourself feel *now,* the stronger will be the motivation of every cell in your body to want to get there and do exactly what you're imaging right now. Feel it. How good are you willing to let yourself feel? *(PAUSE)*

Breathe it throughout every cell in your body . . . breathing deeply in and out . . . letting it grow stronger and stronger.[6]

You have achieved your personal best. You have performed optimally . . . and are pleased with your excellence. Continue through with this image. Picture yourself receiving congratulations, positive feedback, and praise from others. You accept this with sincere thanks. And now you, too, are giving feedback in reward to your team and/or support system. Notice the really good feeling inside. Feel it strongly—it is the high energy fuel that will empower you to reach this and every other victory in the future.

And now take a few moments to reflect upon that greater power that is within you and throughout the universe . . . that is the ultimate source of your energy and creativity . . . of your power and performance.

Focus now on that spark of inspiration that begins each new breath in, and breathe in deeply with each inspiration. As you do, feel that sense of accomplishment and confidence expanding within. Feel the tingling feeling that flows through your body.

---

[5] Imagery adapted from Cassette #50 *Power Vision.* This six-tape set available from Source Cassettes.

[6] Imagery adapted from Cassette #54, *Optimal Performance,* available from Source Cassettes.

RETURNING TO WAKING CONSCIOUSNESS

Now gradually bring this sense of energy to a more active level as you return to an awareness of the space around you. As I count from one to ten, feel the feeling growing even greater within you . . . one . . . breathing it into every part of your being . . . two . . . that feeling of calm energy . . . three . . . you are ready . . . four . . . ready to act . . . just as you planned . . . five . . . as you feel yourself coming up . . . six . . . more and more awake . . . more and more ready . . . seven . . . filled with a secure feeling of confidence . . . eight . . . becoming more and more awake . . . alert and clear . . . feeling your body want to move . . . to stretch . . . nine . . . coming all the way up . . . letting your eyelids open . . ten . . . ready to go into action . . . NOW!

CHAPTER 12

Transformational Imagery for Sports Excellence

JOHN T. SHAFFER

Transformational Imagery is a simple but powerful process. It involves an expanded state of consciousness in that the fully awake mind interacts with the dreaming mind. In this state, it is possible to transform old strategies of living to experience ourselves at our best [1]. I am using sports as a focus to demonstrate the effects of this process. My subject, Bob, had already experienced the more general psychotherapeutic effects of the process and then wanted to apply it to improving his golf game.

The first part of this chapter will give his version of two sessions, and my comments follow. The first section will give the reader the feel of a continuing, inner "plot" and a series of scenes illuminating this plot. How can Bob learn to hit a perfect shot in his mind so that he can hit a perfect shot in reality?

A coach in sports excellence can get the feel of the process by following Bob's experiences and then choose from a variety of exercises that follow. The process can easily be adapted to any sport. As the sports person experiences and shares with the facilitator, the latter will be caught up in the dream plot that begins to emerge. The inner symbols are for the subject to understand and explain to the facilitator. The facilitator's role is to listen carefully to the subject's description and to understand the plot, to follow the client from the inside rather than from the outside point of view. The facilitator is an assistant rather than a mentor, who suggests from time to time a new scene or model and then once again listens and follows the cues.

BOB'S EXPERIENCE WITH IMPROVING HIS GOLF[1]

First Experience

I've had a love-hate relationship with golf for many years. So when John asked what sport I would like to work on, it had to be golf—despite the

---

[1] I am indebted to my friend and colleague for volunteering to take part in this experiment. Bob Greenwell has a Master's Degree in counseling and is a specialist in Transformational Imagery in a general way.

fact that I hadn't been on a golf course for three years or on a practice range for one year.

I had turned my back on golf. I had written it off. It was too frustrating. Either my standards were too high or my talent was too low. But the imagery practice seemed to offer me one last chance.

In the first session, John simply had me picture my golf swing "in my mind's eye." When I did, it seemed awkward and unbalanced. Then he suggested I try to picture a perfect swing.

I couldn't do it! This in itself was a revelation to me. I've seen plenty of perfect swings, in real life and on television. But I could not visualize one. The moment I'd start to get close, a sensation of awkwardness or imbalance would arise, and the actual picture in my mind would be of an off-balance, off-rhythm, jerky, golf swing. I noticed that when I really concentrated on forming an image of a perfect swing, at John's prompting to remember some excellent shot from my past, the image was vague and fuzzy. I couldn't imagine feeling the perfection of the shot in my muscles or my body motion, but I could visualize the perfect flight of the ball.

Then John had me "be the ball." He asked, "How does it feel when you're propelled by a perfect golf swing?" I felt great, from that first powerful instant of crushing impact with the clubhead, to the glorious soaring feeling of flying through the air with direction, purpose, and freedom, to the excitement of homing in with precision on the pin standing in the middle of the green.

So we worked with this perfection. I started with the ball on the tee, anticipating its perfect flight to come. Then I came back to the clubhead at the moment of its perfect impact with the ball. I was the shaft on the club at that perfect moment. I became my hands gripping the club at that moment. Finally I experienced my arms and my whole body at that moment. From there we worked backwards to visualize the backswing and downswing leading to this perfect moment. In that way, I arrived at a visualized swing that was a definite improvement over my first attempts; however, it was still not perfect. *And* it was not stable. That is, I might succeed in visualizing a very good swing, and then just a second later, when trying to repeat the very same swing in my mind, some jerky element or impulse would come in and totally vitiate the swing.

This session was an eye-opener for me, because it was obvious to me that I could not perfect my golf swing in real life until I could consistently visualize a good swing.

In summary, in the first session, I made some progress. First, my visualized golf swing improved but did not attain perfection or consistency. Second, I discovered that I could consistently visualize a perfect flight of the ball. Third, I discovered the amazing fact that I could not consciously control my own inner image of my golf swing.

SESSION II

Session II was designed to work more broadly with my inner images, in order to find out why I couldn't consistently visualize a perfect golf swing, and to then unblock any blockages that might show up.

The first imagery John suggested was for me to be in one of the two hemispheres of my brain, whichever one I chose, or whichever one "happened" to come to mind first. I went into my right hemisphere. John asked me to describe what I noticed or what might be happening. It was like a big cavern, with curved moist rock walls. The most interesting thing was that it was dark on the side that was closest to the center of my head, and then way over to the right and slightly back it became lighter, from some source of light that was out of view. John said, "Be the right hemisphere. How does it feel having all this darkness on one side?" I answered, "I'm very important, because I serve as a hiding place." Then, as myself, I said, "It feels like a place where I can go when I'm afraid, like a little boy—a place like a dark corner where I can cower and be wary and be unseen." John said, "Be the little boy. What's all this mean to you?" I said, "I feel unworthy. Out there toward the light is the hustle-bustle world, and I can never live up to the world's expectations, and I feel safe here in the dark." John suggested that Big Bob (my adult self) go in and talk to Little Bob. So I did. I reassured him that he *was* worthy, and that the light outside was nothing to be afraid of, and that I knew because it was his own future self. John asked, "How does Little Bob feel about that?" Little Bob felt a little less anxious, but this was all pretty new and he was going to take his time to venture forth from his dark corner. John said, "Be the hemisphere. How does it feel about Big Bob coming in and talking to Little Bob in this way?" I answered, "It's about time! This is just what's needed." Then John wondered if perhaps Little Bob would want to allow just a little bit more light into the hemisphere, and Little Bob agreed. Together they asked the light to come more into the interior in some way. A slow, viscous stream of light formed over at the light source and came gently in toward Little Bob. When it got to him, it curled up into a ball (about the size of a softball), a ball of light that he could hold in the palm of his hand and play with. This experience very gently and slightly increased the illumination of Little Bob's area.

John then suggested that I be in the left hemisphere. It was completely different. It was a huge office space with many people and lots of activity, with an overall efficient hum to it. There was a thick wall separating it from the right hemisphere. John suggested, "Be the wall. Ask the wall what it is doing here." The wall responded, "I'm here because I had to protect Little Bob from his own fears, so that he wouldn't be frightened by all the activity and noise over in the left hemisphere; otherwise all this great organization on the left side couldn't have been developed."

About then an image came to the mind of Little Bob in the right hemisphere holding a golf club in his hands and feeling extremely inadequate. He felt inadequate because the golf club was too big and because he would never be able to play golf as well as his father. Then Big Bob talked to Little Bob, telling him that he needs to separate his feelings about his father from his feelings about golf, that his father was not Golf Personified, that golf was bigger than his father.

Then a rather gruesome image spontaneously arose, an image of my father, as seen by Little Bob, with a golf club twisted around his neck and other clubs twisted around his chest and legs, extinguishing him, removing him from the scene. I understood this image to refer not to my actual father, but to a mistaken identification of my father as Personified Golf.

Then I became aware of the people in my left hemisphere being curious about what was going on in the right hemisphere, about what was happening with Little Bob. Some of the people came up to the big wall and opened up slots that they could peer through. They're concerned about Little Bob's welfare. Ultimately, his welfare is their welfare. They're happy something is finally happening over there. Little Bob seems to be stirring from his dark, hibernating corner. John suggested that the people might like to visit the right hemisphere.

I visualized one of the secretaries walking to the rear and coming to a plain, small, little-used door to the right hemisphere and going through. She came to Little Bob, took him by the hand and brought him back through the same door to visit the left hemisphere. Little Bob said, "Wow, this is the left side of my own future brain!" He received a rousing cheer and applause from the multitude of people there. He was impressed and grateful and felt a surge of pride and self-worth. As this was going on, the wall started to evaporate and melted away completely. However, Little Bob still had his area in the right hemisphere where he could cover himself with dark, when he felt the need. Next, John suggested that I build a golf course in the center, between the two hemispheres. It started as a small, luminous dot. But as I kept down-shifting my perspective on it, it grew larger and larger in my vision, becoming as large as a real golf course. As I started to play the course, it was as though the ball itself knew where to go, and the club knew what to do, as if both were animated, and all I had to do was attach myself to the club. Then it was as though Little Bob were holding the club, and then it was as though Little Bob were visualizing the golf course and visualizing Baby Bob holding the club. As the club swung and the ball took off, Baby Bob gurgled with glee.

John checked several things. He asked what the golf course was like, and I said it was absolutely wonderful, challenging but fair. He checked with the inhabitants of my left hemisphere, asking them what they thought of the right hemisphere. They felt that it was totally different from their hemisphere; it was "magical" in comparison, and they liked it.

At this point, John suggested that we leave this scene. There had been a lot of development in it and we had reached a good point. He suggested that I go check out my "golf room" down the "hallway of my mind." A whole new set of images replaced the ones I had been working with. I entered my golf room and looked around and described it to John. It was used very little. There were cobwebs. The walls were lined with display cases, files, and shelves which contained hundreds of my father's trophies and newspaper clippings about my father's accomplishments in golf. John asked, "How do you like that?" I said, "It's all wrong. These things don't belong here. This is *Bob's* golf room. All these things in here belong down the hall in Dad's room." So I immediately ordered the reorganization, and a few big guys came with heavy carts and hauled everything down to Dad's room. I put a sign on the door that emphasized *Bob's* Golf Room. (Anything pertaining to my Dad goes down the hall to Dad's room.)

Next, I had my room thoroughly cleaned and repainted and redecorated. I had video screens installed on two walls, and brought in a collection of videos of beautiful golf courses of the world and of the great golfers of history. In the middle of the room was a small table with a crystal ball on it. It was there to reveal to me the meaning of golf for me. I gazed into it and didn't see any particular image, but simply sensed a grand meaningfulness—that golf symbolized the deep joyousness of life.

John suggested I run a video of the swing of a great golfer. I did so. I still noted some difficulty in visualizing a perfect golf swing, but not as much difficulty as in my first session. When I succeeded in getting a pretty good picture of the great golfer's swing, John had me picture my face on his body and see the same swing. The he had me "walk into" his body, and feel the same swing from the inside. When I did that, I felt a chill, and I was able to sense somewhat the muscular sensations that went with the great swing.

John then suggested another change of scene. He told me to visit my crown. I did, and noted that it was semi-open. I wanted it more open, and so I made an adjustment by rotating a large metal, slotted cap that fit over my crown. John suggested that Little Bob be there too, and he asked how Little Bob liked it.

Little Bob reveled in it, he basked in it, reclining on his back with his arms open, as if he were sunbathing. John asked if he could try an experimental question, and then asked, "At what time in your life has your crown been most open?" Although I remained open to any image that might develop, nothing emerged except the thought that it's been wide open at intermittent times throughout my life. So that experiment didn't reveal any new avenue for us. We refocused on the present moment. Little Bob and Big Bob agreed that we wanted the crown more open all the time. I attached a spring to the crown cap to provide constant pressure to keep it open, except when necessary.

We switched scenes again. John suggested I be on a golf course out in the middle of a fairway. "Now be the golf course," he suggested. "What's your view of Bob's presence there? How is he connected to you?" The golf course replied, "I like him there, but he feels lightweight. He kind of skims the earth, he isn't grounded enough." John suggested that I send an energy pulse of gravity up into Bob's legs. I did so, and then as Bob, I felt a tingling in my calves and started to feel more connected to the earth and to the golf course. There was a little shift as I started to feel that the golf course could be my friend rather than my enemy.

Next John suggested another image. "Be in the center of your head; there are six lines extending out: forward, back, left, right, up and down. How do they meet in the center?" My sense was that they all meet at the same point. John asked, "So, they're all in alignment with each other?" "Yes." John continued, "What is that like?" Well, it feels potent, and feels balanced." That seemed to be as it should be, and we moved to the conclusion of our session.

One other exercise John tried with me was to imagine my "golf coach" in one of my hemispheres. My coach showed up in my left one. John asked, "He or she?" I said, "He" and described him as short and paunchy, a gruff but friendly and no-nonsense guy, wearing a red golf cap. John inquired, "What does your coach think about your inner practice?" I told him that he thought that it was great, but that I especially needed to get the feel of my muscles, and to integrate inner practice with outer practice, actually hitting golf balls. John said, "All right, now go see who your golf coach is in the right hemisphere." I did, and the coach there was a gorgeous, sensuous woman in the nude. (I'm sure John's earlier question, "He or she," cued me to the possibility that the right-hemisphere coach could be a woman.) John asked her, "What do you think of Bob's inner practice?" She said, "It is good, but a little too mechanical. Bob needs to relax more and have more images of beauty and fluidity." John then suggested that the two coaches meet in my center. They did, at first with some antagonism, but then they warmed up to each other and agreed to work together to coach Bob to reach his best golf potential.

John suggested that, with all the experiences of the session in mind, I now imagine playing golf. So I visualized myself on the first tee. I was me, inside my body, addressing the ball with my driver in hand. I let the swing happen, without having a clear visual image of it. I clearly saw the flight of the ball, however, as it shot out, a beautiful drive. Then I was out in the fairway, ready for my second shot. Again, I was only clear on the flight of the ball itself, as it headed straight for the pin, landed about two feet from the hole, and rolled in. I thought, "That's great, but I also need practice chipping and putting, so I can't be making eagles all the time!"

About a week later, I went out to a practice range and hit a small bucket of balls. When I set the first ball up and took my first swing, I half expected something magical to happen—an instant transformation of my swing into PGA mold. It didn't happen. However, there was a difference. The main difference was my sensitivity to my own mental business during my swing. I started to work with my mental images before, during, and after each swing. I learned that a particular image of my right arm and right hand being powerful and controlling the moment of impact resulted in my best shots. A couple of my shots were excellent, even perfect. I tried to ingrain those in my mind in order to strengthen the images associated with them. I left the practice range with the feeling that I had learned a new way to develop consistency and power in my golf game.

One week later, I went to the practice range a second time. First, I practiced my eight iron, then my three iron. It took me a while to get into form. Then, with twelve balls left in the bucket, I took out my driver. Before each shot, I took practice swings until I could feel that I had it just right. Then I stepped up to the ball and quickly took my shot, while the image of a perfect swing (for me) was still afresh. In that way, I hit nine out of twelve excellent shots. That is an improved percentage for me on the practice range, and the other three shots weren't bad either.

I can't directly connect the images that I worked on in my two sessions with John to my golf swing on the practice range. For example, I'm not aware of "being the ball" or of my golf room or of Little Bob when I'm out hitting balls. But I do have a sense of a changed background or of a slightly different mood setting. So far, I haven't been out on a regular golf course to test for any change, but my experience on the practice range is encouraging.

COMMENTS ON THE SESSIONS

Seeing in the mind's eye is an excellent exercise to determine whether a person has the ability to visualize the correct moves. Ordinarily, I would start the first session with the sequence of visiting the hemispheres, but Bob had already done so. Therefore, we proceeded to sensing or feeling one of his best golf shots. When he "became the ball" and worked back to the stroke and the golfer (himself), his thinking mind began to develop the idea of a perfect swing. Previously he had said, "I couldn't imagine feeling . . . in my muscles and in my body."

On the other hand, you may be able to sense a perfect swing. If that is the case, start your perfect inner practice, as outlined later on. See how well you do. If you "see" yourself hitting a perfect shot, walk into the person or be the you hitting the shot. Doing so changes a mind picture to a mind-body experience. This kind of experiencing is the basis for perfect inner practice.

Regardless of your success or failure in this first step of perfect practice, you need to experience the larger dimensions of the sport. You need to experience yourself with all your pluses and minuses. Why did Bob have trouble visualizing his best golf shot? Are you the same or different? If you can hit a perfect golf shot in your mind and it remains stable, why can't you consistently hit that perfect shot in real life? If you can't consciously control your inner life, how can you consciously control your outer life? Thousands of people have experienced, most very easily, the sharp difference between the two hemispheres. Bob, along with about 80 percent of the population I have known, has a right hemisphere of flow and feeling and a left hemisphere of form and activity. You and your subject will experience the hemispheres as they are. Therefore, as facilitator, you will be able to follow and participate as the clues appear.

In this scene, I followed up on the "thick wall separating the hemispheres." I could have done a different facilitation. "Talk to the wall. Does it like being a wall separating the hemispheres? How long have you been there?" (If we had not discovered Little Bob in the right hemisphere, we might have found him in the left because Little Bob knew the wall was there and why.)

Little Bob holding the large golf club is a spontaneous scene arising from the dreaming part of the mind. I did almost nothing in this scene. Bob explained to me what was going on.

Ordinarily, I would have responded to the golf clubs twisted about his father's body. But Bob interpreted it for me himself. I could have done some additional facilitation here, such as: "How do you feel about the scene? How did Little Bob feel about the scene? Is there anything you want to say to Little Bob? How about calling your father into the scene and letting him take part?"

Notice that in the scene in the left hemisphere, I suggested that Bob check with the people about a visit, since they were already opening slots in the wall and peering through. Then notice the spontaneous action: A secretary led Little Bob back to the left hemisphere. The action resulted in considerable integration of right and left hemispheres. However, Little Bob still has his hiding place!

I would like to point out that each person's experience in Transformational Imagery of visiting the hemispheres will contain common elements:

1. The hemispheres are different. The right hemisphere is an I Am Brain, the left hemisphere is an I Do Brain.
2. The hemispheres generally are out of balance. One person had an 80 percent to 20 percent imbalance in favor of the right hemisphere.
3. Most people feel better about one hemisphere than the other.
4. The hemispheres may or may not be well-connected. The hemispheres may or may not know each other very well.
5. Most people will want to change any negative conditions and will have greater and greater success with each visit.
6. The hemispheres in some cases are switched—usually in left-handed people and occasionally in right-handed people. The variation in my experience is approximately 15 percent.

What follows is a brief description of some imagery exercise. In my experiences, they are basic not only in sports excellence, but they are the foundation experiences of Transformational Imagery.

RECOMMENDED PROCEDURE FOR FACILITATORS

Exercises to Maximize Brain Functioning

The following exercises are basic to developing a center where you can practice perfectly. They are repeated from my book entitled, *Be Your Own Coach, Therapist, Healer* [2].

1. Choose a Hemisphere to Visit. "Close your eyes and sense which of the two hemispheres of the brain you would like to visit." (Facilitator waits for a short time.) "Be in the chosen hemisphere and when you can, share with me where you are and what you are experiencing." (If there is no response for a time, the facilitator may ask what is happening.) Then follow the action.

If the subject is having difficulty, the facilitator may ask any of the following:

* How open is it?
* If you feel you are inside the hemisphere, can you move around freely?
* How big is it?
* What colors do you sense, see, or feel?
* How do you feel there?
* Can you talk to anyone or anything?
* Can you touch anything and how does it feel?
* Can you hear, smell, or taste anything?
* Can you imagine being the hemisphere to experience how it feels?

2. Be in the Other Hemisphere. (Facilitator again waits for the subject and responds to the inner story.)

3. Explore Between the Hemispheres. "Be in either hemisphere. Can you sense, see, or feel a passageway between or a connection between the two hemispheres? Are you able to go between the hemispheres?" (The facilitator again waits for the subject's response and follows whatever happens.)

Wait until the subject shares the inner action with you. However, if the subject seems to need help, try any of the following:

* If there's a wall blocking you, ask for a door.
* If it's too narrow, try to widen it the way you want it.
* If it is too rough, try to smooth it out.
* If it's too crooked, try to straighten it out.
* If you can't find a way to get across, ask for help.
* If it is just right, thank the passageway for being there.

You may suggest anything you feel could be helpful. However, if the subject doesn't take to suggestion, drop it. After all, it is the subject's story, not yours.

4. First Experience with the Center Between the Hemispheres. "Be in the center of the pathway between the two hemispheres. Experiment, if you need to do so to determine where the center is. You may just know where it is or you may have to work at it. You may have some difficulty. If so, try for an imagery center of some kind. Now check how you feel in your center. How comfortable is it? Do you feel in balance there, or are you pulled towards one of the hemispheres? What do you feel like doing there, if anything? Do it."

"Now ask the two hemispheres to build you a home base of your own, or to send over to the center some building ideas and materials so you can build it. Explain that you want to be close to both of them so you can learn to work with them and the rest of your body. What response are you getting? Do they feel like doing more? Is there anything you want to improve? Thank the hemispheres for whatever—even for just listening. When you are finished, come out into the here and now." "Log and date. Look over your notes and decide what else you would like to do in the center, if anything. Do you have any furnishings for work and for rest? Do you like the size and shape? Repeat the experience as often as you wish. Log and date."

5. Experiencing an Activity in the Left Hemisphere. "Choose any sport or activity. How does the left hemisphere do it? What's the style or feel of it? How do you feel doing the activity in the left hemisphere? When you have concluded the visit, thank the left hemisphere for showing you whatever, come back into the here and now. Log and date. If you would like to try another activity, do so and then log."

6. Experiencing an Activity in the Right Hemisphere. "Be in the right hemisphere. Choose the same activity you did in the left hemisphere for comparison. What is the feel of this right hemisphere? How does the right hemisphere do the activity? How do you feel doing the activity in the right hemisphere? When you have concluded your visit, thank the right hemisphere for showing you whatever and come back to the here and now. Log and date. If you want to try another activity, do so."

7. First Experience of Doing an Activity in the Center. "Be in your center. From now on we will designate it as the head center.[2] Now do the same activity you first tried in the hemispheres. Ask the hemispheres to send to you in the center their best qualities, so that you can experience both of them at work in your head center. Now try the activity again. Try to experience the unique gifts of the two hemispheres and their efforts to cooperate with you. When you have finished, come out into the here and now. Log and date."

These exercises are very valuable in laying the foundation for the inner perfect practice sessions described below.

8. A Visit to the Crown. Read this to the subject before starting the actual exercise:

> The crown of the head is not an anatomical part of the physical head. It is thought to be situated in the top center of the head close to the soft spot. The Eastern world and many in the Western world believe it is a powerful energy system. I like to think of it also as an entry way into the cosmic world. I generally use it after the center has been established to some degree. Here are the directions for the facilitator.

---

[2] In Transformational Imagery, there are other centers just as significant and meaningful in a different way; e.g., the heart center, the solar plexus center.

"Be in your head center. When you are comfortable there, sense, see, or go up to the top center of your head. How do you experience it? Is it open or closed?" As always, the facilitator follows the clues as they appear.

9. The Hallway of the Mind. The hallway of the mind is used to uncover emotional problems and free a person from their negative effects and to discover healthy emotions as resources. In Bob's case, the golf room was used because he was interested primarily in improving his golf game. I could have used "criticism room," "mistakes rooms," "Father's room," and so on, to encourage him to work through his negative feelings. Or I could have chosen a "confidence room" for developing positive feelings. I recommend that the facilitator begin in this way:

> Close your eyes. Imagine yourself walking down the hallway of your mind to an important room you need to explore. (Pause) What room is it? Tell me about.

In the sports excellence process in Transformational Imagery, the basic model consists of a visit to the two hemispheres and then to the head center. For maximum well being, any or all of the inner staging areas could be used. A visit to the "hallway of the mind," and the "confidence room" represent the positive side. The negative side also needs to be addressed, possibly in the "mistake room." Various blocks, imbalances, and negative emotions could be corrected so that the athlete can experience greater wholeness.

The visits to the hemispheres and the head center, however, bring the best and quickest results. The athlete usually experiences one hemisphere as "stronger and/or better" than the other. This imbalance is at the heart of a slump in performance in any sport. Maximizing brain functioning is absolutely basic. When your hemispheres become acquainted and balanced, it makes a great difference in anything you do. The input of both hemispheres, with the separate, but complementary functioning, is necessary for consistent high-quality performance.

The head center becomes a special place where balance, centeredness, and groundedness are experienced as a reality. The center (roughly the mid-brain area) becomes a perfect practice place for all components of a sport. In addition, when you experience an open crown through which stream cosmic resources, you not only feel your best, but you also do your best in all endeavors.

PERFECT PRACTICE INSIDE THE MIND

After you have visualized hitting a perfect golf shot, practice it in your mind over and over as much as you wish. Do this exercise with all of your clubs. You also may want to sense, see, or feel one of your favorite golf courses in your head center. Practice hitting only your own best shots. Don't waste time on unrealistic dream shots. If you should hit an imperfect shot, imagine something in your memory bank erasing it. Then hit the shot correctly ten times. Finally, hit the shot again into your imaginary hole.

PERFECT PRACTICE AT THE PRACTICE RANGE

Pick a club you wish to use (or let a club pick you for a change). Stand before the ball, close your eyes, and practice the shot you wish to use perfectly in your head center (or an alternate comfortable place.) Sense, see, or feel yourself hitting the shot perfectly ten times. Open your eyes, position yourself in a comfortable stance, and then hit the ball. If the shot is relatively perfect in actuality, hit as many more as you can. Never hit two bad shots in a row. If you hit a poor shot, stop and erase the inferior actual shot from your memory bank. Then practice in your head center again until you hit several perfect shots. Try another practice shot. If it is near perfect, replicate it for as long as you can.

CONCLUDING REMARKS

To illustrate Transformational Fantasy, I have used golf primarily because Bob chose it and because it is an individual game and you can practice all its components. But the process can be used with any sport, and I have done so with baseball, swimming, tennis, gymnastics, skiing, horsemanship, track, and football.

Transformational Imagery is a creative, therapeutic, healing process. It is concerned with the whole person—spirit, mind, emotions, and body. Today, the competitive edge goes to the individual who has developed all of these aspects.

In addition to the competitive edge is the "enjoyment edge"—the feeling of flow that results when all aspects of a person are working harmoniously together: muscles and limbs, and the inner guiding images generally too fast for conscious thought and the spiritual intentions.

REFERENCES

1. J. T. Shaffer, Transformational Fantasy, in *Anthology of Imagery Techniques,* A. A. Sheikh (ed.), American Imagery Institute, Milwaukee, Wisconsin, pp. 325-360, 1986.
2. J. T. Shaffer, *Be Your Own Coach, Therapist, Healer,* The Well-Being Center, St. Louis, Missouri, 1988.

CHAPTER 13

Transformational Fantasy in Sports: A Case Study

ANNA A. SYLVAN

Inability to progress beyond a plateau is common among people training for a sport. Transformational Fantasy was used to help Melissa, a fourteen-year-old equestrian, overcome the fears that prevented her from developing her potential.

Melissa is a typical fourteen-year-old girl. She is outgoing and friendly. She plays the flute and is doing well at school. Melissa also loves horses and would like to compete someday in the Olympics in the equestrian events. She has been riding horses for four years, but two years ago, she reached a plateau and has been unable to advance to the next stage.

Melissa's mother spoke to me of her concern with Melissa's lack of progress, but was unable to give any clue as to what might be the underlying problem. She had noticed that Melissa's moods changed on the day prior to each riding lesson. From a cheerful, care-free teenager, she changed to an anxious, impatient, and often withdrawn individual.

My goals in working with Melissa were to find the cause of her inability to move forward in riding and to help her regain some self-confidence and motivation.

The first meeting lasted one hour during which I tried to establish a friendly relationship with Melissa and learn more about her as a person, especially her love for horses.

Melissa started her "love affair" with horses six years earlier, when she got her first pony from her grandparents. She fell in love with Lucky the first time she saw him and even now, although she has now outgrown her four-legged friend, she considers him her first love. Her childhood was normal and uneventful, with loving and supportive parents. Melissa was cooperative, although not completely convinced that anything could help her become a better rider. She eventually admitted that she felt uptight about her riding lessons and promised to listen to my suggestions.

We met again five days later, one day before her scheduled riding lesson. I immediately sensed her uneasiness, but did not question her about it. Her mother had told me that Melissa typically became defensive and insisted she was fine when questioned on such days. Melissa displayed the same defensiveness when I asked her how she was doing in riding lessons. However, she was a cooperative subject and was able to relax after a short time.

Our first trip was to the left brain. She found the place a hostile, dark field, with no colors or light. At first, she refused to go any farther, but finally agreed to go on if she could find a friend who would hold her hand. I asked her if she had any particular friend in mind, and she decided on Lucky, her pony. Holding him by the mane, she began her exploration, trying to find her way through a pile of twisted and coiled barbed wires that covered the ground.

Suddenly Melissa became quiet. "What is it, Melissa?" I asked. "I am watching her," she answered. "Who are you watching?" I asked. "There is a little girl there. She is sitting on a horse." Melissa hesitated. "Is she riding?" I wanted to know. "No, she can't because of the wires. But she is afraid to move because if she does she is going to hurt herself on the wires. What is she going to do?"

Melissa started crying. She wanted me to help the little girl and I agreed to go back with Melissa to the left brain and rescue the child. She held my hand all the time and step by step, we walked to the horse, and Melissa lifted the girl up and carried her to safety. I told Melissa she was very brave to have done what she did. "I had to," she said. "She was there all alone and no one knew that she was there."

Melissa asked me about the right hemisphere with some reservation, "Is the right brain going to be as scary as the left? If it is, I don't want to go in there." I promised her that the right one would be a much friendlier place and that we would go there the next time we met. But, Melissa had some time that day, and although she was exhausted from her left brain experience, she wanted very much to visit her right hemisphere.

So, our next journey was to her right brain. Melissa did not want to take any chances and decided to go there with her pony again. She found the place a sunny, cheerful meadow, covered with soft grass and flowers. She took a deep breath and smelled the soft aroma of the flowers.

"I love it here?" she exclaimed. "May I go anywhere I want in the right brain?" she asked. I sensed her excitement and curiosity. She displayed the same excitement she had when she told me about Lucky. We were on the right path.

"I want to ride Lucky," Melissa said, "here in the right brain. It is so pretty. Look, the grass is so green and it smells so good!" So, she took off on Lucky and played there for several minutes.

"Melissa," I interrupted, "let's try some jumps on the horse."

"Great! I can see some fences that I can jump over. Look, I can do it! I can really do it. And it isn't as difficult as I thought."

She was ecstatic. She displayed no fear and no inhibitions. She let the horse guide her and trusted herself.

Later Melissa talked to me about the feelings she experienced when she entered the right brain. "It was the most wonderful and happy occasion. I only wish I could feel this way when I ride my real horse." I promised to help her to gain that feeling.

After that first visit to her right hemisphere, Melissa looked forward to our next meeting with real enthusiasm. She found the meadow in the right brain a place of total freedom. She did not fear anything while there and actually started making plans for the Olympics. She said it was the first time she really believed she could make it to the Olympics. "Wouldn't it be wonderful," she exclaimed, "if I could train in my right brain?" I told her that we were going to find the place in her mind that will give her the security and self-confidence she needed to succeed.

Suddenly, Melissa noticed someone in her right brain. It was a little girl riding a horse. I encouraged her to talk to this girl, and Melissa eagerly agreed. They found they had a lot in common. They became friends and promised to ride horses together. Melissa's little friend had her own fears to cope with, and Melissa asked me if I was willing to help her, too. I agreed, of course. The little girl revealed to Melissa a painful childhood experience. When she was six years old, she got her pony from her grandparents. Shortly after that, she sneaked to the barn by herself and tried to ride the pony. She knew she was not allowed to ride without supervision, but her desire was more than she could handle and she decided to take the chance. The next thing she remembered was lying on the ground in shock and in pain. She could not cry and she was afraid to tell anybody what had happened, and so she had carried that pain with her through the years.

Melissa was crying. I hugged her and asked her to hug the little girl who was in pain. They fell into each other's arms, comforting and consoling each other. It was several minutes before Melissa could speak to me. I asked her about the little girl's experience.

"It happened to me so many years ago," she said, "that I had forgotten about." But the little girl could not forget it, and now Melissa understood why she was always afraid to ride horses.

I suggested to Melissa that whenever she felt afraid, she should find the little girl inside her and assure her of her love. Melissa said she would follow the suggestion, and appeared very calm when we said goodbye at the end of the session.

The next session was to be spent cleaning the left brain, and I needed Melissa's cooperation to do it. She arrived a half-hour early so that we could have extra time together.

I said, "Melissa, I want you to take your little friend, and go to your left hemisphere."

"Do I have to?" Melissa was hesitant, but I promised her that she would be all right and suggested she take Lucky along.

The three of them entered the dark, cold place. From Melissa's facial expression, I knew that it was a very difficult task. I guided her step by step, helping her to find her way around.

"It is so dark here, I don't see anything," Melissa objected. "Turn the lights on, Melissa," I suggested. "Oh, yes, it is better now." She appeared calmer. "What do you see, Melissa? I asked. "I can't step anywhere. There are wires everywhere. I don't know what to do." "Well," I said, "why don't you, Lucky and your friend start cleaning the place?"

The suggestion worked. Melissa was able to find a huge dumping place, where they put all the barbed wires. Next, they swept the floor. It was easy as the girls employed some magic and Mr. Wind blew the dust and debris out in a second! I could see that Melissa was having fun. She realized that she is not helpless, but has a power within herself to change and to improve.

"You see," Melissa said, "this place was impossible to ride in. All the wires around and stuff made the little girl scared."

"How is it now?" I asked.

"Well, we could plant some flowers," Melissa suggested. And so, the left brain became a wonderful place where the two girls could ride horses and play together.

It was time to introduce Melissa to another concept—balancing the brains, or finding the Center, where both brains cooperate and function in harmony. Melissa did not have any problems connecting her two hemispheres. She found a doll house in the Center and filled it with her toys. Now she can go there knowing she will find peace and security. I asked her about her feelings. She liked her doll house and she promised to take me with her one day for a cup of tea. Finding the dollhouse was particularly important, because she could take her little friend there in moments of distress.

I asked Melissa if she would like to ride her horse in the middle, and she answered, "I have to open the door to the meadow first. Then I will take Lucky and my friend and we will take a ride."

"Which meadow," I asked, "the one on the left or the one on the right?"

"It doesn't matter," she replied. "I like them both."

Later that week Melissa's mother called and thanked me for what I had done for Melissa. "She is a different child," she said. "There was no anxiety before her riding lesson. She shared her riding experience with the family and didn't mind admitting her mistakes. She is not defensive and took the trainer's advice with pleasure."

The last hour with Melissa was devoted to reinforcing the material that we had covered. Melissa was eager to show me her progress in riding, so I promised to come to watch her riding. Prior to that time, she had refused to have any spectators around while riding a horse. I could see that she had built her self-confidence, and the fear of falling off the horse, although still real, did not bother her any more.

I asked her how she felt about riding now.

"It's easy," she replied. "I see myself as a part of the horse. I am no longer separate from the horse; we are one."

She seemed to understand the concept of excellence. She understood that to succeed one has to:

* work on self-confidence;
* be motivated;
* balance the hemispheres for perfect cooperation; and
* practice mentally and only when the mental picture is perfectly executed, practice in the physical form.

My sessions with Melissa lasted only four weeks. I have heard from her only occasionally, because she is busy preparing for her first competition. Her trainer told me about her incredible progress. She has been moving forward without the problems that he observed before. Her fears have disappeared and she doesn't view her mistakes as personal defeats, but rather as learning opportunities on the way to excellence.

CHAPTER 14

Mental Imagery in Enhancing Performance: Theory and Practical Exercises

ERROL R. KORN

Physical training has long been the foundation for insuring optimal physical performance. Until recently, little attention has been given to mental training. The Russians and former East Germans have been using mental training techniques for several decades with amazing results. Psychotherapists at the Advanced Mental Training Institute in Russia, feel that the ordinary athlete realizes less than half of his/her potential unless the powers of the mind are used [1].

In this chapter, I will define and classify imagery and show how it can work to enhance physical performance and what kinds of physical performance can be enhanced. In the Appendix, specific mental exercises are given for use by individual athletes or groups of athletes.

THE RELATIONSHIP BETWEEN THE MIND AND THE BODY

Any attempt to separate the mind from the body is artificial. To have controlled muscular performance, nerve impulses must arise in the brain before they are distributed peripherally. Injuries and disease to the brain cause muscle dysfunction just as definitely as injuries to the muscles themselves.

The scientific rationale for the use of mental processes, such as imagery, in physical performance date back to studies of more than sixty years ago, when it was demonstrated that if one imagines a physical activity, the muscles involved are stimulated [2]. More recent work has validated these initial findings that the response of imagery was specific to the muscle group necessary to execute the task [3-5].

It was formerly thought that within a few months after birth, humans had a full complement of neurons and new central nervous system neurons did not develop.

However, research by Dr. Solomon Snyder and Dr. Jeffrey Nye demonstrated that human neurons can, indeed, multiply [6], and other research indicates that one of the stimuli for this nerve growth can be mental imagery [7].

There are numerous studies available at this time, both pro and con, with respect to imagery and physical performance, and these are well documented in the other chapters of this volume. However, there are methodical problems with many of these studies and, in order for the scientific evidence to become more valid, a more acceptable model of imagery and sports psychology needs to be developed [8].

For the true scientist, anecdotal evidence holds little credibility. However, when these reports reach staggering numbers some credibility must be given to them. References [4-9] relate many ways that major athletes have used imagery and have, in fact, stated that imagery was a major factor in their success.

The great golfer Jack Nicklaus stated that the mental image was 50 percent of his golf game. He images the ball where he wants it to finish (see End Result Imagery, p. 218) and then he uses, as a mental rehearsal, images of the path, trajectory, and shape of the ball during the shot [9].

John Brodie, former quarterback of the San Francisco 49ers, describes situations that unmistakenly involve alternate states of consciousness, such as dramatic improvement in perception and coordination, and an uncanny type of clarity. In addition, he had the experience of time distortion, leading to the perception of the entire game unfolding as though in slow motion [9].

The British golfer Tony Jacklin describes an alternate state of consciousness that he calls a "cocoon of concentration." In this cocoon he achieves a zen-like state where he is "living fully in the present, not moving out of it . . . involved at what I am doing at that particular moment" [9].

Susan Clements, former national woman sky-diving champion, relates that her dives or maneuvers are possible by the use of mental processes alone [9].

Imagery was a significant part of the training of Arnold Schwarznegger, who talked about the value of mental control over matter, and significantly used End-Result Imagery. He envisioned the physical maneuvers as a follow-through mechanism and to remind himself of the image he already had in mind [9].

Several years ago, the East German shot-putter, Udo Beyer, had a personal record of 68 feet. His coaches did kinesthesiology studies of him and were able to calculate he could potentially perform a 72-foot shot-put. They then created a graphic video image of the form he would need to put the shot 72 feet. In an alternate state of consciousness he watched this image and eighteen months later he was putting 72 feet. This increase of 4 feet in one and a half years is virtually unheard of at this level of world class competition [10].

ACTIVE RELAXATION

To use imagery to its greatest potential, you must first learn how to render your mind completely receptive by quieting, as much as possible, external distractions and internal chatter. The techniques used to produce this state have been given many names; such as, progressive relaxation, meditation, hypnosis, autogenic training, relaxation response, and biofeedback. However, evidence exists that these names do not describe states at all, but rather describe the subjective or psychological responses of those states or the methods used to produce them [11].

The physiologic changes produced by these techniques are remarkably similar no matter what name they are given [12-16]. These changes are the exact opposite of the stress response and thereby are appropriately called relaxation. The essential features needed to achieve these results are: 1) quiet environment, 2) repetitive mental device, 3) passive attitude and, 4) comfortable position [17].

We have associated the steps, sequences, and strategies needed to use relaxation and imagery into a paradigm, that we call AIM [18]. The "A" of the AIM strategy is Active Relaxation. Methods for producing this state appear in Appendix I. Active relaxation decreases oxygen use by the body (a more relaxed state), decreases respiratory rate, decreases heart rate, produces alpha or quiet rhythm on the EEG (electroencephalogram), decreases blood pressure, decreases muscle tension and increases blood flow to the brain [11, 16-22].

In learning Active Relaxation alone, even without the use of imagery, the athlete can derive considerable benefit. Excessive stress is as detrimental to the athlete as it is to all members of society [11, 19]. At both very low and very high levels of stress, performance decreases and only at narrowly defined stress levels is performance optimal. When the athlete experiences relaxation on a daily basis, he/she prevents the adverse effects of the unsustained stress that adversely affects performance.

IMAGERY

Gordon defined imagery as a sensation in the absence of the object or situation that usually results in that perception [20]. For example, if you can imagine an apple without the apple actually being there, you experience a mental image. Under certain situations the dividing line between images and perceptions (seeing an apple when an apple is really there) may be quite vague [21].

Imagery has played a significant role in the development of humanity. Studies of the way children think imply that humans thought in images long before the development of language [22]. In fact, the thinking mode typical of pre-verbal children, primary process thinking, actually relies on images [23].

Thoughts and ideas are encoded in images. Language developed as a response to the human need to make those thoughts and ideas known to others [24]. If the image is the foundation of language, it is not surprising that the phrase, "a failure to communicate," is so familiar. When a person communicates with another, the listener changes the speaker's words into images. Words are a vehicle for communicating images and these images are patterns or symbols within everybody's framework of consciousness. A good example of this is the differences between Socrates and Protagores, who both had different modes of imagery.

> If one is auditory-linguistic, he should never enter into an argument with a motor-linguistic person, as in all topics except for the most concrete facts, either will inevitably fail, completely, to understand the other. Words and their meanings are created and validated in a social context, while images and their meanings are personal creations . . . [25].

Imagery has been erroneously equated with visualization, probably because visual external sensations provide approximately 85 percent of our subjective experience of the external world. However, in addition to a mind's eye, we also have a mind's ear (auditory imagery), a mind's body (kinesthetic imagery), a mind's tongue (gustatory imagery), and mind's nose (olfactory imagery) [26]. For imagery to be most effective, the athlete must use as many of the five senses as he/she can. In fact, in the original studies of imagery and electro-physiology of muscle, it was shown that for motor performance, kinesthetic imagery (touch, pain, temperature, position, sensation, and internal emotions) may be even more important than visual imagery [2].

AIM STRATEGY

In the previous section, I talked about the *AIM* Strategy. AIM is a sequence as well as a strategy; that is, "A" precedes "I," "I" precedes "M."

Active Relaxation the "A" is the most important part of the AIM Strategy. As mentioned previously, relaxation protects us from stress, excessive amounts of which can be detrimental to physical performance. However, "A" serves another purpose. For imagery to be most effective, the individual must be in a state of relaxation; a state produced by active relaxation.

Imagery, End Result ("I"). End result consists of a specific, concrete image of the desired effect as having already taken place. Essentially, this is goal oriented imagery. The tennis player may image his/her serve as already having landed in the appropriate place in the service court. Individual athletes or members of a team, may image themselves as already wearing the championship jacket or ring. A weight lifter may see his name on the scoreboard, next to the successful weight he wishes to lift, indicating he has already accomplished that lift.

Mental Rehearsal ("M"). These are images of an actual or fantasized method by which an effect can be achieved. These are the types of images the athlete uses to enhance performance. For example, the slalom skier imaging the entire course, including all the turns and bumps, or the basketball player mentally imaging successful free-throw shooting.

The fantasized aspect of mental rehearsal is used to increase efficiency. For example, a soccer player wishing to perfect an in-swinger may image that the ball was connected to a curved rod of light extending from where the ball lies at the corner to where he wishes it to end in the net. When the ball is kicked, it follows the curve and destination of the light rod.

A golfer may imagine a string attached to one end of his/her ball and the other to the cup. When he/she imparts energy to the ball by tapping it with a putter, the string can retract into the hole putting the ball with it.

A runner may imagine a cord attached just below his/her navel, the other end wound in the distance, on a gigantic spool. As he/she ran, the spool would retract the cord, thus providing extra speed with less energy use. These "tricks," when practiced mentally, in a relaxed stated, can be used with amazing results during actual performance.

In addition, mental rehearsal ("M") may also consist of rehearsing an event in one's mind without a fantasy aspect. For example, the high jumper imagining every part of the jump, including the pre-preparation, the run to the bar, the actual jump, and the landing.

APPLICATIONS

The major applications of imagery in sports will be discussed in greater detail below. However, numerous other applications of imagery and physical performance are possible [27].

1. Develop the necessary level of competitive tension;
2. Physically improve precision and movement;
3. Increase awareness of body position movement through rehearsal;
4. Increase performance;
5. Help find flaws and isolate mistakes;
6. Improve speed and quality of learning simple and complex motor skills;
7. Increase awareness;
8. Restore energy;
9. Increase self-discovery and help make changes in other areas of one's life;
10. Motivation;
11. Ease anxieties and psychological blocks to performance;
12. Enable memory increases needed to learn the large amounts of information necessary in most sports;
13. Prevent injuries and enhance the immune system to affect healthy recovery from injury;
14. Heighten enjoyment of activity;
15. Decrease fear;
16. Change beliefs and attitudes;

17. Allow accurate analysis of the technical aspects of performance;
18. Teach cues to where to focus during the contest;
19. Enable escape from uncomfortable situations and distraction from anxiety-producing situations;
20. Provide a tool to promote self-awareness and understanding, and;
21. Offer a vehicle to tap new energy sources.

Relaxation

As mentioned earlier in this chapter and also alluded to in other chapters in this volume, the long-term effects of stress, as well as acute stress, cause anxiety and are detrimental to optimal athletic performance. The use of active relaxation *alone* can lead to successful alleviation of these problems [28]. For optimal performance, an athlete should practice active relaxation on a daily basis (see Appendix I).

Also, if he/she has specific anxiety problems related to performance, imagery should be added. The imagery may be as simple as the cues mentioned above (see Appendix I, Part 4), or as complex as a behavior modification type of desensitization rehearsal (for example, in relaxation, the athlete mentally rehearses performing in those situations that would create anxiety, such as, important performances, large crowds, or performing in the visitor's stadium. Rehearsing over and over, in active relaxation, will lead to calm performances when these actual situations arise). Psychologist Charles Garfield says that a major characteristic of peak performers is their ability to be both relaxed and productive, simultaneously [29].

Performance Enhancement

Lane demonstrated that imagery can be used for skill development and error correction [30]. Imaging problems not only allow errors to be discovered, but also afford the opportunity for corrections, resulting in problem correction at the time of actual performance. We agree with Lane that at lower skill levels, it is best for imagery to be guided by a coach or instructor using instructions emphasizing basic skills. Athletes at higher levels may indicate for themselves which elements of the skill they wish to work on and usually will be able to create their own imagery [4, 30].

Consistency and commitment are important. More benefit will be obtained by practicing these methods daily than by practicing them once a week for a longer period of time. Haphazard practice rarely leads to useful results [31].

Ability to control the image is more important than the vividness of the image, the imagery must do what you want it to do. If you are trying to improve free-throw shooting and in your imagery your free throws are missing, in actual practice, they probably will miss as well.

In any stage of skill development, negative thoughts and images may occur. If a negative thought appears, simply think "stop!" If the athlete consistently has uncontrollable imagery, then either this technique is not applicable to his/her training of there are basic, underlying psychological problems, such as fear of failure or fear of success, that may prevent success. These problems may need to be dealt with by other methods.

Sample performance enhancement imagery of both "I" (Imagery End Result) and "M" (Mental Rehearsal), appear in the appendices.

Concentration

Concentration or focused attention can be enhanced with relaxation and imagery. One of the most important techniques in enhancing concentration is the development of cues that can be used on the actual playing surface.

The first part of concentration is elimination of distractions. In nearly every sport there are multitudes of sound, sights, and physical distractions surrounding the event which can impede focus and performance. By preventing distraction, athletes will perform more optimally.

An example of the development of cues is given in Appendix I, Part 4. Cues can be developed for any sport. In golf, for example, you may have the image that, before the game begins, the act of selecting which golf balls you will play with is much like selecting which sights and sounds you will play with. You will only focus on those elements necessary in playing the game well.

In baseball you can use cues: You put on special shoes to play the game. These shoes are specially designed for a specific purpose. In the same way, the shoes are focused to a purpose, you may know that as you put on those shoes you can become more focused and concentrate, specifically, upon your activity and tasks within the game. Any time during the game you desire to have more concentration, merely thinking about your shoes and how they are focused to a purpose can slow you to become more focused in your performance [32].

The second part of concentration is focusing on the specific task that is the crux of optimal performance, for instance, kicking the ball accurately in soccer. Suggestions for soccer concentration may take the form of:

> The playing field is composed of lines and angles. You know the ball travels in the direction that is determined by the precise angle in which the ball is struck. You may find that you know, even without thinking about it, the precise angle at which the ball must be struck in order to travel to the desired place on the field. By taking a deep breath a few moments before you kick the ball, you can develop a deep concentration within you. That concentration can allow your foot to meet the ball at the exact angle you already know will cause the ball to go where you wish it to [32].

Such suggestions tie together images that are already familiar to the athlete with images of future actions. Such cues are more easily accepted and more likely to develop the desired responses. In conversing with the athlete, information will be elicited that will enable the trainer to develop related images. If, for example, the soccer player also enjoyed playing billiards, the trainer might relate the angle of the soccer kick to the rebound of the billiard balls. Taking material from the athlete's repertoire of experiences to create suggestions and images, will make the images more powerful and more successful.

Strength and Energy

There are many sports where strength is important and in all sports energy is important. Garfield related how, in one session, imagery and relaxation methods enabled him to improve vastly his weight lifting performance [29].

Hypnotherapists have used the technique of catalepsy (a process in which a person becomes rigid) to increase strength on a temporary basis. Catalepsy merely consists of forceful contractions of opposing muscle groups. The most graphic example of this is the stage hypnotist's induction of total body rigidity, usually in a small female. While supporting such a rigid subject at the ankles and head on two chairs, a hypnotist can stand on her body.

Aikido and other Oriental martial arts have emphasized the use of mental imagery and meditative states for their effectiveness, including such extraordinary feats of strength as the brick breaking of karate masters [33].

A mental imagery script for energy may be found in Appendix III, Part 2.

Pain and Injury Control/Rehabilitation

By enhancing physical performance, enhancing the effects of training, increasing strength and flexibility, and increasing concentration and present awareness, imagery methods will prevent injuries. Also, if injuries do occur, imagery techniques may be used for enhancement of the healing process, rehabilitation, and pain control [11, 34].

Imagery should not be used indiscriminately for pain control. Although it is a powerful pain control technique, imagery could mask a significant injury. Only after proper medical diagnosis and therapy have been instituted should these methods be used for pain management.

Imagery appears to provide the framework from which relearning motor skills can be maximized. Lang stated, "Evidence suggests that during imagery recall of a just-completed perceptual task, organ changes and muscular adjustments occur that are the patterns observed during the original perceptions [35]. I have previously presented case studies demonstrating how the processes encompassed in the AIM Strategy could be used in physical rehabilitation for the goals of relaxation, maximizing returning function, relief of anxiety, aiding management of depression, increasing motivation, increasing self-confidence, and relieving pain [34].

I use the AIM Strategy for pain management in a similar fashion to enhancing athletic performance. That is, I use A-I-M as a sequence. The athlete is first trained in active relaxation ("A") resulting in a generalized reduction in anxiety/stress level, thereby leading to generalized reduction in pain perception. Associated with this early training, I use relaxation images such as the one in Appendix I, Part 3. Many people do not need more than this for pain control.

Subsequently, if necessary, I provide the ("I") of the AIM Strategy, namely, imagery/end result. The image may be that of the trainee imagining him/herself complete, active, and functional, doing those things and activities he/she was able to do before the injury, and even doing them better. (See Appendix II).

After the trainee has become reasonably proficient in ("I") he/she may learn mental rehearsal ("M"). Mental rehearsal images for pain control appear in Appendix IV. These images can also be found on pre-recorded tapes [36, 37].

FURTHER COMMENTS

All of the effects of imagery in enhancing physical performance, achieving goals, concentration, pain, relief, and injury healing are obtainable and achievable, but they do require practice. The Russians devote as much time to mental training as they do to physical training. We should not expect that any less of a commitment will produce the same kind of results.

That does not mean the novice and occasional athlete need to practice imagery techniques every day. However, for optimal results of imagery, I feel the athlete should devote as much time to the AIM sequence as they do to actual physical practice.

I recommend that all trainees experience ("A") Active Relaxation on a daily basis. This will help the individual in everyday life, as well as with athletic performance.

There is individuality in using active relaxation. Each person has different needs and you will find that some days require more relaxation than others just to reach the same level of calm.

Set aside a particular time of the day that you are most likely to be able to perform relaxation. This develops the habit of using that specific time for relaxation. In the beginning, it is best to set aside separate times for active relaxation and imagery, because the most important element, initially, is relaxation.

After you have experienced active relaxation and can relax easily and quickly, you can then combine the relaxation exercise with imagery by first spending about five minutes exclusively relaxing your body. After that, spend ten minutes with the imagery exercise and then the remainder of the time (total of 20 to 30 minutes) in relaxation, the last segment makes sure the imagery actually sinks into the subconscious mind.

Be certain that you take the necessary time to develop relaxation in your body and mind before you begin your imagery exercises because, by doing this, you will find a much richer experience and will produce faster and more profound results with your imagery. When using ("I") Imagery/End Result, I find that it is more effective to work with one or two goals at a time. One tactic is to work on one goal, exclusively, the first week. Then, in the second week, begin *also* to develop imagery for the second goal. In the third week, work on the new goal only. In the fourth week, the cycle repeats.

When you gain proficiency in developing imagery, you will find that you can close your eyes for a few moments just about anywhere and begin imagining clearly, even in the midst of noise and crowds. When you have developed a specific plan for mental rehearsal and imagery and are repeating specific imagery sequences for reinforcement, it will be easy to take several deep breaths, close your eyes and re-institute a mental picture you are familiar with.

Another anecdotal but quite dramatic story about imagery, as well as commitment, is found in the story of a nineteen-year-old Chinese pianist named Liu Shih-kum. In 1958 he won second place in the International Tchaikovsky Competition, placing only second to Van Cliburn.

He then returned home to China and by the mid 1960s, he was an established concert pianist. Then, Mao Tse-Tung and the cultural revolution came along. Everything Western influenced fell into disfavor and Western music was one of its victims. Pianist Liu, for refusing to renounce the music he loved, was deemed an enemy of the people and thrown into jail. He was locked away where no one could see him and was beaten repeatedly. From the beating he fractured a bone in his right forearm.

For six years he languished in a tiny prison cell and was given no books to read, no paper to write on, and worst of all, no piano.

Then, one day, for propaganda purposes, he was released from jail and requested to perform in Beijing with the Philadelphia orchestra. That request came from Mao, the very man responsible for his fractured arm and jail sentence.

He did play with the Philadelphia orchestra and he played brilliantly, even though he had not touched a piano for six years.

The fact that he survived is, in itself, remarkable; that his hands survived, as though they never stopped playing, was called astonishing. In prison he was denied a piano and even denied paper which might have permitted him to recapture the music he lost. Yet, Liu had something invaluable in the prison cell, something that produced notes of music and a piano keyboard. For more than six years he practiced his music in his vivid disciplined imagination, on a piano no one could see [38].

APPLICATIONS FOR TEAM SPORTS*

One of the most powerful features of group imagery is the cohesiveness and team spirit it can engender [39]. However, group imagery is one of the most under-utilized techniques available to coaches, managers, and others who work with sports teams. In hypnosis literature, group hypnosis was proven to be as, or more, effective than individual hypnosis. Imagery, therefore, may be shown to be, at least, equally effective when used in a team situation.

In team sports, cohesiveness is usually more important than the individual abilities of the members. Any method that will increase this cohesiveness should help team performance. Group practice of relaxation seems to have an enhancing quality. Group consciousness tends to be raised and, furthermore, some individuals whose experiences are not very profound alone have more profound experiences in the group milieu.

Tape recordings or actual live guided relaxation and imagery can be used in a group setting. For examples of this, please see Appendix VIII. End Result Imagery, such as the football team imaging themselves wearing the championship rings, is extremely effective for goal achievement.

Specific skills, to all players, may be taught by specific process images. The entire team may then be subdivided according to specific skills or position. For example, all the goalies on a soccer team can undergo group imagery techniques suitable for their specific positions.

As a word of caution, anyone leading group imagery sessions, as well as anyone leading individual group imagery sessions, should accentuate the positive. A classic story is told of the Hall of Fame pitcher for the then Boston Braves, Warren Spahn, pitching against the New York Yankees in the World Series. The legendary pitcher was on the mound with the score tied, two men on base, and two outs at a critical part of the game and the Series.

The manager walked out of the dugout to give Spahn motivating advice, "Don't give him a high outside pitch." With no time to analyze what the opposite of that ill-fated advice would be, he threw the ball and, sure enough, it was a high, outside fast ball and the smack of the bat signaled the arcing home run that followed, which gave the Yankees the win.

Later, Spahn could not understand why anyone would try to motivate someone with a reverse of an idea. This very interesting story illustrates the fact that negative images and expectations are as damaging as positive ones are constructive. Focusing on negative expectations generally brings about that which we hope to avoid.

This focus on negative expectancy often begins quite early in childhood. When we are first learning to ride a bicycle we may see a rock in the middle of the road

*Co-authored by George J. Pratt.

ahead and try to avoid the rock by thinking, "Look out for the rock, gotta miss that rock, better not hit the rock," and slowly and steadily, most assuredly we run right into the rock.

Coaches will increase the likelihood of a positive outcome if they coach to "pitch the ball low and inside," and provide the images of positive expectation. This positive aspect of this self-fulfilling prophecy cannot be over emphasized. It is a crucial component of the imaging program.

Our "cognition" or thoughts affect our moods and our moods influence our reality [40]. Burns's "Feeling good" points out that people create for themselves what they imagine and say to themselves in their "self talk" [41]. For this reason, it is important for individuals implementing group imaging experiences to provide positive material that the players can develop and maintain positive self-talk, both on and off the playing arena.

In order for a group imagery program to be most effective, the team must be assessed to determine the goals to which the imagery will be directed. When the problems have been isolated and the goals determined, then appropriate images for the group can be constructed that utilize the components of the game, the players individual environments and backgrounds, and other symbols, such as team colors or logos that will serve as cues to remind them of the effects of the imagery sessions.

Finally, we would suggest that the imagery language be choice-oriented. Language such as "maybe you'll" and "perhaps you'll" are better words than "you should" and "you will." Such open-ended and permissive language is less likely to be objected to and interpreted as controlling. Also, the open-ended language and the offering of choices tends to promote more individualization of the imagery by the players.

While imagery may not be a "quick fix" it can have a lasting and winning effect to bring a team closer together. To utilize the body and the mind to the maximum is a winning approach in team sports and suiting up the imagination can be like having a twelfth man on a football team. George Bernard Shaw said "Imagination is the beginning of creation. You imagine what you desire, you will what you imagine, and, at last, you create what you will."

For those interested in a complete outline of an in-depth, specific program in the use of imagery in groups, see [42].

As children, we used mental images to learn physical skills such as walking. We observed others walking, developed a mental image of the activity, fit our own consciousness into that mental image, and then acted upon the image physically, that is, we attempted to walk. As our own physical behavior approached the mental template, we then actually began to walk. Most great athletes, either consciously or unconsciously, use these mental powers to enhance the learning and perfection of physical skills.

APPENDIX

For personal and professional uses, I suggest the trainee first learn a method of inducing active relaxation "A" (Appendix I, Parts 1 and 2) and then fortify this with general relaxation images. (Appendix I, Part 3). Once this has been practiced and perfected, "I" Imagery End Result and "M" Mental Rehearsal, can be added to the experimental session.

Basic Guidelines for Using Imagery:

1. Practice and perfect active relaxation ("A").
2. Use "I"—Imagery, End Result first, because it's usually more powerful and longer lasting. Because it may take longer for end result imagery to be effective for more urgent needs, introduce Mental Rehearsal "M."
3. Have confidence in the imaging process because the initial changes may be subtle and difficult to recognize.
4. Make a commitment to the process if you want the maximum effects of imagery. This commitment means *daily* practice.
5. The creation of an image, in all five senses, is more successful than images in only one sense, such as, visualization alone.
6. It is more important for you to be able to control the image than for the image to be vivid and life-like. The image is a sensory method by which we "program" the unconscious part of the brain to affect the multiple changes required to bring the image or idea to fruition. The image also should be dynamic (moving) rather than static (a still picture).

APPENDIX I — ACTIVE RELAXATION

1. *Active Relaxation*[1] [43]

This is a technique to induce active relaxation and should be modified according to the needs of the individual.

Move into as comfortable a position as you possibly can. The position can be seated with legs uncrossed and arms resting comfortably down by your sides. If you have hard contact lenses, please remove them and loosen all constrictive clothing . . . Simply close your eyes . . .

This is in itself enough to produce a quietness . . . and rest . . . and relaxation. Now, to experience even further comfort and relaxation, begin to breathe deeply . . . and as you do . . . pay particular attention to the sensations you experience as the air leaves your body. Let yourself feel that with every breath you take, every exhalation . . . you are breathing out tension . . . discomfort . . . stress . . . and strain. When you do that, you can feel the muscles in your body relax . . . most

---

[1] Copyright 1980, Errol R. Korn.

prominently in your chest, but also in your other muscles that may be particularly tense, such as shoulders . . . and neck . . . and back. It is just as though when you exhale, you exhale the air . . . and all your troubles . . . all your discomforts . . . and all your anxieties. You may hear noises and sounds in your environment . . . but you can use these noises and sounds to deepen your state of relaxation. In reality, when you breathe out, you really do eliminate tension . . . discomfort . . . and stress. Experience then what really does take place. With your breath, you eliminate toxins and waste products. Your lungs are one of your most efficient eliminators of waste . . . so just let yourself feel that with every breath you take . . . you are becoming more comfortable. With this process alone . . . you may be surprised to find that you can eliminate almost all the tension and discomforts . . . that you have accumulated. However, if there are still residual areas of discomfort or tension . . . you can eliminate them progressively . . .

Put your consciousness . . . your mind . . . into your toes. Consciousness does not have to be where most of us think it is, that is, in the head. We only perceive our consciousness in our head because the brain, the most concentrated organ of our consciousness, resides in your head. Even place your consciousness . . . or attention . . . anywhere in your body you want to. If you were to stub your toe . . . your consciousness would travel there instantly. At this time . . . just place your awareness there . . . not because you have to . . . but because you . . . want to. With your consciousness in your toes . . . simply let yourself experience whatever it is you experience when you think of the word . . . relax. It may be a heaviness . . . or lightness . . . or tingling . . . or numbness . . . or warmth . . . or coolness . . . or maybe something else. But even if you feel there has been no change, rest assured that at some level of your consciousness there is a change . . . a lessening of tension in that toe. It may be that this change is too subtle for you to experience at this time . . . but no matter whether you perceive it or not . . . it still takes place.

Let the relaxation spread, now, to the toes of the other foot . . . and whatever it is you feel . . . just let it spread upward through your feet . . . through the lower portion of your legs and into your knees . . . as though you were standing knee-deep in a swirling . . . warm . . . relaxing whirlpool tub. Now, allow the comfort and relaxation to spread upward into your thighs . . . and into your groin area. Let it spread through your pelvis and buttocks . . . into your abdomen and all the way up to your waist . . as though you are now standing waist-deep in that warm . . . comfortable . . . water. Allow your entire body, from your waist down, to be relaxed . . . comfortable . . . loose . . . and limp. In fact . . . you may be surprised to find parts of your body feeling so relaxed . . . you lose awareness of those parts. That's perfectly alright. Those parts are still there and functioning . . . just as your lungs and heart function when you are not aware of them. You can regain the awareness whenever you want to.

— (long pause) —

Now . . . let the comfort and relaxation spread upward into your upper abdomen and mid back . . . and into your chest . . . both front and back, so breathing, which has become relaxed to this point . . . becomes even more comfortable and relaxed.
— (long pause) —
Now, let the soothing wave of relaxation move into your shoulders, an area in which most of us hold a great deal of tension. Just let your shoulders . . . drop. If you are sitting . . . feel them being pulled down by gravity and . . . if you are lying down . . . just feel your shoulders melting into the floor.
— (long pause) —
Let the looseness and warmth and comfort travel from your shoulders . . . all the way down your arms . . . past your elbows . . . into your wrists . . . hands . . . and fingers. Feel your arms just dangling without substance . . . loose . . . and limp . . . like a rag doll.
— (long pause) —
Now . . . allow the comfort to spread into another area in which most of us hold a great deal of tension . . . your neck. Feel your neck become loose . . . and limp . . . and comfortable.
— (long pause) —
Feel the comfort spread into another area in which we hold much tension . . . and rarely realize it. Feel how good it feels to let the tension go from this area . . . so good you not only feel it in the local area . . . but also the rest of your face . . . head . . . and neck. The area I am referring to is your . . . jaw. Feel how good it feels to just let your jaw drop downward.
— (long pause) —
And now . . . let the comfort spread into your face . . . around your eyes . . . letting your eyes become relaxed . . . to the area of your temples . . . your forehead . . . and the top of your head. Allow your entire head and face to become comfortable . . . and relaxed.
At this point . . . your entire body should be loose . . . limp . . . and relaxed. If there is any residual discomfort present . . . take a few more breaths . . . and concentrate on that area of discomfort . . . until that part of the body is as comfortable and relaxed . . . as the remainder of your body.
Now . . . begin to take a few deep breaths again . . . and become aware of what it feels like when you inhale. Remember the importance of the substances that you take in with your breath. You take in food . . . but you can survive a long period of time without food. You take in water . . . but you can survive several days without water. However, you can only survive a few minutes . . . without that which you take in through the breath. Feel energy going back into your body . . . entering a body that is fully relaxed . . . and feel it not just in your lungs . . . but feel it spread from your lungs into every single cell of your body. Feel the energy and remember you can feel energetic and vigorous . . . at the same time . . . that you remain comfortable . . . and . . . relaxed. As you feel the

energy coming in . . . become more aware of the room that you are in, the time and place that you're experiencing. Become aware of your body and especially any body parts of which you may have lost awareness. And, whenever you are fully ready, you can open your eyes, feeling the benefits of all that you have just experienced.

2. *Alternate Method of Relaxation Using Benson's Relaxation Response* [17]

A. Sit quietly in a comfortable position.

B. Close your eyes.

C. Breathe through your nose. Become aware of your breathing. As you breathe out, say the word "one" silently to yourself. Continue the pattern: Breathe in . . . out, "one;" in . . . out, "one;" etc. Breathe easily and naturally.

D. Continue for 10 to 20 minutes. You may open your eyes to check the time, but do not use an alarm. When you finish, sit quietly for a few minutes, first with your eyes closed, and later with your eyes open. Do not stand up for a few minutes.

E. Do not worry about whether you were successful in achieving a deep level of relaxation. Maintain a passive attitude and permit relaxation to occur at its own pace. When distracting thoughts occur, try to ignore them by not dwelling on them and return to repeating "one." With practice, the response should come with little effort. Practice the technique once or twice daily.

3. *Safe Place Image*[2] [44]

The safe place is a general image used to intensify the benefits of active relaxation in overcoming the detrimental effects of the stress response. Think of the words peace . . . safety . . . comfort . . . and . . . happiness. Now . . . let your mind spontaneously take you to a place . . . that means as many of these things as possible to you. It may be a place that you go to frequently . . . or one that you have visited only in the distant past . . . or . . . maybe one that is totally imaginary. Stay with the first place that comes to your mind. Anything else is tricks being played on you by the conscious part of your mind . . . the part of your mind that says you can't do something . . . or puts judgement on things . . . or that leads you to an external, rather than an internal, experience. The first place . . . the one that came to you spontaneously . . . is the place to stay with . . . because that place appeared to you from deep down . . . inside . . . and is associated at some level of your being with comfort . . . with relaxation . . . with peace . . . and . . . with safety.

Appreciate the scene with all your senses. See it . . . or imagine it as vividly as you can. Hear the silence . . . appreciate the aromas . . . touch and feel the environment . . . and objects therein . . . and appreciate the tastes. Perceive above you . . . beneath you . . . and all around you . . . exploring in fine detail all the ingredients of the scene . . . whether it is outside . . . or inside a building.

[2] Copyright 1980, Errol R. Korn, M.D.

As you practice this image . . . this place becomes associated with the important . . . deep . . . parts of your mind . . . with the concepts of peace . . . safety . . . comfort . . . happiness . . . and relaxation. Over time, these associations will strengthen . . . to the point where you can go to this place mentally . . . and dissociate completely from what is happening to you in your waking state. You could feel comfort . . . when usually you would feel anxiety or pain. Later . . . as your practice increases . . . even in your waking state . . . simply *thinking* about this place . . . could institute all of the feelings of comfort . . . peace . . . safety . . . and relaxation that you experience now. Also, you could practice this image just by thinking of it several times . . . a day . . . in your usual waking state. Remember . . . every time you practice . . going to the safe place . . . the place becomes imprinted in your mind. As time goes by, it will become easier . . . to achieve the benefits of this image. Even more important is that each time the concepts and images become . . . more permanently fixed in your mind . . . and when they are there . . . they become active . . . creating changes in your life that are . . . beneficial . . . to you and lead you toward a realization of those changes.

4. *Cues*[3] [45]

A cue is a rapid technique to quickly bring back the image, the result of the image, and/or the state of experience (such as relaxation) that you experienced while you were training the cue. You use the cue when you are in a relaxed state, alone, to train relaxation or when you are in a relaxed state with the appropriate imagery to train that image.

Use one of the methods above (1 or 2) to induce relaxation. When you are in the relaxed state, if you want to cue relaxation, just use the safe place image, in 3 above. If you want to cue something else, just put yourself in a scene in which you are experiencing what you would like to cue. For example, you wish to feel great strength and energy. It may be a scene where this happened recently or one from the distant past. Or . . . if you wish . . . you can use a completely fantasized situation.

As you practice, bring this place to mind vividly. Use all your senses . . . see everything there is to see . . . listen to sounds . . . feel the sensations . . . and feel your own internal emotions. Appreciate any aromas . . . and tastes. Put yourself as completely into this place . . . as possible.

The more vividly you imagine yourself in this place . . . the more your mind will believe it is real . . . and . . . will associate this place with what it is you wish to achieve.

Now . . . that you are in this state of comfort and relaxation . . . a state in which you are building up a tremendous amount of energy, to be used when you return to your usual waking state . . . take your non-dominant hand . . . the left one in

[3] Copyright 1988, Errol R. Korn, M.D.

most people . . . and touch your thumb and a finger together . . . and don't let them come apart until I instruct you to do so.

As you spend these moments in this physical position, with your thumb and finger touching . . . your mind interprets this physical maneuver to be a signal of the way you feel at this moment . . . relaxed and comfortable. It also interprets this to be a signal of any goal you happen to be imaging at this moment.

In the future, after practicing this cue several times while in this relaxed state, just touching your thumb and finger together . . . while you are in your usual waking state, can bring on the experience you are now having. Eventually . . . with practice and use . . . this degree of comfort can be as profound as that you experienced while practicing in this relaxed state.

Now . . . let your thumb and finger move apart and allow your hand to completely relax.

5. *Enhancing Imagery*

For those of you who want to enhance your imagery, please refer to Dr. Sheikh's et al. article in this volume (Chapter 9). For an additional exercise, please use the one below[4] [45].

If you have difficulty conjuring an image, the following practice will be helpful for you. You may want to first . . . imagine a pet or a very good friend you had as a child. See that person or pet in a usual setting . . . allow the person or pet to move around . . . and interact with the person or pet. Also, experience any sounds you hear . . . touch . . . feel . . . and . . . smell.

— (long pause) —

Now develop a new image of the home you live in or any home that you have had in the past that you have a particular fondness for. Look . . . move around . . . hear . . . see . . . feel . . . and smell. If there is anything in the house to taste . . . by all means . . . go ahead and taste it.

— (long pause) —

Now, imagine a very special outfit or set of clothes that you have now . . . would like to have in the future . . . or have had in the past. Feel yourself put on the clothes and . . . look at yourself in the mirror . . . wearing the clothes . . . and imagine them from all angles and perspectives.

APPENDIX II — "I" — IMAGERY, END RESULT[5]

The "I" — Imagery, End Result — can be used for any type of goal, not only improvement in sports and physical performance, but also business performance, creativity, health maintenance, weight control. In fact, its use is virtually

---

[4] Copyright 1988, Errol R. Korn, M.D.

[5] Copyright 1988, Errol R. Korn.

unlimited. Imagine yourself sitting in front of a television set. You are very comfortable . . . in a comfortable chair. The scene in which you find yourself may be completely imaginary . . . or . . . it may be in a favorite room in your house . . . and . . . in a favorite chair.

Now . . . begin to think of a goal that you wish to achieve and think of it so you are in a scene . . . or . . . situation . . . which you could only be in if you had already achieved your goal.

Imagine seeing yourself . . . on this television screen . . . as though you are already this kind of person.

If your image is not very clear . . . you may begin to use the coarse and then . . . if necessary . . . the fine tuning mechanism of the television set. You may change channels if you wish. You can use any television control. All these methods are available to you . . . to enable you to clearly imagine your goal as having been achieved.

In this image use all your senses. See everything there is to see . . . particularly your attitudes and movements. Also, hear the sounds . . . and feel the temperatures . . . textures . . . and movements. Smell the aromas . . . Taste anything there is to taste.

If you are imagining looking at yourself in this scene, if you can do so now . . . instead of looking at yourself . . . actually feel your own consciousness emerge with . . . and become that person you are looking at. If you are not able to do this right now, you will be able to do it in the future. If you are able to accomplish this merging . . . then . . . you will experience the scene of the results of your action from the first person . . . rather than from the somewhat . . . second person viewpoint.

As you practice this technique in this state of relaxation . . . it becomes . . . imbedded deeply in your mind . . . and behavior changes that are necessary for you to enable you to achieve your goal [46].

APPENDIX III — MENTAL REHEARSAL

1. *Goal Setting*[6] [47]

I'd like you now to get a clear vision or . . . at least . . . a mind's eye image of a goal. You can use this exercise for one goal now and at later dates for other goals. Now imagine distractions . . . excuses . . . stumbling blocks . . . keeping you from reaching your goals. The distractions . . . excuses . . . and . . . stumbling blocks may be real ones or you may just imagine the words, excuses . . . stumbling blocks . . . distractions. You may imagine these interfering factors as people . . . or events . . . or actual blocks or boulders over which you stumble.

Now . . . imagine a large cylinder . . . large around enough for you to walk comfortably through and not very long. It can be transparent . . . so you can see

---

[6] Copyright 1988, Errol R. Korn.

outside . . . however . . . the cylinder prevents the distractions and excuses from pulling you away from your goal . . . and . . . prevents the stumbling blocks from interfering with your smooth passage towards your goal.

As you enter the cylinder, you may feel yourself being gently pushed from behind by an unseen . . . though strong . . . and gentle . . . force.

As you move through the cylinder you can look out at the distractions and excuses and stumbling blocks . . . but realize they no longer have any power over you.

— (long pause) —

As you find yourself approaching the midway point of the cylinder . . . instead of being gently pushed . . . you now feel your goal creating a magnetic force that gently pulls you toward it. And . . . at the end of this experience . . . you and your goal will be one.

— (long pause) —

If you practice this image in your relaxed state . . . you eventually will use it even in your waking state . . . just by thinking about it.

2. *Increasing Motivation and Energy*[7] [48]

All of us . . . no matter how physically trained we are . . . and no matter how happy we are . . . can experience some sluggish, let-down periods during physical activity and competition. If this happens . . . you can receive an energy boost by imagining a large, soft object . . . a friendly hand in the small of your back, pushing you forward . . . thus making your strides more effortless.

. . . or you may feel a string or rope attached to the front of you . . . being wound upon a long, large spool, way in front of you . . . pulling you effortlessly along your path.

. . . or you may want to imagine that your are walking on a cloud . . . so your feet don't even touch the ground.

All of these are quick methods to increase energy . . . decrease fatigue . . . and give you the mental and physical lift that you need to make you perform at your maximum ability.

3. *Positive Attitude*[8] [49]

Now . . . you are going to learn how to reset your attitude gauge. A positive attitude propels you forward, whereas a negative attitude keeps you stuck.

In your mind now, develop a picture of a gauge or scale. This scale could have numbers or just lines. Imagine the middle of the gauge as zero, with a negative side to the left and a positive side to the right. Next to the gauge is a lever . . . and as you move the lever upward . . . the gauge pointer moves to the right or to a more positive attitude. Likewise, as you push the level downward . . . the gauge moves to the left or more negative in attitude.

---

[7] Copyright 1988, Errol R. Korn, M.D.
[8] Copyright 1988, Errol R. Korn, M.D.

Now . . . allow yourself to imagine the gauge to be anywhere it wants to be. We have found, where the gauge appears spontaneously in your imagination . . . is a fairly good estimate of where your mood really is at this moment.

Experiment now, moving the lever downward first . . . so the gauge actually moves toward that of a more negative, pessimistic attitude. When you can do this . . . move the lever up . . . so the gauge moves toward a more positive attitude.

— (long pause) —

Now, spend several moments moving the lever back and forth, so you really get control over the gauge . . . and . . place the lever in such a way that the gauge remains in a positive mode.

— (long pause) —

Although it may sound silly at first as you practice this technique with the gauge and lever . . . the image actually becomes indelibly impressed upon your mind and becomes associated with the overall positivity of your attitude. If you find your attitude, at particular moments in time, decreasing to negativity . . . by closing your eyes and going through a short relaxation . . . you can then begin to move the lever to positivity. The more you move the lever to the positive side . . . and . . . the more you see it at the positive side . . . as manifested by the gauge being positive . . . the more your attitude will be positive.

After you have practiced this technique for a period of time, you may find that just by imagining the gauge and lever in your usual waking state . . . will confer attitude control on the short-term and eventually, the long-term. Remember, the more you practice this image of the gauge and the lever . . . the more indelibly intertwined it becomes with your attitude. The more you practice, the more proficient you will become. Use this every day . . . even in your usual waking state . . . to develop control and direction over your attitude.

4. *Positive Attitude II*[9] [49]

Negative thoughts can act like heavy weights to slow you down . . . increase the negativity of your attitude . . . and set you up for unhappiness. Here's a quick image you can use to unload these negative thoughts.

This technique is cognitive therapy . . . a technique that is very powerful in changing thought process . . . a powerful method to lead you to become a more positive, pessimistic person.

If you feel worn out . . . negative . . . and unhappy . . . imagine you are carrying a load of weights on your back. This is an analogy to Atlas carrying the entire world on his shoulders.

Imagine now . . . one by one . . . you begin to unload the weights . . . and . . . as you do, your posture becomes straighter, your back becomes straighter, your energy level builds, your outlook and expression become brighter, a smile begins

[9] Copyright 1988, Errol R. Korn, M.D.

to form on your face and you begin to move and walk around more breezily and easily.

As you remove these weights and become a more optimistic and happy and positive person, your mind interprets this mental maneuver to be a signal of the way you want to feel; happy, healthy, positive, and comfortable.

In the future, after practicing this image several times in your relaxed state . . . simply imagining unloading the weights while in your usual waking state can bring on optimism . . . happiness . . . and . . . lightness of effort. Eventually, with practice and use, this degree of optimism can be as profound as the positivity you experienced while practicing the technique in this relaxed state.

APPENDIX IV — PAIN MANAGEMENT I[10] [50]

1. *Exercise 1:* Imagine either a set of switches, somewhere in the middle of your body . . . in your chest or abdomen . . . or a rheostat or dimmer switch.

— (long pause) —

Entering the bottom of the switch are wires from all parts of your body . . . or . . . if you have one specific part of your body that you need to make comfortable . . . these wires can come from that part of the body. Imagine one wire emanating from the top of the rheostat or dimmer switch into your brain . . . the area in your body where pain registers and is perceived. This imagery light switch . . . or switches . . . or dimmer switch . . . controls the amount of pain sensation which eventually leaves the top of the switch . . . to be perceived in your brain. Imagine there is a large amount of pain energy coming through the switch . . . allow the switch and the wires to vibrate . . . feel their vibration . . . let the switch and the wires be colored with very vibrant colors and even hear the vibration. As you do this exercise, you may actually begin to feel the pain increase. That's okay . . . you're learning control . . . even if this control is in the opposite direction to which you wanted . . . at first.

— (long pause) —

Do this technique several times . . . now . . . turn the switch up so that more sensation goes through . . . and then turn the switch down so that less sensation goes through. Even if you don't feel any change in your pain at this time . . . rest assured that practice will send the message to your subconscious mind that this . . . indeed . . . is the means you want to develop to control your aches and pains.

— (long pause) —

If you practice this image in your relaxed state . . . you will eventually be able to use it even in your waking state . . . just by thinking about it.

[10]Copyright 1988, Errol R. Korn, M.D.

2. *Exercise 2*: Imagine a pail or bucket next to your dominant hand . . . the right hand in most of us. In this bucket, imagine a solution of a very powerful anesthetic agent . . . similar to novocaine . . . except that it has no allergic responses . . . and . . . it works by just placing your hands in the bucket.

Place your hand in the bucket so it is completely immersed in the solution, up to your wrist. Move your hand and fingers around in the solution. Begin to feel whatever it is you feel as the solution becomes active. It may be numbness or tingling . . . or it may be just a subtle change in sensation. Do this long enough until you feel a comfortable numbness in your hand.

— (long pause) —

Now . . . remove your hand from the solution and place it on the part of your body you would like to make comfortable. As you do this . . . feel the comfortable feeling move from your hand to that part of the body you want to be more comfortable. Leave your hand in this place until all the comfort has been transferred from your hands to that part of your body.

— (long pause) —

Now . . . slowly make a fist with your hand and as you do so, feel any residual discomfort in that part of your body you are making more comfortable . . . close your fist and hold the discomfort in your hand.

Now . . . place your hand to your side and open it to flick or throw away the discomfort.

At this point . . . you can repeat the entire procedure . . . that is, place your hand in the pail or bucket until it becomes comfortably numb . . . move your hand to the part of the body you wish to make more comfortable . . . and feel the comfort move completely from your hand into that part of your body . . . begin to make a fist with your hand and pull out any residual discomfort from your body.

You can do this as many times as you need to for as many places on your body that you need to, until you are as comfortable as you need to be . . . at this point in time.

At the end of this experience . . . normal sensation can return into your hand while the comfortable feeling can remain on the part of your body you wish to be more comfortable, for a long period of time. As you practice this technique in a state of relaxation . . . the technique becomes imbedded deeply in your mind . . . and will be more powerful . . . and more efficient as time passes.

APPENDIX V — MEMORY ENHANCEMENT[11] [51]

Events that are very striking when they occur leave deeper marks on our memories . . . and make these memories indelible. If you want to remember someone you have just met . . . you can relive or rehearse the meeting . . . and by

---

[11]Copyright 1988, Errol R. Korn, M.D.

reliving the event, it becomes indelibly imprinted on your mind. There is a metaphor that associations are like fishing hooks . . . they catch buried memories lurking below your consciousness.

Now . . . let's imagine an actual fishing hook, fishing for buried memory below your consciousness. Just for practice . . . think of a meal you had in the last week or two . . . one that you don't remember at the present time. Imagine the fishing hook going into the pool of memories . . . catching the memory . . . and reeling up the memory. The memory is the recollection of the contents of the meal. When retrieved, it may appear as a picture . . . or you may have hooked and retrieved the actual meal itself.

Practice this technique further for memories you would like to recall . . . such as the answer to a question you may not have been able to retrieve . . . someone's name . . . a particular fact . . . or anything else that is important to you. Remember again . . . by practicing these techniques while you are in the relaxed state . . . they will become more easily usable to your waking state. The more you practice . . . the more potent they become.

APPENDIX VI — DEALING WITH NEGATIVE EXPERIENCES [18]

From negative experiences, some people feel that subsequent attempts will also fail . . . thereby initiating a self-fulfilling prophecy. For example . . . if you have failed in a performance in any individual field event in track and field . . . you may have a bit of self-doubt on the next performance. These self-doubts can be mental land mines . . . just waiting for your next footstep.

You can use imagery to mine sweep these experiences and prevent them from interfering with your future actions. In this experience, you will learn to selectively forget the unsuccessful experience . . . you can learn everything you need from the experience . . . then forget about it.

Now . . . picture a negative experience that you have had . . . preferably related to your performance in an athletic endeavor . . . although . . . it can be related to anything in your life. For the next few minutes, picture this and learn from it what you can.

To clear your mind of the negativity of the event . . . imagine the event being placed in a trash bag . . . just as any item that is no longer useful. Mentally bundle the unpleasant experience . . . and . . . with the rest of the trash . . . drop it into the trash chute. Hear the bag fall and land in the receptacle far away from you. When you close the door of the chute, you have closed the door on that negative event . . . and . . . the memory of it is as far away as the bag . . . and . . . it gets further away as time passes.

APPENDIX VII — MENTAL REHEARSAL FOR SPECIFIC EVENT[12]

This is the most common type of mental rehearsal for your athletic performance. You can use this mental rehearsal in two ways. First, by going through your event, game, or strategy while in a relaxed state you can actually train yourself to perform in such a way that the desired goal will take place. Also, while you are doing this, you are training your ability to be able to use these techniques to ensure better performance at the time of performance. Therefore, just prior to your performance, especially in an individual event, but also in team events, take a few moments and replay in your mind the imagery you have been working with in the relaxed state.

Imagine yourself, now, at the scene of your event. As you have done with previous imagery exercises, put all of your senses into this scene. See everything there is around you. Feel the ground at your feet . . . the temperature . . . the surfaces around you. Also . . . feel your emotions. Note whether you are anxious . . . excited . . . motivated . . . lethargic . . . or whatever other feelings you have. This is a beginning to changing those sensations to the ones that would be most productive for you.

Hear the sounds.

Now . . . in a very slow . . . methodic way . . . maybe even in slow motion . . . picture yourself performing the event. Picture it from the first thought of the event . . . through the entire event . . . and after the event. Make sure that you have successfully completed the event . . . or game . . . so that your desired outcome has taken place. Remember . . . if you image losing . . . then you will lose. It is important that you image winning . . . or . . . the successful completion of your goal in any individual event. Do this several times now while continuing to relax.

— (long pause) —

The more you practice these steps in this safe . . . relaxed . . . place . . . the more you train yourself to be able to perform just as well . . . when the actual event does take place.

Now, you can further train yourself to be able to handle unexpected situations by using imagery as well. Begin to notice something that you hadn't counted on. Maybe it's a change in temperature . . . a change in strength or direction of wind . . . a different opponent . . . a hostile crowd. Just as you did before . . . put all of your senses into the scene. Notice in this image . . . how well you handle these unexpected changes in conditions. Feel the elation . . . and . . . satisfaction you have from overcoming these obstacles.

[12]Copyright 1988, Errol R. Korn, M.D.

APPENDIX VIII — IMAGERY FOR TEAMS*

I would like each of you to take five, six, or seven deep breaths. Now I would like you to get as comfortable as you can while you take one more, slow, deep breath, with your eyes either open or closed, as your prefer. Imagine a large rubber-band twisted until it is knotted up and tight. Perhaps imagine a rubber-band airplane like one you might have played with when you were a child and imagine it tightly wound up and knotted. Now with that image in your mind, imagine how your own body can be as wound up and knotted with tension and stress as that rubber-band can be. In that same way, imagine your body tightened and tense while you actually tense all the muscles in your body . . . that's right, go ahead right now and tense all your muscles including your face, toes, fingers, and stomach. Hold your breath while you do this.

Now, whether your eyes are relaxed and open or more comfortably closed, imagine how that rubber-band loosens and becomes unwound and relaxed when you release it . . . and as you imagine that rubber-band loosening and relaxing its tension, relax . . . release, and loosen your own tension as you exhale. Very good.

Take a few more deep breaths and as you exhale each breath imagine more and more the release of stress, tension, and pressure. You may notice you feel more relaxed and perhaps you may notice your heart is beating a bit slower. You might even feel a warmth, coolness, or a little tingling sensation in your feet or hands . . . that's perfectly normal and if you feel your breathing slow a bit, that's okay too.

Now you can continue to leave your eyes relaxed and comfortably closed if it feels good and, if it helps you, imagine a favorite place you have when you want to relax. Go ahead and imagine that favorite place right now. It may be the mountains, it may be a special room at home, it may be a beach or your favorite chair, it doesn't matter where your favorite place of relaxation is, just imagine that place right now as you take a few deep, slow, comfortable breaths.

As you imagine your favorite place of relaxation, I would like you to imagine colored ribbons, your team colors. Imagine them now circling your place of relaxation. If your favorite place of relaxation is outdoors the ribbons might be attached to trees or bushes, laying on the ground, or even floating in the air, gently suspended by a very fine group of supporting ties.

You may imagine the ribbons encircling your favorite place of relaxation as an imaginary fence that guards your relaxation spot, protecting you from both back and front and from side to side. While you are in your favorite spot of relaxation you can be as comfortable, relaxed, and confident as you can be, knowing that the ribbon surrounds you and guards you from being disturbed while you are in the center of your favorite place of relaxation.

*Co-authored by George J. Pratt.

Now I would like you to focus on the multicolored ribbon surrounding and guarding you against unnecessary and unwanted distractions . . . Imagine what that ribbon feels like in your hands . . . Imagine grasping the ribbon in your hands and imagine the sound it might make as you squeeze it and then release it. You may even notice as you release it you can also release even more stress and tension. Perhaps as you squeeze the ribbon it makes a sound like a crumbling piece of paper or it may only make a soft sound you can barely hear. It really does not matter what the sound is like, because you know that the ribbon and the colors of the ribbon can remind you of the comfort and relaxed security you would feel in your favorite relaxation area.

In fact, you may notice that when you see these colors at any time, they can remind you of how relaxed and comfortable you can be anywhere, at anytime. You don't even have to think about how the colors of the ribbons can remind you of the secure comfortable feeling of your relaxation spot. I would like you to be aware of how good this feeling of relaxation is right now and that you can return to the same feeling of comfort and relaxation anytime you wish . . . You may wish to practice this sort of imagery on your own, as well as when we are all together as we are right now, feeling comfortable and relaxed and together inside the ribbons right now. Very good.

COMMENTS ON THE ABOVE

This is a condensation, the complete imagery session would contain much more repetition and variations on the central theme. This also represents only one imagery session in a series, each session is built on the ones before it and draws on the previous material and reinforces that material.

Each group imagery session usually involves a five-point procedure that incorporates the following steps:

1. Relaxation. A state of relaxation, preferably in a quiet, distraction free setting.
2. At some level the autonomic nervous system is introduced to demonstrate the effect of this concentration and focus. For example, pulse rate and rate of breathing are normally autonomic body functions which can be deliberately changed to some degree through a relaxation state.
3. Positive mental imagery is introduced, both as mental rehearsal and imagery to the end result.
4. Imagery is used to access past successes to break slumps or to overcome performance anxiety. For instance, if a baseball player is having a batting slump, imagery can be developed which recalls the player's best batting season and provides a positive reference point to help the unconscious mind rehearse correct body-to-hand coordination.

5. Imagery is used to develop "cues" and to create relaxation or focus during specific times while in competitive play. Cues are symbols, actions, or events which trigger either a conscious or unconscious relaxation response. An example may be three deep breaths while in the huddle or a few seconds of eye closure in imaging a relaxing scene just before stepping into the batter's box. This provides a powerful extension of group imagery experience that can be accessed at any time, and even on a real-time basis.

REFERENCES

1. S. Ostrander and L. Schroeder, *Super Learning,* Dell, New York, 1979.
2. E. Jacobson, Electrical Measurements of Neuromuscular States During Mental Activities, *American Journal of Physiology, 96,* pp. 115-121, 1931.
3. B. D. Hale, The Effects of Internal and External Imagery on Muscular and Ocular Concomitants, *Journal of Sports Psychology, 5,* pp. 379-387, 1982.
4. D. V. Harris and W. J. Robinson, The Effects of Skill Level on EMG Activity During Internal and External Imagery, *Journal of Sports Psychology, 8,* pp. 105-111, 1986.
5. M. P. Anderson, Assessment of Imaginal Processes: Approaches and Issues, in *Cognitive Assessment,* T. V. Merluzzi, C. R. Glass, and M. Genest (eds.), Guilford Press, New York, pp. 149-187, 1988.
6. P. Radetsky, The Brainiest Cells Alive, *Discover,* pp. 83-90, April 1991.
7. A. Ahsen, Neural-Experimental Growth Treatment of Accidental Traumas, Debilitating Stress Conditions and Chronic Emotional Blocking, *Journal of Mental Imagery, 2,* pp. 1-22, 1978.
8. S. M. Murphy, Models of Imagery in Sports Psychology: A Review, *Journal of Mental Imagery, 3/4,* pp. 153-172, 1990.
9. G. Leonard, *The Ultimate Athlete,* Abon, New York, 1977.
10. M. Spino, Beyond Jogging: The Interspace of Running, *Celestial Arts,* Millbrae, California, 1976.
11. E. R. Korn and K. Johnson, *Visualization: The Uses of Altered States of Consciousness and Imagery in the Health Professions,* Dow Jones/Irwin, Homewood, Illinois, 1983.
12. E. R. Morse, J. S. Martin, M. L. Furst et al., A Physiological and Subjective Evaluation of Meditation, Hypnosis and Relaxation, *Psychosomatic Medicine, 5,* pp. 304-324, 1977.
13. G. L. Paul, Physiological Effects of Relaxation Training and Hypnotic Suggestion, *Journal of Abnormal Psychology, 74,* pp. 425-537, 1969.
14. S. M. Barmark and S. C. B. Gaunitz, Transcendental Meditation and Hypnosis as Altered States of Consciousness, *International Journal of Clinical and Experimental Hypnosis, 27,* pp. 227-239, 1979.
15. L. C. Walrath and D. W. Hamilton, Autonomic Correlates of Medication and Hypnosis, *American Journal of Clinical Hypnosis, 17,* pp. 190-196, 1975.
16. A. P. Shapiro, G. E. Schwartz, and D. C. E. Ferguson, Behavioral Methods in the Treatment of Hypertension, *Annals of Internal Medicine, 86,* pp. 626-636, 1977.
17. H. Benson, *The Relaxation Response,* Morrow, New York, 1975.
18. E. R. Korn and G. J. Pratt, *Hyper-Performances: The AIM Strategy for Releasing Your Business Potential,* John Wiley and Sons, New York, 1987.

19. Y. U. L. Hanin, O Sprochnoi Diagnostike Sostoiaiia Lichnosti V Grupe, *Teorija I Praktika Fizizheskoi Kul'tury, 8,* 1977.
20. R. Gordon, A Very Private World, in *The Nature and Function of Imagery,* P. W. Sheehan (ed.), Academic Press, New York, pp. 63-80, 1972.
21. C. W. Perky, Environmental Study of the Imagination, *American Journal of Psychology, 21,* pp. 422-452, 1910.
22. E. R. Korn, The Uses of Relaxation and Mental Imagery to Enhance Athletic Performance, in *Imagery, Volume 4: Recent Practice and Theory,* M. Wolpin, J. E. Shorr, and L. Krueger (eds.), Plenum, New York, 1986.
23. M. J. Horowitz, Image Formation: Clinical Observations of Cognitive Model, in *The Nature and Function of Imagery,* P. W. Sheehan (ed.), Academic Press, New York 1972.
24. I. U. Begg and T. D. Wilton, Imagery in Verbal Communication, *Journal of Mental Imagery, 2,* pp. 165-186, 1978.
25. W. Lay, Mental Imagery, *Psych RES, Monographs and Supplements, 92,* pp. 1-59, 1897.
26. E. R. Korn, Imagery in a Clinical Hypnosis Primer, G. J. Pratt, D. T. Wood, B. M. Almann (eds.), John Wiley and Sons, pp. 73-89, 1988.
27. G. Hendricks and J. U. Carlson, *The Centered Athlete,* Prentice-Hall, Englewood Cliffs, New Jersey, 1982.
28. E. W. Krenz, Improving Competitive Performance with Hypnotic Suggestions and Modified Autogenic Training: Case Reports, *American Journal of Clinical Hypnosis, 27,* pp. 58-63, 1984.
29. C. C. Garfield, *Peak Performance: Mental Training Techniques of the World's Greatest Athletes,* Tarcher, Los Angeles, 1984.
30. J. F. Lane, Improving Athletic Performance Through Visual Motor Behavior Rehearsal, in *Psychology in Sports: Methods and Applications,* R. M. Suinn (ed.), Burgess, Minneapolis, Minnesota, 1980.
31. G. Larsson, Routinization of Mental Training and Organization: Effects on Performance and Well Being, *Journal of Applied Psychology, 72,* pp. 81-91, 1987.
32. G. J. Pratt and E. R. Korn, Using Hypnosis to Enhance Athletic Performance, in *Hypnosis: Questions and Answers,* B. Zilbergeld, M. G. Edelstein, and D. L. Araoz (eds.), W. W. Norton, New York, 1988.
33. R. Windle and M. Samko, Hypnosis, Eriksonian Hypotherapy and Aikido, *American Journal of Clinical Hypnosis, 34,* pp. 261-270, 1992.
34. E. R. Korn, The Use of Altered States of Consciousness in Imagery and Physical and Pain Rehabilitation, *Journal of Mental Imagery, 7,* pp. 25-34, 1983.
35. P. J. Lang, Bio-Informational Theory of Emotional Imagery, in *Psychophysiology, 16,* pp. 495-512, 1979.
36. E. R. Korn, *Pain Management with Relaxation and Mental Imagery,* (Audio Tape) PCA Press, La Jolla, California, 1982.
37. E. R. Korn, Free Yourself from Pain, *Prevention Magazine* (Audio Cassette) Rodale Press, Emmaus, Pennsylvania, 1988.
38. M. De Michele, *Executive Speaker,* August 1986.
39. I. D. Yalom, *The Theory and Practice of Group Psychotherapy,* Basic Books, New York, 1970.
40. A. T. Beck, A. J. Rush, B. F. Shaw, and G. Emery, *Cognitive Therapy of Depression,* Guilford Press, New York, 1979.
41. D. D. Burns, Feeling Good, William Morrow and Company, 1980.
42. J. Chelostedt, Sports Psychology at a Ski Academy: Teaching Mental Skills to Young Athletes, *Sports Psychologist, 1,* pp. 56-68, 1987.

43. E. R. Korn, Visualization Techniques and Altered States of Consciousness, in *Anthology of Imagery Techniques,* A. A. Sheikh (ed.), American Imagery Institute, Milwaukee, Wisconsin, 1986.

44. E. R. Korn, Imagery, in *A Clinical Hypnosis Primer,* G. J. Pratt, D. S. Woods, and B. M. Alman (eds.), John Wiley and Sons, New York, 1988.

45. E. R. Korn, Boosting Your Immune Power, *Prevention Magazine* (Audio Cassette), Rodale Press, Emmaus, Pennsylvania, 1988.

46. E. R. Korn, Super Memory, *Prevention Magazine* (Audio Cassette), Rodale Press, Emmaus, Pennsylvania, 1988.

47. E. R. Korn, Stop Procrastinating Now, *Prevention Magazine* (Audio Cassette), Rodale Press, Emmaus, Pennsylvania, 1988.

48. E. R. Korn, Walking for Health and Happiness, *Prevention Magazine* (Audio Cassette), Rodale Press, Emmaus, Pennsylvania, 1988.

49. E. R. Korn, Be a Positive Person, *Prevention Magazine* (Audio Cassette), Rodale Press, Emmaus, Pennsylvania, 1988.

50. E. R. Korn, Soothing Aches and Pains, *Prevention Magazine,* (Audio Cassette), Rodale Press, Emmaus, Pennsylvania, 1988.

51. E. R. Korn, Super Memory, *Prevention Magazine* (Audio Cassette), Rodale Press, Emmaus, Pennsylvania, 1988.

CHAPTER 15

Improving Imaging Abilities

ANEES A. SHEIKH, KATHARINA S. SHEIKH, AND L. MARTIN MOLESKI

A number of studies have demonstrated that significant changes in experiential, behavioral, and physiological measures can be produced in subjects who experience vivid images, but not in those who can muster only weak ones [1-3]. The crucial question that comes to mind at this point is: Are weak imagers condemned to remain so, or can they learn to reduce or even eliminate their handicap?

Already in 1883, Sir Francis Galton, in his *Inquiries into Human Faculty*, indicated that practice in forming mental images can strengthen this ability [4]. Galton referred to a French educator who trained his students to visualize objects so clearly, that they could draw these images. He began by urging his students to examine the object carefully, so that they could form a clear visual image. Next, he directed them to "draw" it in the air, so that they might retain "muscular memories" of it. Finally, he required them to draw the object from memory. He claimed that after his students had been trained in this manner for three to four months, they could summon images with ease and hold them steady enough to draw them.

Imagery researchers agree that everyone has the capacity to image. Marks comments, "While the ability to generate and employ mental imagery varies across people, the potential to do so is probably universal. Given appropriate and optimal conditions of thinking and performance, it is likely that all persons could utilize imagery-encoded information [in 5, p. 61]. Kroger and Fezler state, "Many believe that once sensations have been experienced, they are retained somewhere within the system and that the ability to recall and reexperience the situation and its associated sensations is available to all of us, although we rarely take advantage of these possibilities" [in 5, p. 61]. Imagery ability is an innate potential like drawing or the use of language, or any other skill that improves with practice. Since the potential is there, it is possible to develop it through training. Of course, not all people can become superimagers, any more than they can learn to draw like Leonardo da Vinci or write like Shakespeare, but everyone can improve his/her skill over what it is at the present [6]. In short, the main ingredient in improving imagery appears to be "practice, practice, and more practice" [6, p. 139].

Conversely, neglect eventually will lead to the inability to summon images. Korn states, "Any system or ability that is not nurtured tends to atrophy. When we do not utilize the birthright of imagery experience, we eventually 'forget' the experience entirely" [5, p. 62].

The next question that arises is: Have researchers provided evidence that practice can improve imagery ability, and have they identified specific methods? Unfortunately, systematic research in the area of the enhancement of imagery has been very limited, but a number of useful suggestions and some indirect evidence are scattered throughout the literature. The purpose of this brief review is to bring these together and to offer recommendations for further research.

METHODS FOR IMPROVING IMAGERY VIVIDNESS

The salient factors that seem to lead to improved imagery vividness include: relaxation, concentration, body position and sensory input, sensory training, practice in imaging, multimodal training, convincing the client, developmentally determined images, increased right-hemisphere activity, somato-affective states, overcoming resistances, drugs, and certain developmental factors. This section provides a brief discussion of all of these factors.

Relaxation

Relaxation appears to be one of the most important prerequisites for the experience of vivid imagery [7, 8]; for, it seems to allow the process of becoming aware of internal states to begin.

Imagery, a symbolic mode of representation, to be distinguished from the verbal symbolic mode [9], is produced throughout the waking hours. But generally we are unaware of our imagery because it has to compete with the live broadcasting of everyday experience. We constantly are bombarded by stimuli, and the preoccupation with filtering out the superfluous ones among them renders us unaware of the internal stimuli which are of a relatively less dramatic nature. Furthermore, in Western cultures, the tendency has been to emphasize verbal, rational, secondary thought processes at the expense of imaginal experience—most people literally lose sight of their imagery.

During relaxation, the noisy, hectic world is shut out, and the inner world, the realm of imaginal experience, has a chance to become the focus of attention. Gendlin notes, "Imagery comes very well and very richly during highly relaxed states" [8, p. 71]. Singer concludes that relaxation is "conducive to the occurrence or awareness of imagery and ongoing daydreaming" [10, p. 226]. Relaxation reduces "hyperalertness to external stimulation that would blur the vividness of imagery and overload the visual system which must handle both imagery derived from long-term memory and incoming stimulation" [10, p. 226]. Bakan, too, focuses on the central role of relaxation: "It is evident to people who work with imagery that relaxation is conducive to the experience of imagery." He explains, "The left hemisphere appears to have a closer relationship to more activity than does the right hemisphere. Perhaps imagery activity, associated with the right hemisphere, is incompatible with a high degree of motor activity" [7, p. 40]. It may be more accurate to say that imagery is incompatible with *changes* in sensory input or in motor activity. Many long-distance runners have reported that they have experienced highly vivid imagery, often of a creative or problem-solving nature, while running. Their imaginal experience appears to be related not to speed or distance, but to length of time: Generally it occurs when they maintain a steady pace. This finding is in harmony with Shapiro's observation relative to the psychology of meditation. He states that meditation involves habituation to any single stimulus that has been the primary focus of attention [11].

Numerous relaxation procedures have been developed over the years. For detailed information about these methods the reader is referred to other sources [5, 12, 13].

Concentration

Relaxation is a necessary preliminary step to visualization; it clears the mind and dispels distracting muscular tension. But another prerequisite for vivid imagery is the ability to concentrate. Generally, an endless procession of thoughts files through our mind, and we seem to have little control over their occurrence or their nature. But obviously this lack of thought control must be overcome by anyone who wishes to focus on one image.

Yoga offers a variety of suggestions to develop the powers of concentration:

1. Concentration on a small external object: The student attempts to think only of the object, and each time a different thought intrudes, he/she pushes it aside and returns to the object.
2. Counting breaths: The student tries to ban all thoughts and to focus on counting breaths. Every time a thought does arise, he/she returns to the count. One way of dealing with these unbidden thoughts is to cut them off as quickly as possible, before they have a chance to unfold. Another approach is to let the intrusive thought pass unheeded, as if they belonged to someone else. A Zen metaphor likens thoughts to birds flying across the sky of one's mind—one simply watches them appear and then disappear [12].

Regular practice of such exercises enables a person to better ward off intrusive thoughts and to hold an image for a longer period [12, pp. 111-113]. Detailed discussions of numerous exercises in concentration are available elsewhere [12, 14, 15].

Body Position and Sensory Input

The supine body position has been found to facilitate the experience of vivid imagery, and it probably was by design that Freud directed his patients to the analytic couch. Pope has stated that the recumbent posture can markedly increase the experience of visual imagery and influence the flow of consciousness and the quality of our imagining experience [16]. Kroth reported that individuals who were reclining, free-associated more freely, more spontaneously, and generally more effectively than those who sat up [17]. Unfortunately, Kroth did not present data on imagery per se. Morgan and Bakan determined that subjects who were lying down produced reports that rated much higher in vividness of imagery than subjects who were sitting [18]. In a subsequent study, Berdach and Bakan elicited memory material from subjects in a reclining or sitting position, and they found that the reclining subjects produced earlier and more copious memories than the comparison group [19].

Segal and Glickman produced some very objective evidence by means of the Perky phenomenon [20]. Subjects, who were either lying down or sitting, gazed at a blank white screen onto which they were directed to project certain images. Unknown to them, the experimenter projected comparable images onto the screen. The investigators found that reclining subjects were much less likely to become aware that an external image had been projected. That is, their own images were sufficiently vivid to preclude awareness of the external ones.

A number of researchers have proposed explanations why imagery is enhanced in the reclining position. Berdach and Bakan suggest that this is so due to the decrease of tension in the head and neck muscles, a condition that prevails also at the onset of rapid eye movement sleep [19]. Singer points out that the reclining position is associated with sleep and hence with dreaming and daydreaming. Most people report that the greatest part of their daydreaming occurs while they are preparing for sleep [21].

Rychlak proposes that the effect may be due not to the reclining position as such, but rather to the reduction in complex external stimulation that accompanies this posture—a black ceiling simply is not very distracting [22]. As Richardson indicates, imagery is more likely to manifest itself when we are awake and when external stimuli are not functionally operative [23].

Sensory Training

On the basis of extensive interviews of women who had been rated as excellent hypnotic subjects, Wilson and Barber concluded that a hallmark of these individuals is their profound fantasy life [24, 25]. These people (who constitute approximately 4% of the population) fantasize much of the time, and they do so very intensely—that is, they generally can "see," "hear," "smell," "feel," and fully experience what they are imagining.

These fantasy-prone individuals experience more vividly in all the sense modalities not only their fantasies but also the real world around them. Wilson and Barber hypothesize

> that vivid sensory experiences, vivid memories, and vivid fantasies are causally interrelated as follows: individuals who focus on and vividly feel their sensory experiences, have relatively vivid memories of their experiences; and individuals with vivid memories of their experiences are able to have relatively vivid fantasies because they can use their vivid memories as raw material from which they can creatively construct their fantasies [25, p. 380].

This relationship is corroborated by what is known about the manner in which creative persons approach the world. It seems that they experience the world with a certain innocence and consequently more intensely. Vivid sensory experience engenders vivid sensory-based memory, which in turn provides the material for vivid fantasies.

In other words, it appears that sensory training leads to improved imagery abilities [4, 23, 25]. Samuels and Samuels state, "The better people train their minds to perceive external images, the easier it becomes for them to image internal images as well" [12, p. 114]. For instance, "learning to see directly affects the ability to visualize. In seeing the images are external; in visualizing the images are internal. But the process and effects are similar" [12, p. 116].

Many psychologists believe that congenitally blind persons have no visual images. Similarly, those who see blindly will have difficulty in forming visual mental images. And it is indeed possible to see blindly. All of us probably have had the experience of walking right past a friend on the street without noticing him/her, because we were preoccupied by our thoughts. Another type of blind seeing occurs when we view an object solely with regard to a specific function and ignore all its other attributes. For example, when we are tired, we may regard a chair only as a place to rest and not notice anything else about it [12].

Samuels and Samuels suggest that the first step in developing the ability to see is becoming fully alert and aware as we look around, and, of course, this suggestion is applicable also to the cultivation of the other senses [12]. A number of specific exercises toward that end have been proposed:

1. It is beneficial to focus upon the various traits of an object, one after the other. One should take note of the way the light strikes the object, the highlights and shadows, and the color variations it creates. One should focus on the texture of the object, its color, its perspective, and its many other properties [12].
2. It is very helpful to stare at an object and to attempt to experience it. This means trying not to react verbally or to label, but rather to admit the object into one's consciousness [12].

3. The ability to perceive is improved by looking at an object from different physical perspectives and from different mental points of view. For instance, one could consider an apple from the viewpoint of an artist, a hungry man, a migrant worker picking an apple, etc. With each shift, different aspects of the object will come to the fore. Witnessing this rich procession of attributes helps one to become aware of the labels and associations that one unconsciously uses in ordinary seeing; and this awareness prompts one to break out of the habitual manner of viewing familiar things and to see them again with a degree of innocence [12].

4. Hooper believes that clarity of perception can be improved by attentively sketching and photographing objects from various angles [6].

5. Petitclere suggests that it is useful to describe an object that one can feel, but not see [in 6].

6. McKim uses puzzles and games to improve visual recognition. For instance, he may present five playing cards, of which four contain errors and one is correct. In order to find the minor errors, such as a spade which is upside down or a 10 written 01, the player must pay close attention to details. Analogous puzzles targeting the other senses could easily be devised. For example, a succession of tones could be played, and the player would be required to identify the one that was a different pitch. Also, different fabrics or spices could be presented to a blindfolded person for identification [26].

7. Parmenter maintains that one can improve one's powers of observation by pretending to be a reporter on a news assignment [in 6].

Numerous other exercises designed to sharpen one's awareness of the world have been outlined and the interested reader can find those elsewhere [6, 12, 26, 27].

Practice in Imaging

Practice in imaging seems to yield improvement in imaging ability, and a number of apparently useful exercises have been devised for that purpose.

1. McKim proposes the following: A person closes his/her eyes and visualizes a wooden cube whose sides are painted red. Then he/she images two parallel vertical cuts through the cube, dividing it into thirds, and two more vertical cuts perpendicular to the first ones, dividing it into ninths. Next, he/she visualizes two parallel, horizontal cuts through the cube, dividing it into twenty-seven cubes. Now, he/she tries to imagine how many cubes are red on three sides, on two sides, on one side, and how many cubes are unpainted on all sides [26].

2. McKim suggests the use of two-dimensional designs which can be folded together to make three-dimensional figures. The task consists of mentally folding a design and then indicating which one of several test figures has been created [26].

3. McKim recommends sketching to promote thinking schematically. The student starts with free doodling, then he/she progresses to disciplined doodling, then to realistic drawing, and finally to drawing his/her images. Later still, he/she draws things which are felt rather than seen, such as objects concealed in a bag. McKim's exercises focus on vision; however, they could be adapted without difficulty to involve the other senses. The guiding principle which runs through all these procedures is that practice promptly followed by feedback will improve performance [26].

4. Parmenter, a reporter, found the search for similes to sharpen his powers of observation. He stumbled upon this technique during an airplane trip—as he discerned a certain feature in the landscape, he asked himself, "What does it recall?" And he attempted to answer in a different material, species, or modality every time. For example, a winding road reminded him of a tortoise shell hairpin, and he compared a brook to worm tracks in wood [in 6].

5. Lazarus has found the blackboard exercise to be effective [27]. The student relaxes, closes his/her eyes, visualizes a blackboard, and imagines writing a letter "A" on it, followed by "B" and so forth. Throughout the process, the student tries to retain a clear image of all the letters on the board. Initially, most people find that, as they add more letters, the beginning ones tend to fade. But with practice, the clarity of the letters improves.

6. Lazarus also recommends the light bulb technique. The student closes his/her eyes and imagines a dim light bulb suspended in front of him/her. While focusing on the light, he/she attempts to make it grow brighter and brighter until it illuminates everything, and then dimmer and dimmer [27].

7. Another technique involves careful study of a common object. The student scrutinizes the object until he/she is familiar with it. Then he/she closes his/her eyes and pretends to still be studying the object. He/she tries to see it as clearly as possible and studies it as he/she did the real object. Next, he/she opens his/her eyes and reexamines the real object to compare the difference between it and its image. Then he/she closes his/her eyes again and repeats the exercise, taking care to add to the image those traits which were missed the first time [27].

8. Lazarus also claims to have used the seashore exercise with success. The student relaxes, closes his/her eyes, and imagines that he/she is strolling along a quiet beach on a balmy day. He/she is wearing a swim suit, and he/she feels the warm sun on the skin and the sand between the toes. He/she smells the fresh sea air and listens to the waves breaking on the sand. He/she summons other soothing images associated with a stroll on the beach and enjoys the serenity that accompanies them [27].

9. Samuels and Samuels recommend the following sequence for improving visualization ability: A) With the eyes closed, imagine a two-dimensional object, such as a geometrical shape. Then close the eyes and try to visualize it. B) Repeat Exercise A with a three-dimensional object. C) Visualize your childhood room. D) Image a large object, such as a house, and move around and through it. E) Visualize a complicated, three-dimensional object from various angles. F) Return to the childhood room of Exercise C, and imagine that you are doing several things in it, such as picking up items, switching the lights off, etc. G) Visualize a person. H) Image yourself as if you are looking in a mirror [12].

There is some evidence that hypnotic suggestions can lead to more vivid imagery; hence, many of the above exercises may be more effective when they are performed under hypnosis [5, 12]. Also, some clinicians claim that listening to concrete descriptions of scenes, either recorded ones or ones presented live by the therapist, can stimulate imagery.

Many other procedures have appeared in the popular literature. But "what is lacking for all these techniques is information on how they work. As parlor games, they are fun and harmless. However, before they are included in school curricula or mnemonics workshops, some efforts must be made to measure their effectiveness" [6, p. 147].

Multimodal Training

Related to the ideas discussed in the preceding section are Cautela and McCullough's suggestion concerning the involvement of all sense modalities:

> Vividness must not be equated solely with visual imagery, for the greatest effectiveness is obtained when the client reports a vividness in all sense modalities. For example, if a client had trouble imagining or visualizing an airplane, the sound of the plane would be described, the kinaesthetic feeling of the takeoff or the seatbelt, the physiological responses such as increased heartbeat or shortness of breath, and the appropriate affective state such as anxiety or exhilaration. It is emphasized that the client not simply imagine the scene, but try to feel that he is actually experiencing it. Recent research suggests that the largest and most consistent physiological responses occur in response to imagining somato-motor and visceral responses and to imagining "being there" rather than just imagining detailed descriptions without affective components [28, p. 236].

Convincing the Client

Imaging ability probably is universal; yet, some clients claim that they lack it. An important preliminary step with such individuals is convincing them of the contrary. Korn proposes a simple yet effective procedure [5]: The client is directed to imagine that the therapist is a window washer contracting to clean the windows of the client's residence. In order to quote a price, the window washer must know how many windows are involved. The client is asked to furnish this information. In response to this request, the client's eyes will turn to the side opposite the nondominant hemisphere, which may indicate stimulation of the nondominant hemisphere, and if the client is questioned at this point, he/she will reveal that he/she actually was counting the windows. But,

> how can one count the windows without visualizing them, even if the image is not clear and tends to be a mind's eye image? This will demonstrate to even the most recalcitrant of subjects that imagery is not only possible, but that he or she uses it every day for the solution of many of life's problems [5, p. 62].

Shorr mentions another method of demonstrating to clients that they are capable of producing imagery: "When people tell me they never have images, I ask them to imagine several scenes . . . So far this has resulted in no failures" [28, p. 157].

Developmentally Determined Images

Images of past key events seem to be effective in rendering the individual aware of his/her images in general. Even those individuals who do not have vivid imagery, with some encouragement and concentration, can visualize developmentally determined images from significant life situations in the past. These images tend to open up the general imagination and fantasy processes [30].

Enhancing Right-Hemisphere Activity

Research on cerebral specialization has revealed that:

> the left hemisphere seems to be more concerned with the temporal analysis of incoming information which it labels verbally, for storage and later retrieval and manipulation in recall or problem solving. The right hemisphere on the other hand, seems to deal with organizing incoming information on the basis of complex wholes, and acts as a synthesizer rather than analyzer [31, p. 112].

Paivio proposes that verbal or mathematical processes, which involve sequential processing, occur in the left hemisphere; spatial or imaginal processes, which entail parallel processing, take place in the right hemisphere [9]. Oyle expresses the differentiation of the hemispheres in this manner: "The self is hermaphroditic. Each of us is two individuals, a male and a female. The former is rational, can speak, and think thoughts. The female side makes the pictures, dreams, mental images, and empirical reality" [32, p. 99]. Ley stresses that the right hemisphere "seems to predominate in a variety of states of consciousness, such as dreaming (day and night), hypnosis and meditation, as well as in religious and drug-induced states, in which emotional and imagery components are salient" [33, p. 42].

Since right-hemisphere functions are linked to imagery, enhancement of the former would be expected to produce amelioration of the latter. Thus, participation in activities that generally are regarded as right hemispheric, such as music, art, poetry, dancing, humor, and meditation, would be expected to lead to enhanced imagery production. Although some support for this contention can be found in the literature, there is an obvious need for further empirical validation.

Oyle suggests two general approaches to imagery enhancement that are relevant to this section:

> The left hemisphere can be put at rest by a variety of techniques. These have by and large been formalized as religious rituals, hypnotic suggestions, or sensory deprivation among others. Another way to shift the balance in favor of the image-making right brain is to overload the thinker in the left brain" [32, p. 87].

This may be accomplished by the use of Zen Buddhist koans, insoluble problems, like "What is the sound of one hand clapping?" Oyle feels that "if the thinker is quiescent or overloaded to the point of exhaustion, energy flows from the right cerebral hemisphere to form an image" [32, p. 87].

The Role of Somato-Affective States

Imagery has long been thought to have a direct relationship to emotions. Many psychologists have noted that images possess an amazing ability to effect extensive affective and physiological changes [3, 34]. A recent memory image may elicit an emotional response and a physiological arousal whose intensity rivals and even surpasses that of the reaction to the actual event [35, 36]. Bauer and Craighead state:

> A basic assumption underlying the use of imagery techniques in behavioral therapy has been that the patterns of physiological response to imagined and real stimuli are essentially isomorphic. For example, Wolpe [37] suggested that the pattern of arousal elicited by visualization of fearful scenes in desensitization directly corresponded to that brought about by actual contact with an anxiety-eliciting stimulus [38, p. 389].

Recently, attempts have been made to integrate three fundamental aspects of all human experience [39-41]. These include: the image (I), the somatic response—including emotional arousal (S), and the meaning—including affective significantion (M). It seems that all significant images are a triadic unity (ISM). Clinicians often work with the image component of this triangle. They ask the client to concentrate and to repeatedly project an image that originally had been weak or vague, until it becomes vivid, precise, detailed, and stable. Through the image, the individual attempts to recreate the original experience, that is to reexperience the affect and meaning and the accompanying bodily responses, which form the memory in its entirety. If the concept of the ISM is valid, then focusing on any aspect of this triangle, not only on the image, should bring the entire experience into relief. In other words, concentrating on the image's meaning or on the affect and bodily response it evokes, should render the whole event more real. For example, if the focus is on an aggressive image, the production of bodily responses involved in aggression may help to make the image more vivid.

Support for the ISM approach to the enhancement of imagery can be found in the research of several investigators. For instance, Ley considers imagery and emotions to be inseparable: "Given sufficient, affective potency, stimulus salience, and the vast and elusive differences in imaging ability and cognitive styles (i.e., 'picture' thinkers vs. 'word' thinkers), imagic and emotional stimulus components may be inextricable in practice" [33, p. 47]. Perhaps these imagic and emotional components are inextricable because they are bound together by the meaning they convey. Gendlin, who has developed a form of therapy called "focusing" which relies substantially on imagery, recommends emphasizing the somatic component to enhance imagery; for, he has observed that a by-product of doing so is increased *meaning* for the individual.

> In summary, I believe that whatever your way of working with imagery may be, you will find your method enhanced quite powerfully, if you employ focusing. . . . Imagery and body-sense are inherently related, but on different planes. It is much more powerful if one not only works with the body and imagery, but devotes specific attention to the formation of something directly sensed in the body, yet implicitly meaningful [40, p. 72].

Lang's brain-formation theory of emotional imagery is also relevant here [42]. Lang conceives the image in the brain to be a "conceptual network, controlling specific somatovisceral patterns, in constituting a prototype for overt behavioral expression" [in 5, p. 73]. He believes that instructions to the client would be more effective if they consisted not only of the usual stimulus propositions, but also of response propositions. Therefore, a statement such as, "The wooden walls of the small room surround you, closing you in . . ." would change to "You tense all your muscles of your forehead, squinting . . . your eyes . . . dart left and right to glimpse the exit" [in 5, p. 73].

Overcoming Resistances

In some cases, the inability to image or to image vividly may be a function of certain kinds of resistances on the part of the client. These resistances may affect imaging ability in specific areas, or they may inhibit the total imaging process. Such resistances need to be identified and understood before proper evolvement of imagery can take place. Shorr offers an explanation for these resistances: "It is inevitably the fears, anxieties, or frustrations inherent in people's internal conflicts, which lead to the curtailment of an imaginary capacity, in order to shrink the boundaries of their self-hood to more manageable dimensions" [43, p. 15].

A detailed discussion of various types of resistances is beyond the scope of this chapter and the reader is referred to other sources [5, 30, 44-47].

Drugs

It has been known for centuries, for instance by participants in religious rituals, that certain psychoactive drugs stimulate mental imagery [48]. For example, the religious rites of the American Indians culminated in the ingestion of psychoactive drugs, such as peyote and psilocybin, that prompted intense religious experiences mediated by remarkably vivid imagery [49, 50]. In the 1960s, thousands of American youths made the expansion of their minds and conscious awareness a top priority. The means they most commonly used were LSD, marijuana, and cocaine, and their major shared experience was intensification of sensory awareness through hallucinations [51].

Subject accounts indicate that the drug experience often involves an attitudinal shift or change in level of awareness that fosters the production of imagery or the greater awareness of imagery. For example, ordinary awareness has been compared to spotlighting: This focused lighting is like our linear, logical thinking—specific and task oriented. Drug-induced awareness represents a shift toward floodlighting; it is more global, more panoramic [52]. The analogy parallels comparisons of left- and right-brain functioning, which are different but complimentary types of perception [7]. Holt too links the attitudinal changes, such as weakened defenses, which accompany drug-induced conditions, to increased imagery [53].

The image-enhancing quality of certain drugs may be due also to their relaxing effect on the system. For instance, Segal found that subjects who were under the influence of tranquilizers displayed a stronger Perky effect than those who were not [54].

Obviously, drugs are not a recommended means of enhancing imagery. Nevertheless, it is possible that some subjects who have experienced vivid imagery by means of drugs, will be more highly motivated to enhance their imagery, simply because they already have had a taste of the experience.

Developmental Factors

Qualls and Sheehan believe that "the origins of imaginal skills and the readiness to spontaneously utilize imaginal capacities lie in the imaginative make-believe play and fantasy experiences of childhood" and that "early childhood may represent a sensitive period for the development of imaginal abilities" [55, p. 91]. Investigators have identified a number of factors that seem to enhance make-believe play in children that in turn may lead to better imagery abilities later in life:

1. Positive interpersonal experiences early in life are beneficial [56].
2. Security of attachment is an important factor [56].
3. A parental model who enjoys artistic pursuits and verbal and other forms of inventiveness enriches the child's play activities.

4. Opportunities for space and time to be alone, accompanied by the approval of a parent figure, contribute to meaningful play [56].
5. The child should be encouraged to engage in role-taking activities and to *behave* toward an object as if it were something other than what it actually is [57].
6. Storytelling by parents and other significant individuals can be helpful [58].
7. Television viewing in moderate degrees can also be a useful catalyst for imaginative play. However, the presence of an adult to encourage the creative use of television rather than passive viewing, is very important [59].
8. Both sociodramatic play, which involves themes and events within the realm of the child's everyday experience (e.g., playing school or pretending to go to the doctor), and thematic fantasy play, whose themes and events are remote from personal experience (e.g., fairy tales), are effective in stimulating the child's imaginal abilities [55].

DIRECT RESEARCH EVIDENCE

Although numerous techniques to enhance imagery have been proposed, research directly investigating their efficacy is extremely limited. However, the results of the few existing studies are encouraging.

Walsh, White, and Aston found that imagery training can be beneficial and that marked improvements can take place in a relatively short time [60]. They identified vivid and weak imagers by means of the Betts Test and then formed three groups, each consisting of six vivid and six weak imagers. Every group met for twenty minutes on four successive days. One group was not exposed to any imagery-related activities. Another group discussed the therapeutic uses of imagery but did not undergo any formal training. The experimental group practiced visual, kinesthetic, and auditory imaging on the first day, gustatory and olfactory on the next day, tactile and organic on the third day, and an exercise which involved all seven modalities on the last day. Also, they were assigned exercises to practice at home between sessions.

The posttest revealed no significant change in the first two groups. Of the third group, the vivid imagers revealed no change, but the weak imagers exhibited a very significant change. Not only did they rate their imagery as markedly more vivid, which may represent simply a response to the demand characteristics of the situation, but also, when they were asked to imagine their favorite food, they salivated as copiously as untrained vivid imagers.

Richardson and Patterson felt the need to extend and refine the study of Walsh et al., for a number of reasons [61]. First, Walsh et al. had not separated the effects of sensory-awareness training from the effects ascribable to relaxation. Richardson and Patterson took care to do so. Second, the earlier study invited the question whether training in a single major modality (vision) would suffice to produce the reported amelioration in imagery vividness. Consequently,

Richardson and Patterson exposed two groups to multimodal training, and they gave the other group practice solely in the visual modality. Third, Walsh et al. had conducted the evaluation only immediately after the training period. Richardson and Patterson added a follow-up test administered two months after the conclusion of training. That is, Richardson and Patterson evaluated the relative effectiveness of three training procedures: multimodal imagery training with relaxation (RMM), multimodal imagery training by itself (MM), and visual imagery training with relaxation (RV).

They found an increase in imagery vividness for the RMM and MM training groups both on experiential (Betts Questionnaire) and on physiological (salivation) measures. However, the posttest two months later did not reveal significant differences. It is possible that weak imagers need periodic refresher training sessions to maintain their gain in imagery vividness and to prevent the relapse to their habitual modes of thought [2].

There are several other recent studies which have implications for the enhancement of imagery, that the reader may wish to consult [62, 63].

THE ISSUE OF IMAGERY CONTROL

The success of imagery procedures is determined not only by the ability to form images but also by the ability to control them. If the individual can produce vivid images but is unable to control them, the prospects for effective use of imagery techniques are dim. "In fact, the most difficult state in which to cause behavioral change is one in which the client experiences intensely vivid imagery but cannot control or maintain adaptive thoughts and continues to revert to maladaptive images" [28, p. 237]. According to Richardson, the combination of high vividness and high controllability correlates the most with behavioral change, while the combination of high vividness and low controllability correlates the least with behavioral change [23].

Quite typically, an individual who lacks control over his/her images, will experience difficulty in focusing on beneficial images. He/she may begin by imagining a very positive situation but then find himself/herself constantly interrupted by aversive thoughts; for example, he/she may visualize himself/herself skiing downhill on a sunny day, only to fall. Cautela and McCullough propose a number of procedures that seem to aid in controlling and redirecting negative imagery:

1. The individual is reminded that the fantasy is his/hers, that he/she has created it and hence also can change it in any way. Then he/she is asked to describe the scene again but with a positive outcome (e.g., he/she skis down the hill without a mishap). Sometimes this exercise suffices, and the person is able to control his/her imagery.

2. If the above exercise is not effective, then undesirable images are modified gradually by shaping. For instance, the individual proceeds to imagine falling down while skiing, but the fall does not hurt. He/she visualizes the skiing scene repeatedly, and each time he/she images that he/she is able to maintain better balance or stop before falling.

3. The person keeps a log of all the situations which cause tension, anxiety, or depression. After a week of recording these incidents, he/she learns to identify them quickly. He/she attempts to relax in the face of aversive thoughts and to interrupt them at the onset, when they are easier to control and stifle [28].

CONCLUDING REMARKS

A survey of the literature relevant to the enhancement of imagery reveals that investigators share the persuasion that everyone possesses the potential for imaging. Furthermore, it appears that even if the imaging ability has withered due to neglect, it can be revived. The literature contains a number of methods that have been used for stimulating mental imagery. Nevertheless, little research has been carried out to establish the efficacy of these various methods and also to determine their relative merit under different circumstances.

Furthermore, it appears that investigators have been disproportionately fascinated by visual imagery. Although visual images are the most common kind, they are not the only type or even the preferred one for some individuals. Undoubtedly, the other modalities deserve more of the investigators' attention than they have hitherto received.

Also, researchers seem preoccupied with the issue of vividness, and although they recognize the importance of control of imagery, they have made little attempt to explore this area. More sophisticated measures of control as well as scientifically developed procedures to improve control are sorely needed.

If the increase of interest over the last ten years in imagery-related topics can be used as an indicator, then it seems virtually certain that within the next ten years a host of pressing questions will be answered, and clearer guidelines will be available.

REFERENCES

1. D. F. Marks, Imagery and Consciousness, *Journal of Mental Imagery, 2,* pp. 275-290, 1977.
2. A. Richardson and C. C. Taylor, Vividness of Mental Imagery and Self-induced Mood Change, *British Journal of Clinical Psychology, 21,* pp. 111-117, 1982.
3. A. A. Sheikh and R. G. Kunzendorf, Imagery, Physiology, and Psychosomatic Illness, in *International Review of Mental Imagery,* Vol. 1, A. A. Sheikh (ed.), Human Sciences Press, New York, pp. 95-138, 1984.
4. F. Galton, *Inquiries into Human Faculty,* Macmillan, London, 1883.

5. E. R. Korn, *Visualization: Uses of Imagery in the Health Professions,* Dow Jones-Irwin, Homewood, Illinois, 1983.
6. R. Sommer, *The Mind's Eye: Imagery in Everyday Life,* Delacorte Press, New York, 1978.
7. P. Bakan, Imagery, Raw and Cooked: A Hemispheric Recipe, in *Imagery: Its Many Dimensions and Applications,* J. E. Shorr, G. E. Sobel, P. Robin, and J. A. Connella (eds.), Plenum, New York, pp. 35-53, 1980.
8. E. T. Gendlin, *Focusing,* Bantam Books, New York, 1981.
9. A. Paivio, *Imagery and Verbal Processes,* Holt, Rinehart, Winston, New York, 1971.
10. J. L. Singer, *Imagery and Daydream Methods in Psychotherapy and Behavior Modification,* Academic Press, New York, 1974.
11. D. L. Shapiro, The Significance of the Visual Image in Psychotherapy, *Psychotherapy: Theory, Research, and Practice, 7,* pp. 209-212, 1974.
12. M. Samuels and N. Samuels, *Seeing with the Mind's Eye,* Random House, New York, 1975.
13. A. A. Sheikh (ed.), *Imagination and Healing,* Baywood, New York, 1984.
14. D. Goleman, *The Varieties of the Meditative Experience,* E. P. Dutton, New York, 1977.
15. S. Ostrander, L. Schroeder, and N. Ostrander, *Superlearning,* Dell, New York, 1979.
16. K. Pope, How Gender, Solitude and Posture Influence the Stream of Consciousness, in *The Stream of Consciousness,* K. S. Pope and J. L. Singer (eds.), Plenum, New York, 1978.
17. J. A. Kroth, The Analytic Couch and Response to Free Association, *Psychotherapy: Theory, Research, and Practice, 7,* pp. 206-208, 1970.
18. R. Morgan and P. Bakan, Sensory Deprivation Hallucinations and Other Sleep Behavior as a Function of Position, Method of Report, and Anxiety, *Perceptual and Motor Skills, 20,* pp. 19-25, 1965.
19. E. Berdach and P. Bakan, Body Position and Free Recall of Early Memories, *Psychotherapy: Theory, Research, and Practice, 4,* pp. 101-102, 1967.
20. S. J. Segal and M. Glickman, Relaxation and the Perky Effect: The Influence of Body Position and Judgments of Imagery, *American Journal of Psychology, 60,* pp. 257-262, 1967.
21. J. L. Singer, Experimental Studies of Daydreaming and the Stream of Consciousness, in *The Stream of Consciousness,* K. S. Pope and J. L. Singer (eds.), Plenum, New York, 1978.
22. J. Rychlak, Time Orientation in the Positive and Negative Free Phantasies of Mildly Abnormal versus Normal Highschool Males, *Journal of Consulting and Clinical Psychology, 41,* pp. 175-190, 1973.
23. A. Richardson, *Mental Imagery,* Routledge and Kegan Paul, London, 1969.
24. T. X. Barber, Changing "Unchangeable" Bodily Processes by (Hypnotic) Suggestions: A New Look at Hypnosis, Cognitions, Imagining, and the Mind-Body Problem, in *Imagination and Healing,* A. A. Sheikh (ed.), Baywood, New York, pp. 69-127, 1984.
25. S. C. Wilson and T. X. Barber, The Fantasy-Prone Personality: Implications for Understanding Imagery, Hypnosis, and Parapsychological Phenomena, in *Imagery: Current Theory, Research, and Application,* A. A. Sheikh (ed.), Wiley, New York, 1983.
26. R. H. McKim, *Experiences in Visual Thinking,* Brooks/Cole, Monterey, California, 1980.
27. A. Lazarus, *In the Mind's Eye,* Rawson Associates, New York, 1977.
28. J. R. Cautela and L. McCullough, Covert Conditioning, in *The Power of Human Imagination,* J. L. Singer and K. S. Pope (eds.), Plenum, New York, pp. 227-254, 1978.

29. J. E. Shorr, *Go See the Movie in Your Head,* Popular Library, New York, 1977.
30. A. A. Sheikh, Eidetic Psychotherapy, in *The Power of Human Imagination,* J. L. Singer and K. S. Pope (eds.), Plenum, New York, pp. 197-224, 1978.
31. A. Richardson, Verbalizer-Visualizer: A Cognitive Style Dimension, *Journal of Mental Imagery, 1,* pp. 109-126, 1977.
32. I. Oyle, *The New American Medicine Show,* Celestial Arts, Millbrae, California, 1979.
33. R. G. Ley, Cerebral Asymmetries, Emotional Experience, and Imagery: Implications for Psychotherapy, in *The Potential of Fantasy and Imagination,* A. A. Sheikh and J. T. Shaffer (eds.), Brandon House, New York, pp. 41-65, 1979.
34. A. A. Sheikh and N. C. Panagiotou, Use of Mental Imagery in Psychotherapy: A Critical Review, *Perceptual and Motor Stills, 41,* pp. 555-585, 1975.
35. A. Ellis, *Reason and Emotion in Psychotherapy,* Lyle Stuart, New York, 1962.
36. M. J. Horowitz, *Image Formation and Cognition,* Appleton Century Crofts, New York, 1970.
37. J. Wolpe, *Psychotherapy by Reciprocal Inhibition,* Stanford University Press, Stanford, California, 1958.
38. R. Bauer and E. Craighead, Psychophysiological Responses to the Imagination of Fearful and Neutral Situations: The Effects of Imagery Instructions, *Behavior Therapy, 10,* pp. 389-403, 1979.
39. A. Ahsen, *Basic Concepts in Eidetic Psychotherapy,* Brandon House, New York, 1968.
40. E. T. Gendlin, Imagery is More Powerful with Focusing, in *Imagery: Its Many Dimensions and Applications,* J. E. Shorr, G. E. Sobel, P. Robin, and J. A. Connella (eds.), Plenum, New York, pp. 65-73, 1980.
41. A. A. Sheikh (ed.), *Imagery: Current Theory, Research, and Application,* Wiley, New York, 1983.
42. P. J. Lang, Imagery in Therapy: An Information Processing Analysis of Fear, *Behavior Therapy, 8,* pp. 862-886, 1977.
43. J. E. Shorr, *Psychotherapy Through Imagery,* Thieme-Stratton, New York, 1983.
44. A. Ahsen, *Eidetic Psychotherapy: A Short Introduction,* Nai Matbooat, Lahore, 1965.
45. A. Bry, *Visualization: Directing the Movies of Your Mind,* Barnes and Noble, New York, 1972.
46. J. E. Shorr, Clinical Uses of Categories of Therapeutic Imagery, in *The Power of Human Imagination,* J. L. Singer and K. S. Pope (eds.), Plenum, New York, pp. 95-121, 1978.
47. M. M. Watkins, *Waking Dreams,* Harper and Row, New York, 1976.
48. P. McKellar, Imagery from the Standpoint of Introspection, in *The Function and Nature of Imagery,* P. W. Sheehan (ed.), Academic Press, New York, pp. 36-61, 1972.
49. C. Castaneda, *The Teachings of Don Juan: A Yavui Way of Knowledge,* Simon and Schuster, New York, 1968.
50. C. Castaneda, *Journey to Ixtlan,* Simon and Schuster, New York, 1972.
51. T. Leary, R. Metzner, and R. Alpert, *The Psychedelic Experience,* University Books, New York, 1964.
52. C. Tart (ed.), *Altered States of Consciousness,* Doubleday, New York, 1969.
53. R. R. Holt, On the Nature and Generality of Mental Imagery, in *The Function and Nature of Imagery,* P. W. Sheehan (ed.), Academic Press, New York, pp. 6-33, 1972.
54. S. J. Segal (ed.), *Imagery: Current Cognitive Approaches,* Academic Press, New York, 1971.
55. P. J. Qualls and P. W. Sheehan, Imaginative, Make-Believe Experiences and Their Role in the Development of the Child, in *Mental Imagery and Learning,* M. L. Fleming

and D. W. Hutton (eds.), Educational Technology Publication, Englewood Cliffs, New Jersey, pp. 75-97, 1983.

56. R. B. Tower, Imagery: Its Role in Development, in *Imagery: Current Theory, Research, and Application,* A. A. Sheikh (eds.), Wiley, New York, pp. 222-251, 1983.

57. E. Saltz, D. Dixon, and J. Johnson, Training Disadvantaged Preschoolers on Various Fantasy Activities: Effects on Cognitive Functioning and Impulse Control, *Child Development, 48,* pp. 367-380, 1977.

58. J. Hilgard, *Personality and Hypnosis: A Study of Imaginative Involvement,* University of Chicago Press, Chicago, 1980.

59. J. L. Singer, Imagination and Make-Believe Play in Early Childhood: Some Educational Implications, *Journal of Mental Imagery, 1,* pp. 127-144, 1977.

60. F. J. Walsh, K. D. White, and R. Ashton, *Imagery Training: Development of a Procedure and Its Evaluation,* unpublished research report, University of Queensland, 1978.

61. A. Richardson and Y. Patterson, An Evaluation of Three Procedures for Increasing Imagery Vividness, in *International Review of Mental Imagery,* Vol. 2, A. A. Sheikh (ed.), Human Sciences Press, New York, 1986.

62. H. J. Crawford and C. McLeod-Morgan, Hypnotic Investigations of Imagery, in *International Review of Mental Imagery,* Vol. 2, A. A. Sheikh (ed.), Human Sciences Press, New York, 1986.

63. J. Heil, Visual Imagery Change During Relaxation Meditation Training, doctoral dissertation, Lehigh University, 1982, *Dissertation Abstracts International, 43,* p. 2338B, 1982.

Contributors

ERIC BUCKOLZ, Ph.D., received his doctorate in Motor Learning from the University of Alberta in 1972 and has been at the University of Western Ontario for the past 17 years. His theoretical research has focused upon factors which influence decision speed and errors, and upon "response interference." His applied research has dealt with cue utilization in sports, the influence of "set" upon sprint start reaction time, and the impact of practice upon peripheral processing speed and accuracy.

ALAN J. BUDNEY, Ph.D., received his doctorate in Clinical Psychology from Rutgers University in 1989, completed an internship at the United States Olympic Training Center in 1988 and a postdoctoral training fellowship at the University of Vermont in 1993. Currently Dr. Budney is an Assistant Professor of Psychiatry and Psychology at the University of Vermont, College of Medicine. He is interested primarily in the development and evaluation of behavioral treatments for drug dependence, in the investigation of the mechanisms of action, and in the evaluation of sport performance enhancement techniques.

JOANN DAHLKOETTER, Ph.D., is a sports psychology consultant in private practice in San Francisco. She is a world-class triathlete and a distance runner herself, and she works with all levels of athletes from recreational to Olympic, providing motivation and concentration training, and biofeedback and stress management for peak performance. She has appeared on ABC's Wide World of Sports, has written for a variety of national fitness magazines, (*Runner's World, Triathlon Magazine, Sports Illustrated,* and *Newsweek*) and has been on the faculty of the University of California at Berkeley Extension.

MARIE-CLAUDE DURAND, B.A., received her B.A. from the University of Toronto in psychology. Currently, she is undertaking graduate studies in kinesiology at the University of Western Ontario. Her interest is in sports psychology, especially in how mental imagery facilitates the learning and performance of motor skills. She has co-authored a review paper on the effects of combining imagery practice with physical practice.

LANCE B. GREEN, Ph.D., received his doctorate from the University of Northern Colorado. Subsequently he accepted an appointment at the University of Hawaii-Hilo, which included teaching courses in the psychosocial aspects of sport and serving as pitching/associate head coach of the baseball team. Currently he is assistant professor in the Department of Exercise and Sport Sciences at Tulane University and Associate Chair and Director of the Exercise Science Program. His research interests lie in the psychophysiological components of physical activity and the social and philosophical aspects of sport participation.

BRUCE D. HALE, Ph.D., received his doctorate from Penn State in physical education with emphasis in sport psychology. At this time, he is an academic-athletic counselor for the Academic Support Center and an affiliate Assistant Professor in Exercise and Sport Science at Penn State University. Also, he is registered as an educational sports psychologist with the Sports Medicine Committee of the U.S.O.C., and he is a consultant certified by the Association for the Advancement of Applied Sport Psychology. He has worked with hundreds of college and elite athletes on performance enhancement strategies and is a sport psychology consultant for U.S.A.C. Roller Skating, U.S.A. Wrestling, and U.S. Rugby.

CRAIG HALL, Ph.D., received his doctorate from the University of Alberta in 1977, and then he joined the Faculty of Kinesiology at the University of Western Ontario. He is interested primarily in the relationship between imagery ability and motor behavior. Most recently his research has focused on how elite and novice athletes use imagery, the effects of positive versus negative imagery, and how imagery can be used in conjunction with other mental rehearsal strategies. He has published over thirty articles on the various roles of imagery in the learning and performance of motor skills.

JEFFREY J. JANSSEN, M.S., received a masters degree in sports psychology from the University of Arizona. At this time he is a performance enhancement consultant in the Exercise and Sport Science Department of the University of Arizona and a member of the Association for the Advancement of Applied Sport Psychology. Mr. Janssen is the coauthor of *Mental Toughness Training for Softball.*

ERROL R. KORN, M.D., is in private practice and on the staff of Scripps Memorial Hospital and Chula Vista Community Memorial Hospital in Chula Vista, California. Dr. Korn is well known for his work involving imagery and altered states of consciousness, particularly in regard to pain and stress management, and peak athletic performance. He has lectured throughout the country, and his publications include numerous articles and the books *Visualization: The Use of Imagery and Altered States of Consciousness in the Health Professions* and *Hyper-Performance: The A-I-M Strategy for Business Success.*

ERIC W. KRENZ, Ph.D., received his doctorate from the University of Utah, specializing in sport psychology. Currently he is a Lecturer in the Department of Health Science at California State University, Fresno. Dr. Krenz has over ten years experience as a consultant and lecturer in stress management and the mental preparation of athletes for competition. Dr. Krenz has worked with athletes in a wide range of sports, including figure skating, gymnastics, baseball, football, basketball, track/field, and rodeo. Dr. Krenz's work with Modified Autogenic Training has received national and international attention.

VICKIE D. KRENZ, Ph.D., M.S.P.H., received her doctorate in health education and her M.S. in public health from the University of Utah. Currently she is an Associate Professor of Health Science at California State University, Fresno. Her interests include health promotion for optimal performance among athletes.

NEIL McCLEAN, Ph.D., is a Lecturer in Psychology at the University of Western Australia. He is a registered Clinical Psychologist and a member of the Australian Psychological Society Board of Sport Psychology. He acts as a consultant to several professional sporting teams and has worked with athletes from a wide range of sports. He was one of the sport psychologists appointed to the Australian Olympic Team for the 1992 Olympic Games in Barcelona.

CRAIG H. McQUEEN, M.D., is an orthopedic surgeon in private practice and has specialized in sports medicine for over twenty years. He is also an orthopedic consultant to such organizations as the University of Utah Athletic Department, Ballet West, Ririe Woodbury Dance Company, Park City Ski Patrol, and Deer Valley Resort. In addition, Dr. McQueen was the medical director of the 1984 National Figure Skating and Olympic Trials. Currently he is the regional physician for the U.S. Nordic Ski and U.S. Tennis Teams and team physician for the World U.S.A. Junior Figure Skating Team. Dr. McQueen is nationally and internationally known for his work in the areas of sports psychology and the mental preparation of athletes.

EMMETT E. MILLER, M.D., is a physician, mathematician, musician, and poet who has won international acclaim as a pioneer in humanistic psychology and the emerging "new medicine." His outstanding audio-cassettes, which weave his soothing and inspiring voice through a rich tapestry of music and nature sounds, are in widespread use by medical centers, wellness clinics, and individual health professionals. Dr. Miller is the author of two books: *Self-Imagery* and *Software for the Mind.*

L. MARTIN MOLESKI, M.A., received a masters degree in psychology from Marquette University, and subsequently he studied acupuncture and other Eastern approaches to healing. He was on the staff of Marin County General Hospital, California, for several years until the time of his death.

SHANE MURPHY, Ph.D., received his doctorate in clinical psychology from Rutgers University. For five years he was sport psychologist for the United States Olympic Committee, and he was the U.S. Team Sport Psychologist at the Olympic Games in Seoul and Albertville. At the present time he is Associate Director of the U.S.O.C. Division of Sport Science and Technology. In that role he is responsible for shaping policy for the application of science to Olympic sport. Dr. Murphy has published numerous articles and chapters on sport psychology, and he has served on the editorial board of *The Sport Psychologist* since 1989.

ALAN RICHARDSON, Ph.D., has a doctorate from the University of London, England, and has conducted research and lectured at universities throughout the British Isles, in Continental Europe, the United States, and Australia. At this time, he is Emeritus Professor of Psychology and Senior Honorary Research Fellow at the University of Western Australia. Dr. Richardson has published widely on the topic of mental imagery: an influential book, *Mental Imagery*, published in 1969, review papers on the topic of mental practice, and numerous other research papers. Also, he has made important theoretical and empirical contributions to the social psychology of immigrant assimilation and adjustment. In 1981, he was elected a Fellow of the Academy of the Social Sciences in Australia.

HARVEY L. RISCHE, Ph.D., A.C.S.W., received his doctorate from the University of North Texas. Now he works in a psychiatric clinic and is in private practice. His interest in hypnotherapy and athletics led him to the area of sports psychology. He has helped athletes from the recreational to the professional level use their mental abilities to enhance their performance. The challenge of helping athletes benefits psychotherapy with nonathletic patients, since many techniques can be applied to patients troubled by other life stressors.

DARLENE SCHMIDT, B.Ed., obtained her Bachelor of Education degree from the University of Regina in 1983. She then taught secondary-school physical education. Her involvement in high-school athletics as an educator and a coach, and her extensive personal participation in numerous sports, fostered an interest in sport psychology. Currently Ms. Schmidt is a graduate student in sport psychology at the University of Western Ontario. Her work has focused on mental imagery, more specifically, on the effects of positive versus negative imagery on athletic performance.

JOHN T. SHAFFER, D.Min., is a psychotherapist in private practice and the Director of the Well-Being Center in St. Louis, Missouri. He is past president of the American Association for the Study of Mental Imagery and the organizer of several significant conferences on imagery. He has presented numerous lectures and workshops in this country and Canada and is the coeditor of *The Potential of Fantasy and Imagination.*

ANEES A. SHEIKH, Ph.D., is Professor of Psychology at Marquette University and Clinical Professor of Psychiatry and Mental Health Sciences at the Medical College of Wisconsin. He is internationally recognized for his contributions to the field of mental imagery. A former editor of the *Journal of Mental Imagery*, he now edits the *Imagery and Human Development Series*. His books include *The Potential of Fantasy and Imagination, Imagery: Current Theory, Research and Application, Imagination and Healing, Imagery in Education, Anthology of Imagery Techniques, Psychophysiology of Mental Imagery, Dream Images, Eastern and Western Approaches to Healing, and Death Imagery*. He is past president of the American Association for the Study of Mental Imagery.

KATHARINA S. SHEIKH, M.A., was formerly on the faculty of Clara Schumann Schule, Bonn, Germany, Cardinal Stritch College, and St. Francis de Sales College in Milwaukee. She is the president of the Institute for Human

Enhancement. For her undergraduate work, she attended the University of Western Ontario and the University of Strasbourg, France, and she holds graduate degrees from the University of Toronto and Marquette University. Her publications include the books *Imagery in Education Eastern and Western Approaches to Healing,* and *Death Imagery.*

RICHARD M. SUINN, Ph.D., has been team psychologist at the Summer and Winter Olympic Games. He has consulted with U.S. Biathlon, Cross-Country Ski, Alpine Ski, Ski Jumping, Women's Athletics, Marksmanship, and Modern Pentathlon Teams. He is head of the Psychology Department, Colorado State University, on the Board of Directors of the American Psychological Association, and president-elect of the Association for the Advancement of Behavior Therapy. He is the originator of visual motor behavior rehearsal, a method for visualization training. He has lectured on sport psychology in Japan, China, Singapore, Mexico, and Canada. His books include: *Seven Steps to Peak Performance, Psychology in Sports,* and *Anxiety Management Training.*

ANNA SYLVAN, has studied eastern philosophy, comparative religions, holistic health, and sport psychology for the last fifteen years. She has conducted numerous seminars on meditation techniques, holistic life, and related subjects.

ROBERT L. WOOLFOLK, Ph.D., is Professor of Psychology at Rutgers University. He also has served on the faculties of Princeton University and the University of Texas at Austin. He is the author of three books and numerous research articles.

Index